THE BOOK KNOWN AS Q

ROBERT GIROUX

THE BOOK
KNOWN AS Q

A Consideration of
Shakespeare's Sonnets

VINTAGE BOOKS
A Division of Random House
New York

First Vintage Books Edition, September 1983
Copyright © 1982 by Robert Giroux
All rights reserved under International and Pan-American
Copyright Conventions. Published in the United States by
Random House, Inc., New York, and simultaneously in
Canada by Random House of Canada Limited, Toronto.
Originally published by Atheneum in 1982.

Library of Congress Cataloging in Publication Data
Giroux, Robert.
The book known as Q.
Reprint. Originally published: New York :
Atheneum, c1982.
Includes bibliographical references and index.
1. Shakespeare, William 1564-1616. Sonnets.
2. Sonnets, English—History and criticism.
I. Shakespeare, William, 1564-1616. Sonnets. 1983.
II. Title.
[PR2848.G57 1983]   821'.3   83-5737
ISBN 0-394-71728-7

Manufactured in the United States of America

IN MEMORIAM

MARK VAN DOREN &~ JOHN BERRYMAN

Preface

THIS BOOK is concerned with a curious anomaly: late in Shakespeare's life (seven years before his death), at the height of his fame, the publication of his sonnets in the 1609 quarto, known as Q, was met with silence. In its original form Q was not only not reprinted, it went underground for a century. It was almost unknown to seventeenth-century writers; only in a satirical verse play of Suckling's do a few echoes of the sonnets reappear around 1640.[1] Yet the sonnets were well known in Elizabethan literary circles eleven years before their publication, and were circulating privately in manuscript, as Francis Meres revealed in 1598. Two of the sonnets, which in Q bear the numbers 138 and 144 (the final sonnet is 154), appeared in an anthology in 1599. How does one explain this interest in the sonnets in the 1590s and their failure, or absence from contemporary records, in 1609?

I have approached the subject as a book publisher, a

---

[1] Sources and Notes, page 307.

vii

publisher of poets, and an amateur who had the good fortune to be trained by a superb Shakespeare scholar and charismatic teacher, the poet Mark Van Doren. This book is dedicated to his memory and that of another poet and scholar, John Berryman; we were fellow-students under Mark at Columbia College. They are absolved of all responsibility for the opinions expressed in these pages, which are mine alone. (As John's friends have long known, it was his conviction that the Elizabethan playwright William Haughton was not only Shakespeare's collaborator on *The Taming of the Shrew* but also the friend in his sonnets.)

I am happy with my status as an amateur, which the Oxford English Dictionary defines as "a lover" who "cultivates anything as a pastime, as distinguished from one who prosecutes it professionally." After forty years of intimacy with Shakespearean scholarship, I can only regard with amusement those who profess the idea that one cannot interpret the sonnets as biography, and insist that they are "pure" literature, whatever that is. Poets, after all, are not pure spirits; from my experience, I would say they are all too human. This critical aberration of some scholars is discussed in "The Antibiographical Fallacy" (page 46). Not all the sonnets are biographical; only a few are—and they are crucial to an understanding of the man Dr. Johnson called quite simply "our poet."

One of the many extraordinary things about Shakespeare is that around 1594 he seems to have lost all interest in "authorship" as a role. Earlier he was clearly intent upon making his name as a poet, perhaps in part as a result of Robert Greene's scurrilous attack late in 1592, calling him (among other things) one of the "rude grooms" and "apes" who "supposes he is as well able to bombast out a blank verse" as, say, Christopher Marlowe. The line in sonnet 112—"Which vulgar scandal stamped upon my brow"—is a reference to Greene's attack of 1592, and the coined verb "o'er-greene" (as spelled in Q) reinforces the allusion two lines later. Shakespeare was attacked because he was a successful new playwright, and poor Greene was jealous and resentful. But making one's name as a playwright was nothing in comparison to being accepted as a poet, and *that* is what in 1592 Shakespeare was determined to be.

In April 1593 he published *Venus and Adonis,* a long poem of 1,194 lines, which had immediate and widespread success. It made his name as a poet. A year later, his second and longer poem of 1,855 lines, *The Rape of Lucrece,* met with almost equal success as a "graver" work. Yet he seems never to have had any interest in publishing his plays, which the world regards as his crowning achievement. Of course the plays were not his property, in a technical sense; they were owned by the acting company he helped form in 1594 and in which he was a shareholder. In his seeming lack of authorly pride as playwright, Shakespeare was notably different from Ben Jonson, whose plays were owned by the same company. It appears that Jonson's insistence on the publication of his plays in a handsome and expensive folio in 1616, the year of Shakespeare's death, influenced the surviving shareholders to issue the First Folio in 1623, after much delay. (Its publication was actually announced in 1622 in the Frankfurt Book Fair catalogue.) The format and design of Jonson's

folio, except for the title-page, which has a classic orna-
mental frame instead of a portrait, were followed faithfully in the First Folio.

It is likely, as W. H. Auden was convinced, that the
publication of the sonnets in 1609 horrified Shakespeare.
They were not, like his two narrative poems, a bid for
reputation; he was long past that stage. The appearance of
these privately circulated and very personal poems so late
in his career might well have been an embarrassment to
their author, considering their nature. He may also have
felt betrayed by the badly supervised and sloppily edited
text of Q. There is a plausible explanation of the silence
that greeted the sonnets in 1609. This and my few discoveries as a publisher and common reader will, I hope, be
apparent in the pages that follow.

The argument of this book is soritical. If you are convinced (as I am) that sonnet 26 is a statement in verse of
what Shakespeare wrote, in 1594, in his dedicatory letter
in *The Rape of Lucrece,* the conclusion—since the letter
names a name—is inevitable. If you do not see the resemblance between poem and letter, all arguments are unavail-
ing. As with most readers of the sonnets, I did not start out
with convictions about, or even interest in, identities. I
have remained interested only in what Shakespeare wrote,
and my conclusions have been derived only from what he
wrote.

With one or two exceptions, I reproduce Elizabethan
poems and documents in modern spelling, which has the
value of eliminating the pitfalls of condescension, false
quaintness, and possible misreadings. Yet occasionally it is
crucial to see the text of Q and consult the sonnets in their

original form. For that and other reasons, Q is reproduced in facsimile beginning on page 227.

All students of the sonnets owe an enormous debt to the indefatigable labours of Hyder Edward Rollins in compiling his two-volume New Variorum edition of the *Sonnets* (1944), which contains overwhelming proof of E. K. Chambers's dictum, "More folly has been written about the sonnets than any other Shakespearean topic." I have tried not to add to the folly.

I am grateful to Wesleyan University at Middletown, Connecticut, for giving me the needed impetus to write this book; their invitation in 1978 to present one of a triad of lectures in homage to Paul Horgan, Professor Emeritus, Author in Residence, and Director of their Center for Advanced Studies from 1962 to 1967, inspired my paper "The Book Known as Q." I am also grateful to The Friends of the Olin Library, who co-sponsored the lecture. Many of my ideas were developed and expanded in the Archibald Smith Lecture[2] at the Baylor School, Chattanooga, Tennessee, in the spring of 1981.

I wish to acknowledge the generous help and advice of the following persons, who read the manuscript at various stages: Catharine Carver, Budwin Conn, Leon Edel, Robert Fitzgerald, Harry Ford, Carmen Gomezplata, Paul Horgan, Franklin Kissner, Nancy Miller, Charles Phillips Reilly, Richard Sewall, and Thomas A. Stewart. To Lynn Warshow I am indebted for her helpful redaction of the text. To Robert Phelps I am grateful for the source of the quotation from Colette; to Bruce High for overseeing publication of the Baylor School lecture; to Joan Massey for her help in typing various drafts; and to Mrs. Theodore

McClintock for the index. I am greatly indebted to Harry Ford for his interest in the book from the start, for its excellent design, and for his unfailing professionalism; and to Charles Reilly for his encouragement at the beginning and his assistance at difficult intervals.

A final word about the title of this book. I am well aware that the siglum Q applies to all quarto texts, and I neither say nor mean to imply that the 1609 edition of the sonnets is the *only* book so known. The use of Q provides a convenient way of differentiating between the book issued in 1609, and the individual sonnets which—like 138 and 144—were circulating ten or more years earlier. The bibliographical, printing, and format aspects of Q have important implications, not only in my analysis of Thorpe's dedication but throughout this book. If the reader consults the text of Q reproduced here, and in the end rereads all the poems, I shall have achieved my aim.

CONTENTS

THE POEMS I

THE PATRON

THE PEDANT

THE PLAY

Contents

THE PUBLISHER

THE POEMS II

THE POET 221

ILLUSTRATIONS

THE POEMS I

'Tis better to be vile than vile esteemed . . .

SONNET 121

The Story of Q

T HE BOOK known as Q, from its quarto size, is one of
the most famous, and mysterious, books in the history
of publishing. This rare book, only thirteen copies of
which are extant,* was published in 1609 in the paper-
covered and unbound form usual for the period. It has
eighty unnumbered pages. In the unlikely event that an
unknown copy were to come on the market, it would fetch
an astronomical price. The surviving copies differ slightly
in overall dimensions, as a result of having been variously
cropped before being cased in fine eighteenth- and nineteenth-century bindings.

Q contains not only the 2,155 lines of William Shakespeare's 154 sonnets (one of which has twelve, and another fifteen, lines, instead of the usual fourteen) but also
his narrative poem of 329 lines in forty-seven stanzas,
entitled "A Lover's Complaint." A few critics have refused
to acknowledge this poem as Shakespeare's, including

---

* Six are in England (two at the British Library, two at the Bodleian,
one at Trinity College, Cambridge, and one at The John Rylands Library, Manchester); six are in the United States (two at the Folger
Shakespeare Library, two at the Huntington Library, one at Harvard, and
one at the Elizabethan Club, Yale); and one is at the Bibliotheca Bodmeriana, Geneva.

3

some who accept the sonnets, yet its provenance is exactly that of the sonnets. The tides of Shakespearean scholarship can shift surprisingly: in 1930 the formidable scholar E. K. Chambers believed the authorship of "A Lover's Complaint" to be "open to much doubt,"[1] while in 1960 George Rylands called it a "little-appreciated Elizabethan masterpiece"[2] by the author whose name it bears in Q. Recent critics dispute not its Shakespearean authorship but its early or late dating; its relation to a contemporary poem has become a focus of interest (page 210).

In 1609 an author's "rights," as we know them, scarcely existed. The licence required for publishing a book could be obtained only by a member of the Stationers' Company, the guild of printers. If a guild member gained possession of a manuscript, and the wardens allowed it to be entered in the register at the Stationers' Hall, he—not the author— became the copyright owner. Q was entered for Thomas Thorpe on 20 May 1609 as "a Booke called Shakespeares *sonnettes.*"

The mystery begins: publication of the sonnets apparently met with total silence; there was no second edition of what unquestionably ranks with the greatest poetry in the language. On 19 June 1609 Edward Alleyn, the star of the Lord Admiral's Men, the actors who were the chief rivals to Shakespeare's company, recorded in his household accounts the purchase of Q for five pence; no other undisputed reference to the newly published book is known. It is astonishing that Q was never reprinted in Shakespeare's lifetime, in contrast to his two earlier books of verse, *Venus and Adonis* (1593) and *The Rape of Lucrece* (1594), both of which went into numerous editions.

A not widely known fact is that Q went underground

for one hundred years. The sonnets did not reappear in their original form until 1711, when the London publisher Bernard Lintott, having obtained a copy of Q formerly in the possession of the playwright William Congreve, incorporated the 1609 text into a collection of Shakespeare's poems. The sonnets have never since been out of print.

Most of the sonnets had been used in corrupt and fraudulent form twenty-four years after Shakespeare's death in *Poems: Written by Will. Shakespeare, Gent.* This pirated volume was published in 1640 by John Benson, known chiefly as a printer of broadsides and ballads. He incorporated material from many sources—songs from the plays; the 1601 poem, "The Phoenix and the Turtle"; "A Lover's Complaint"; and everything else he could lay hands on, except *Venus* and *Lucrece,* which were protected by other publishers' copyrights. Apparently Benson saw his opportunity when Thomas Thorpe, the copyright owner of Q, died in 1639. Benson suppressed eight sonnets completely, and rearranged and bowdlerized the rest, changing pronouns to make it appear that poems addressed to "him" were meant for "her." Nowhere does Benson use the word "sonnet": the verse form was thoroughly out of fashion by 1640. He transformed 146 sonnets into 72 new poems, running two, three, and even five sonnets together as if they were written as a single poem. He also invented 72 titles, like "A Bashful Lover," "Careless Neglect," and "Upon the Receipt of a Table-Book from His Mistress," which readers took to be Shakespeare's. Benson added a preface falsely stating that the contents had been written in the last years of the poet's life and that, "himself then living," Shakespeare had vouched for the purity and authenticity of Benson's text. In addition, the book presents as Shakespeare's more than ten poems not written by him. Edward Capell, the eighteenth-century editor, called Benson's book "rubbish."[3] If awards were given for rascality in publishing, John Benson would deserve a prize.

"There are *no* contemporary allusions to it [Q]."[4] This statement by J. W. Mackail seems unbelievable, especially when one remembers the phrase about Shakespeare's "sugared sonnets," but it turns out that none of the allusions to the sonnets is an allusion to Q. In 1598 Francis Meres published *Palladis Tamia: Wits Treasury,* which described Shakespeare as one of "the most passionate among us to bewail and bemoan the perplexities of love." It included the informative and often quoted contemporary estimate of the poet: "The sweet witty soul of Ovid lives in mellifluous and honey-tongued Shakespeare—witness his 'Venus and Adonis,' his 'Lucrece,' his sugared sonnets among his private friends, &c." This fascinating allusion to the sonnets in manuscript form, like the publication of two sonnets—"When my love swears that she is made of truth," and "Two loves I have, of comfort and despair"—in the 1599 anthology *A Passionate Pilgrim,* cannot be called references to Q, which they preceded by ten and eleven years respectively. Edward Alleyn's notation of his purchase of Q in the summer of 1609, though indeed a contemporary allusion, was not discovered until 1881.

In 1963 Paul Morgan[5] unearthed in the Balliol library another possible inscribed allusion to Q, though not an undisputed one. It could be interpreted as a reference to Shakespeare's poetry in general, including his narrative and dramatic poems, rather than to Q alone. The inscription was presumably written during Shakespeare's lifetime by Leonard Digges, the Hispanophile who contributed a commendatory poem to the First Folio. On a fly-leaf of Lope de Vega's *Rimas,* published in Madrid in 1613, Digges inscribed this undated note, apparently while in Spain: "Knowing that Mr. Mabbe was to send you this book of sonnets, which with Spaniards here is accounted of their Lope de Vega as in England we should of our Will Shakespeare, I could not but insert this much to you, that if you like him [Vega] not, you must never never read a Spanish poet."

The mysterious silence that greeted the appearance of Q went long unnoticed, and no one proposed a plausible explanation until 1922, when Frank Mathew suggested: "The neglect of the *Sonnets* of 1609 can only be explained by concluding that they were quickly suppressed."[6] This was seconded in 1926 by J. M. Robertson: "[Q] is now a very rare book yet the natural presumption would be that in 1609, at the height of Shakespeare's contemporary fame, it would have found a considerable sale if it were not interfered with; and that a second printing would have followed in a few years . . . There is fair ground for a presumption that . . . [Q] was stopped."[7]

In 1944 Hyder Edward Rollins, editor of the monumental New Variorum edition of the sonnets (to whom I am indebted for many things, including the use of the siglum Q), asked: "Unless Q *was* quickly suppressed, how can one account for the total silence of Shakespeare's contemporaries about the mysterious figures of the dark woman, the male friend, and the rival poet?"[8] It is also strange that Robert Burton of Christ Church, known in 1599 as a "devourer of books" (including *Venus* and

Lucrece), had no copy of Q in his enormous library. He nowhere mentions it in his great compendium, *The Anatomy of Melancholy,* published in 1621, packed with all kinds of quotations from classical and contemporary literature, and containing a vast section entitled "Love-Melancholy." In *Robert Burton's Knowledge of English Poetry* H. J. Gottlieb asserts that Burton "had no copy of the *Sonnets,* nor does he quote or allude to them."[9] It is also worth noting that John Milton, a Londoner whose life overlapped that of Shakespeare by eight years—he contributed a sonnet on Shakespeare to the prefatory matter of the Second Folio in 1632—shows absolutely no knowledge of Q.

There is no direct evidence for the suppression of Q; it is all indirect, negative, and circumstantial, like the scarcity of surviving copies. But circumstantial evidence is evidence. If Q were not suppressed, it would be reasonable to suppose that the author might have had a hand in its publication. Is there any evidence of this? Shakespeare, who had turned forty-five the month prior to Thorpe's registration of the sonnets, and lived seven years more until his death in 1616, apparently had nothing to do with the production of Q, because, among other reasons, it was so badly proofread. This contrasts with the texts of *Venus* and *Lucrece,* both of which are impressively free of printing errors, carry his signed dedications, and apparently had careful reading, having been printed in London by Richard Field, his fellow-Stratfordian. Q, on the other hand, is riddled with errors.

The worst, and perhaps most revealing, gaffe is the two pairs of parentheses, enclosing blank space, inserted on consecutive lines at the end of the twelve-line sonnet 126 (see page 283). It is an overcorrection, constituting a mistake, rather than an ordinary misprint. Someone other than the author (perhaps the publisher, Thorpe, or the printer, Eld) counted the lines, concluded that the couplet was missing, and decided to indicate its omission. He did not realize that the poem has a different rhyme scheme from the rest, or that the twelve lines function as a coda or *envoi* to the first series of sonnets.

In sonnet 146, generally ranked among the greatest sonnets, the compositor went wrong at the start of line 2. The opening quatrain is printed in Q as follows:

> *Poor soul, the center of my sinful earth,*
> My sinful earth *these rebel powers that thee array,*
> *Why dost thou pine within and suffer dearth,*
> *Painting thy outward walls so costly gay?*

We can only guess at the missing words that the compositor apparently lost when he absentmindedly repeated the words "my sinful earth." George Steevens's clever emendation, *"Starved by* these rebel powers that thee array," was inspired by the rhyme-word "dearth."[10] Other editors have suggested "A prey to," "Ruled by," "Leagued with," "Thrall to," "Resist" (which requires a full stop, rather than Q's comma, after "array"), and "Racked by." Purists simply insert dots of elision at line 2.

Perhaps the most interesting mistake in Q is that the couplet ending sonnet 36,

> *But do not so, I love thee in such sort*
> *As, thou being mine, mine is thy good report.*

reappears, word for word, at the end of sonnet 96. It is unlikely that this is a printer's error; the duplications are too far removed from each other—sixty sonnets apart—for the compositor to have been responsible. If the author had seen proofs, he would have caught this borrowing from himself and would probably have written a new couplet for sonnet 96. This repetition, which could have slipped past an inattentive patron receiving the sonnets say, one a week, confirms the thesis that the author never intended the poems for publication. It also strengthens the critical view that Shakespeare's couplets are, with a few notable exceptions, the weakest parts of the sonnets.

The couplet of sonnet 112, as it is printed in Q, with "y'are" standing for "you are," is meaningless:

> *You are so strongly in my purpose bred*
> *That all the world besides me thinks y'are dead.*

Edmund Malone first emended it to read, "That all the world besides [except] you thinks me dead."[11] Steevens disagreed; he combined "me" and "thinks" into a verb, and deleted "y' " as an error. The Steevens solution is now generally accepted, often without commas: "That all the world besides, methinks, are dead."[12]

The most blatant printer's error—which stands out because each sonnet in Q begins with a large, bold-face initial capital—occurs in sonnet 122, in which the poet acknowledges a gift of blank-books or writing-tablets. In the opening line, the compositor doubled both the capital and comma: "*T*thy gift,, thy tables, are within my brain . . ."

Sonnets 12, 35, 54, 69, and 77 contain garbled words or phrases. "And sable curls or silvered ore with white" (12.4) can be straightened out by changing "or" to "all" and "ore" to "o'er." The meaningless line "Excusing their sins more than their sins are" (35.8) is usually corrected by changing "their" to "thy." The closing line of sonnet 54, "When that shall vade, by verse distills your truth," is usually emended to "my verse"; some editors also change "vade," meaning depart or perish, to "fade." In sonnet 69, there is a fault of rhyme in line 3, where "due" is misprinted as "end." In sonnet 77, sometimes called the "Schoolmaster" sonnet, whose theme is the reverse of sonnet 122—the poet's gift of a writing-tablet to the youth—the noun in the tenth line, "Commit to these waste blacks," requires correction to "blanks."

In the third quatrain of sonnet 25, which is thought to refer to Sir Walter Ralegh's disgrace, there is a failure of rhyme due to hasty composition or misreading by the printer:

> *The painful warrior famousèd for worth,*
> *After a thousand victories once foiled,*
> *Is from the book of honour rasèd quite*
> *And all the rest forgot for which he toiled.*

Editors usually change "worth" to "might" or "fight."

The total number of errors in Q has been variously estimated, depending on differing views in matters of punctuation, at a minimum of fifty-three and a maximum of eighty-four, but the foregoing examples will suffice. They led the chief arbiter of Shakespeare problems, E. K. Chambers, to classify the text as "not a very good one. . . . There are sufficient misprints," he concluded, "to make it clear that the volume cannot have been 'overseen' . . . by Shakespeare."[13]

Not overseen by Shakespeare, unauthorized for publication, probably suppressed, almost invisible for one hundred years—these interesting discoveries about Q provoke at least two questions: How *did* it get published? What was Shakespeare's reaction? One would suppose it to be much more difficult to answer the second question than the first, but when W. H. Auden touched on both matters in a BBC broadcast in 1964,[14] he said he was sure he knew the answer to the second:

> How the sonnets came to be published—whether Shakespeare gave copies to some friend who then betrayed him, or whether some enemy stole them—we shall probably never know. *Of one thing I am certain* [italics mine]: Shakespeare must have been horrified when they were published.

The Story in the Sonnets

The greatest mystery of Q is not its strange publishing history, its possible suppression, its weird dedication, or even the identities of the male friend, the dark-eyed and dark-haired woman, and the rival poets. It is the poems themselves. In 1609—when Shakespeare, a gentleman of means near the end of his writing career (*The Tempest* was performed at court in 1611), was apparently in semiretirement at Stratford—the publication of these highly personal sonnets probably disturbed their author profoundly. The sonnets to my mind not only belong to a much earlier era, they were not even written as a book, nor were they intended for many other eyes (Auden thought *no other*

eyes). Why hadn't Shakespeare destroyed the manuscripts? How did they get out of his hands into Thorpe's?
We do not know. If the answers were available, they
might tell us how the poems got published, but they probably would not help us to date their composition, or resolve another nagging question: are the poems expressive
of homosexual love?

There is also the unsolvable problem of the correct
order of the sonnets, on which depends in part our understanding of the story in Q. This problem arises from the
obvious fact that Q was not a book prepared by its author.
Shakespeare clearly did not create it as a unified work, as
he did each of his plays and narrative poems.

There are those who interpret the sonnets by numerology, implying that the poems in Q were most carefully
arranged by the poet. Many Elizabethan poets were fasci-
nated by, even addicted to, numerology: there are 108
sonnets in Sidney's *Astrophel and Stella,* because in the
Odyssey there were 108 suitors for Penelope (Stella's real
name being Penelope); A. K. Hieatt[15] has shown that
Spenser's "Epithalamion" was constructed on numerological lines, and so on. But common sense protests when a
numerologist critic[16] of Q tells us that by omitting sonnet
136 (because it contains the line "Then in the number let
me pass untold") the remaining 153 sonnets form an
equilateral triangle with a base of, presto, 17! (This is
significant in his eyes, because the opening poems in Q are
the seventeen "Marriage" sonnets). Almost any finished
work offers an ingenious reader numerous possibilities for
the extraction of *post hoc* mathematical marvels. If Shakespeare had intended that sonnet 136 should not be
counted, wouldn't it have been simpler for him to omit it

than to have written a clue to omit it? (This reminds one of the story, perhaps apocryphal, that George Kittredge of Harvard, at a banquet honouring Shakespeare, proved by means of clever anagrams that Francis Bacon had written the menu.) If Shakespeare did organize his sonnets according to a numerological plan or, as Leslie Hotson maintains, according to the Penitential Psalms,[17] then Q is indeed a finished work and the order of the sonnets is sacrosanct. Unfortunately for these theories, the order of the sonnets in a few instances is demonstrably awry.*

The sonnets in Q, in my opinion, are an accumulation—"a kind of portfolio," to use the phrase of J. Dover Wilson[18]—written over a period of at least three years, to judge from internal evidence. Yet they have a surprising degree of coherence, falling into three sections—the first 126 sonnets to the young man, ending with the *envoi;* a new series to the raven-haired mistress (127–152); and, at the end, the two so-called "Bath" sonnets (153–4).

An emotional development and progression can be charted within the first poems—from impersonality to infatuation and love to disillusionment, bitterness, and resignation. Some critics argue that all the sonnets in the first group may not be addressed to the same young man, but it is ludicrous to suppose the poet would have sustained such passion and intensity of feeling for several persons. To leave no doubt that he is writing for one person only, Shakespeare asserts in sonnet 76:

---

* H. C. Beeching: "36–39, if they are rightly placed, do not explain their position; 75 would come better after 52; 77 and 81 interrupt the series on the Rival Poet." (*Sonnets*, 1904, p. lxv.) C. H. Herford: "The three *absence* sonnets 97–99 betray a frank and joyous confidence hard to reconcile with the desolate 'farewell' note of the previous group and with the silence which follows." (*Works of Shakespeare*, 1899, X.)

Why write I still all one, ever the same,
And keep invention in a noted weed
That every word doth almost tell my name,
Showing their birth, and where they did proceed?
O know, sweet love, I always write of you,
And you and love are still my argument
So all my best is dressing old words new . . .

He reasserts it in sonnet 105:

> *. . . all alike my songs and praises be*
> *To one, of one, still such, and ever so.*

Throughout Q there is unevenness in the quality of the poems—ranging from those that achieve perfection (Auden picks forty-nine such sonnets[19]) to the only sonnet (145) written in octosyllabic and comparatively plodding verse. (Because it contains the words "hate away," it has been suggested that the poem was written to Anne Hathaway!) Yet Vladimir Nabokov called 145 "this elegant little sonnet."[20] At their best, as in 71, "No longer mourn for me when I am dead," the sonnets convince readers that nothing greater has been written in English. Perhaps for this reason, some critics find it difficult to accept an early dating for their composition. But there is an explanation: genius.

I believe that all the poems, with a single exception, belong to the earliest years of Shakespeare's career, 1592 to 1594–5. I believe they contributed, as early work, to his development at a crucial period. They define a formative experience of his life. What precisely was this experience? It starts with the first poems in Q, the so-called "Marriage" sonnets.

If, as many believe, Shakespeare began to write the sonnets as commissioned work, the contract must have covered only the first seventeen poems. Their theme is such that, in the ordinary course of events, a poet would not be likely to take it up—persuading a young man to marry and have children. Why should a poet care whether another man, particularly one he does not seem to know very well, marries and has a child? The youth's parents or relatives might care, but it is unlikely a poet would undertake such an assignment except for a reward or favour. John Jay Chapman concluded that the sonnets "were almost certainly paid for."[21] If they were, the person who commissioned them received value only up to sonnet 18, for at this point the subject of marriage is dropped and never raised again.

A curious thing happens within the first seventeen poems. Up to sonnet 10 they are wholly impersonal—the words "I," "my," "mine" do not occur—but sonnet 8 records a very personal reaction: the young man is addressed as "Music to hear." In the following sonnet the poet has concluded that the young man loves no one ("No love towards others in that bosom sits"), thereby providing a theme for sonnet 10—"Grant if thou wilt, thou art beloved of many,/ But that thou none lovest is most evident." Five lines later the poet first uses personal pronouns—"O change thy thought, that *I* may change *my* mind"—and takes a bold step in the couplet, "Make thee another self, *for love of me*." With these words the poet connects himself to the youth, in terms of affection, for the first time.

Sonnet 11 reverts to the impersonal tone, as if the previous one had gone too far; it has no "I" or "me," and the

marriage advice is revived. Yet for the remainder of the
sequence, the first person appears in every sonnet, formally
at first ("When I do count the clock," introducing a central theme, Time), until in the first line of sonnet 13, the
poet openly addresses the youth as his love—"O that you
were yourself, but love, you are," and again in line 13 as
"Dear my love."

In sonnet 15, one of the richest poems in this series, he
introduces another theme, Immortality, dropping the marriage motif and for the first time using a theatre image:
"this huge stage presenteth naught but shows." The argument upholding the order of the sonnets as printed in Q is
supported by sonnets 15 and 16, which, like two earlier
sonnets 5 and 6, are *linked* poems, merging one into the
other. The obviously correct order of these four early sonnets, and of the many other linked poems later, strongly
reinforce this conclusion.

The order of the poems as printed in Q is *on the whole*
right, though imperfect. Even if one acknowledges dis-
crepancies in the order of some of the sonnets, it seems
wiser to accept the numbering as given than to attempt the
chaos of rearrangement, which foolhardy critics have not
hesitated to do. (It was an affectation of nineteenth-century
scholars to use roman numerals for the sonnets; all the
numbers in Q—beginning with 2, since the first sonnet
bears no number—are arabic.) Shakespeare concludes the
"Marriage" sonnet sequence, which started so formally
and impersonally, with the words "in my rhyme," merging
the themes of Marriage and Immortality. All sonnet-
sequences traditionally promised the beloved immortality;
this conceit from classic literature had been revived in the
sonnets of Petrarch and imitated by the Elizabethans. The

difference with Q is that the poet's promise to the unnamed friend has indeed been kept.

Certain critics believe that sonnet 126, the twelve-line *envoi*, was intended to follow 17. I disagree, but had it ended the "Marriage" series and these 18 were all of Q that had survived, we should have been left a story along these lines: an ambitious and aspiring poet, early in his career (when he most needs help), undertakes, at the request of a fatherless family ("Is it for fear to wet a widow's eye?"), to persuade the reluctant heir to marry and perpetuate the family line. The heir appears to be interested in poetry and poets, else why would the family encourage so unlikely and literary a device? The poet embarks on his commission, fashioning the first poems with great skill to catch the young man's interest. There is brilliant artificial writing up to sonnet 10, when something appears to have happened: a note of sincerity, tenderness, and conviction has entered the lines.

If lovers of poetry had not caught this note, if the poems were merely the formal conceits of "friendship" insisted on by such critics as Sidney Lee, they would have lost most readers long ago. Sonnet 18, "Shall I compare thee to a summer's day?" is universally regarded as one of the great love poems in English. Readers with normal sexual tastes, with no knowledge of the poem's context, inevitably read sonnet 18 as a lover's poem to his lady:

Shall I compare thee to a summer's day?
Thou art more lovely and more temperate:
Rough winds do shake the darling buds of May,
And summer's lease hath all too short a date.
Sometimes too hot the eye of heaven shines

And often is his gold complexion dimmed,
And every fair from fair sometime declines,
By chance or nature's changing course untrimmed.
But thy eternal summer shall not fade
Nor lose possession of that fair thou owest,
Nor shall death brag thou wanderest in his shade
When in eternal lines to time thou growest.
   So long as men can breathe or eyes can see,
   So long lives this, and this gives life to thee.

On learning that this is, in fact, a love poem addressed by the poet to a young man, what is the reader to conclude?

The Love in the Sonnets

One of the few helpful insights into the question of homosexuality in the sonnets is provided by C. S. Lewis, who concludes that Shakespeare's language "is too lover-like for ordinary male friendship; and though the claims of friendship are sometimes put very high in, say, the *Arcadia*, I have found no real parallel to such language between friends in sixteenth-century literature. Yet, on the other hand, this does not seem to be the poetry of full-blown pederasty. Shakespeare, and indeed Shakespeare's age, did nothing by halves. If he had intended in these sonnets to be the poet of pederasty, I think he would have left us in no doubt: the lovely *paidikà*, attended by a whole train of mythological perversities, would have blazed across the pages."[22]

The poem that is most explicitly homosexual is sonnet 20, addressed to the young man:

A woman's face with Nature's own hand painted
Hast thou, the Master-Mistress of my passion,
A woman's gentle heart, but not acquainted
With shifting change, as is false women's fashion;
An eye more bright than theirs, less false in rolling,
Gilding the object whereupon it gazeth.
A man in hue all hues in his controlling,
Which steals men's eyes and women's souls amazeth.
And for a woman wert thou first created
Till Nature, as she wrought thee, fell a-doting,
And by addition me of thee defeated,
By adding one thing to my purpose nothing.
  But since she pricked thee out for women's pleasure,
  Mine be thy love, and thy love's use their treasure.

This is a poem of love, but apparently not physical love, since the poet's conclusion is that nature "me of thee defeated" by having added "one thing to my purpose nothing." These words do not represent the feelings of an active homosexual. On the contrary, the punning couplet at the end is the poet's humourous way of saying that physical love between him and the young man is out of the question.

Yet this disclaimer by the poet does not settle the matter for everyone. Stephen Spender argues that it still leaves in doubt the role and reaction of the young man. Shakespeare's early years in Stratford were conventional, or at least heterosexual, since at eighteen he had married the older, and pregnant, Anne Hathaway. He was the father of three children before he was launched on his relatively late-starting public career, when nearly twenty-eight. But the social and sexual mores of his aristocratic young patron, the Earl of Southampton, with whom Shakespeare apparently came in contact around 1592, were those of a different world. The poems in Q describe the young man as prone to "lascivious faults," and he is openly criticized in sonnet 96 for his lax morals: "Some say thy fault is youth, some wantonness . . ." (For the evidence of Southampton's homosexuality, see page 98.) As Spender points out, "Writers who see the sonnet as a simple 'clearing' of Shakespeare read it as though it were addressed by the poet to himself or to a bardolatrous posterity. When one remembers that it was written to a young man of lascivious faults, one has to consider that the poet was anticipating some reaction, the nature of which we can only guess."[23]

As for the possibility that Shakespeare was bisexual, Martin Seymour-Smith advocates the theory that the poems in Q may be described "as a heterosexual's homosexual experience." In his fine edition of the sonnets, he concludes: "It is likely that on at least one occasion Shakespeare did have some kind of physical relationship with the Friend. The sonnets addressed to him, particularly 33–36, are difficult to explain on any other hypothesis. The sense of guilt is too clearly stated. . . ."[24] This was also the view of Samuel Butler in 1899, though his conclusions were simplistic and unwarranted: "Between sonnets 34 and 35," wrote Butler, "there has been a catastrophe" for Shakespeare, a trap into which the young man lured him (sonnet 34) to "travel forth without [his] cloak."

Butler then invents: "Hardly had he [Shakespeare] laid the cloak aside before he was surprised according to a preconcerted scheme, and very probably roughly handled."[25] This is as foolish as Valéry Larbaud's shocked reaction to Butler's suggestion: "To suggest the word 'pederasty' with reference to so pure a glory!"[26] For Larbaud it was even unthinkable that "the Great National Poet" could have been an *unwilling* homosexual.

It is true that sonnets 33–36 express a sense of guilt over some "disgrace" and "strong offense." The poems chide the friend for "thy trespass" and "thy sensual fault," adding the ominous words that "loathsome canker lives in sweetest bud." They come to a climax in 36, with the poet's resolve "that we two must be twain," and that

> *I may not evermore acknowledge thee*
> *Lest my bewailèd guilt should do thee shame,*
> *Nor thou with public kindness honour me,*
> *Unless thou take that honour from thy name.*

These are strong words, suggesting that something serious has occurred, but the language of the poems is unspecific and open to many interpretations. It may have been a crisis over the young man's seduction by the poet's mistress, the double betrayal that is recounted in 40–42. But in this situation why should the poet feel "bewailèd guilt," since his friend and mistress are the guilty ones? Similarly, how could the poet "do shame" to his patron in such a situation? Are these lines another reference to the "vulgar scandal" of Greene's scathing attack on Shakespeare contained in sonnet 122? It is worth noting that the poet's resolve to go his separate way is not carried out. This resembles the crisis recounted in sonnets 78–86, over the rival poets, followed by the apparently unshakable resolve, "Farewell, thou art too dear for my possessing," after which no separation occurs. That the relationship was occasionally stormy is certainly clear, but that it was homosexual in a physical sense remains unproved.

William Empson, commenting on Seymour-Smith's "interesting and vigorous treatment" of the sonnets, points to the contradiction inherent in his thesis "that homosexual feelings, unlike heterosexual, cannot transcend self-love; whereas critics have chiefly admired the fatherly generosity of Shakespeare's attitude to the Friend, which is lacking in his attitude to the Mistress." Mr. Empson then confronts, head on, what he considers an evasion. He feels that modern critics of the sonnets "do not care to mention" what supposedly happened: "Mr. Seymour-Smith, I think, assumes that anal coition took place, with the Earl as the girl; and this is what Dr. Rowse *et al.* feel it urgent to rebut, though the available bit of evidence [sonnet 20, presumably, though Empson does not specify] is slightly off the point." Empson concludes: "So far I agree with the majority and Dr. Rowse: the Earl was prone enough to women, and what he expected of his poets was flattery. I expect he was practically as virgin as the Queen who served as his model in the affair. . . ."[27] It is interesting that Shakespeare, in the linked sonnet immediately following 20, drops the Master-Mistress image and becomes quite conventional. Far from developing the theme of homosexuality, he says in 21 that he does not have the problem other poets face, of having to indite a love poem to "a painted beauty." He can tell the truth: "O let me, true in love, but truly write."

Readers who believe that Shakespeare nowhere else in

his work deals with homosexuality are mistaken. It is explicit in *Troilus and Cressida,* when Thersites tells Patroclus that he is gossiped about as "Achilles' male varlet." Patroclus: "Male varlet, you rogue! What's that?" Thersites: "Why, his masculine whore " (v, i, 19–20). In *The Merchant of Venice,* the feeling between Antonio and Bassanio is so intense that the former, believing he is about to die, gives Bassanio a farewell message for Portia:

> *Say how I loved you, speak me fair in death;*
> *And when the tale is told, bid her be judge*
> *Whether Bassanio had not once a love* [i.e., Antonio].

Bassanio's reply is that, if fate allowed him to make a choice, Portia would lose:

> *Antonio, I am married to a wife*
> *Which is as dear to me as life itself,*
> *But life itself, my wife, and all the world*
> *Are not with me esteemed above thy life.*
> *I would lose all, aye, sacrifice them all*
> *Here to this devil* [Shylock], *to deliver you.*
>
> > [*IV, i,* 275–87.]

Portia, disguised as their lawyer, is at hand listening to every word. Renaissance literature perpetuated the classic view that the claim of male friendship was greater than that between spouses. As G. B. Harrison has pointed out, "It was a common belief in Shakespeare's time that the love of a man for his friend, especially his 'sworn brother,' was stronger and nobler than the love of a man for a woman."[28] For example, Lyly's *Endimion,* whose popularity was at its height at the start of Shakespeare's career, rates friendship above love: "Friendship [is] the image of eternity, in which there is nothing movable. . . . Love ebbs, but friendship standeth stiffly in storms."[29]

In his biography of Tennyson, Robert Bernard Martin doubts that post-Freudian concepts explain the poet's love for Arthur Hallam. "Love is [now] described as either homosexual or heterosexual with little awareness that it may consist of a good deal that defies these categories . . . Even in relationships that are deeply sexual, there are many other factors that have little to do with sex. Sympathy, companionship, likeness of interests, and even habitual proximity often form a great part of love, although they are obviously sexual in prompting. It was surely these feelings that were at the heart of Tennyson's friendship with Hallam."[30] Yet in Q the poet is explicit in calling the young man his "love"; for this reason I concur in W. H. Auden's conclusion that "we are confronted in the sonnets by a mystery, rather than by an aberration." This mystery arises from the fact that an ordinary homosexual explanation of the sonnets is unsatisfactory: it does not account for the contradiction between the poet's boast, "mine be thy love," and his equally firm rejection of "thy love's use."

What kind of love poems, then, are they? My own conclusion, based on the poet's gradual self-discovery revealed by the first twenty sonnets, and on sonnets 104, 108, 121, and 144 in particular, is that Shakespeare experienced real love. Iris Murdoch, in a novel having nothing to do with our poet, marvellously defined the genuine article as "the real, the indubitable and authoritative Eros: that unmistakable seismic shock, that total concentration of everything into one necessary being, mysterious, uncanny, unique, one of the strangest phenomena in the world."[31]

An indispensable element of the mystery is also contained in Marcel Proust's definition: "What Leonardo said of painting can equally well be said of love, that it is *cosa mentale,* something in the mind."[32] Shakespeare tells us in sonnet 104 that, when he first saw the young man, he experienced a kind of vision, and it is interesting that the power and freshness of the vision is strong even after three years. This is his recollection:

> *To me, fair friend, you never can be old,*
> *For as you were when first your eye I eyed*
> *Such seems your beauty still. Three winters cold*
> *Have from the forests shook three summers' pride,*
> *Three beauteous springs to yellow autumn turned*
> *In process of the seasons have I seen,*
> *Three April perfumes in three hot Junes burned*
> *Since first I saw you fresh . . .*

The deliberate, unusual, and brilliant "eye I eyed" has the onomatopoeic effect of "Ay, ay, ay!"—an outburst* induced not only by the beauty of the young man but by the poet's shock at recognizing his fate. Something momentous in his life has occurred.

Their first meeting also seems to have endowed the youth in his eyes with a superior, almost sacred, character. The word "sacred" is not an exaggeration. In sonnet 108,

---

* "Eye I eyed" has been a stumbling-block for critics, even superior critics, who have failed to grasp its meaning. For example, Edward Hubler called the phrase one of Shakespeare's "spectacular failures . . . The modern reader wonders how Shakespeare brought himself to do it." And J. B. Leishman characterized the poem as "one of the most beautiful of the sonnets, despite the careless (I cannot think deliberate) 'eye I eyed' in the second line." But how could such a bizarre sequence of words not be deliberate?

whose theme is "the first conceit of love," he uses the word "hallowed" to describe their original encounter:

> *. . . thou mine, I thine,*
> *Even as when first I hallowed thy fair name.*

Such an experience is called a vision, and a mystical vision is said to be akin to the experience of falling in love. The one who has the vision can be fully aware of its erotic character, but his desire is subordinated to the sacredness of the beloved, whom he regards as infinitely above himself. If such visions are rare, they can nevertheless be genuine. The most famous example in classic literature is Dante's account of his love for the unattainable Beatrice in *La Vita Nuova*. In modern fiction Jay Gatsby's adoration of Daisy Buchanan is of the same order; she is so superior in his eyes that she becomes as unreachable as, at the end, the ever-receding symbolic light on the elusive farther shore. Visions of this nature cannot survive a physical sexual relationship. They may also be based on a misconception of the character of the beloved, and the vision can be destroyed when its true nature is revealed. This kind of reversal is, I believe, one of the developments in Q.

It is obvious that the outcome of Shakespeare's original vision was Q. It can be called his only book of love poems, and it is remarkable how many kinds of love all the poems express, including those to the mistress, as well as to the youth—infatuation, admiration, slavish devotion, lust, rapture, eros, philia, and transcendence. R. P. Blackmur has defined the "devouring general theme" of Q as "infatuation: its initiation, cultivation, and history. . . . The whole collection makes a poetics for infatuation."[33] The poems also reveal contradictions within the kinds of love expressed for the two principals—deep affection for the young man by whom the poet is ultimately disillusioned, but whom he never abandons; and obsessive passion for the mistress he neither trusts nor respects. They also express compassion, when the friend robs him of his mistress ("Take all my loves, my love, yea take them all"); and resignation and near-despair when he thinks the leading rival poet's great verse has won the prize. As C. S. Lewis summed it up, "However the thing began—in perversion, in convention, even (who knows?) in fiction—Shakespeare . . . ends by expressing simply love, the quintessence of all loves whether erotic, parental, filial, amicable, or feudal."[34] To these I would add a special kind of amicable love, which Aristotle calls *useful friendship*. It is not usually applied to Q, perhaps because it seems too prosaic, but I believe it to be operative in the poems owing to Shakespeare's social and financial vulnerability at this stage of his life. Aristotle defines a friendship of utility as unequal if either party possesses some superiority over the other.[35] Shakespeare's relation to the young man was of course unequal, and from this arises much of the pain, bitterness, and disillusionment he suffers. He humbly acknowledges in sonnet 87 that inequality is characteristic of their love:

> *For how do I hold thee but by thy granting,*
> *And for that riches, where is my deserving?*

and in 49:

> *To leave poor me thou hast the strength of laws,*
> *Since why to love [me] I can allege no cause.*

28

"This self-abnegation, the 'naughting,' in the *Sonnets* never rings false," C. S. Lewis concluded. "This patience, this anxiety (more like a parent's than a lover's) to find excuses for the beloved, this clear-sighted and wholly un-embittered resignation, this transference of the whole self into another self without the demand for a return, have hardly a precedent in profane literature. In certain senses of the word 'love,' Shakespeare is not so much our best as our only love poet."[36]

Two sonnets reveal, each in a different way, that Shakespeare was well aware of the unusual nature of the love expressed in the sonnets. In sonnet 144 he bluntly expresses its dual nature:

> *Two loves I have, of comfort and despair,*
> *Which like two spirits do suggest me still:*
> *The better angel is a man right fair*
> *The worser spirit a woman coloured ill.*
> *To win me soon to hell my female evil*
> *Tempteth my better angel from my side,**
> *And would corrupt my saint to be a devil*
> *Wooing his purity with her foul pride.*
> *And whether that my angel be turned fiend*
> *Suspect I may, but not directly tell;*
> *But being both from me, both to each friend,*
> *I guess one angel in another's hell.*
> > *Yet this shall I ne'er know, but live in doubt,*
> > *Till my bad angel fire my good one out.*

The ever-present sexual punning is evident in line 12; "hell" in the slang of the day could mean the sexual

---

* "Side" reads "sight" in Q, but appears correctly in *The Passionate Pilgrim.*

organs. This poem was famous enough by 1599 to be printed in *The Passionate Pilgrim*.

The other revealing sonnet, 121, has never to my knowledge been recognized as dealing with the subject of sex, but I interpret it as Shakespeare's response to the "reproach of being" homosexual. What other meaning can one attribute to the poet's statement that he was considered "vile"? It was fashionable to have a mistress; that would not have been a cause of criticism. The sonnet's first bitter lines assert that it might be better to *be* vile than to be thought so unjustly. Sonnet 121 can be called Shakespeare's only angry sonnet. He is angry because he has been wrongly accused of being "vile," reproached for his "sportive blood" or sensual nature, spied on and gossiped about ("Or on my frailties why are frailer spies?") until he explodes in a magnificent assertion, unique in his writing: "No! I AM THAT I AM—and they that level / At my abuses reckon up their own. . . ."

This crucial sonnet is worth closer examination for many reasons. It is one of the few sonnets in Q not addressed to anyone; it is solely about the poet's own feelings. It is the most personal poem to be found in Shakespeare, in the sense that it wholly and exclusively concerns *him*. Its tone is one of rage over something by which he feels affronted and insulted. The poem seems to have been written in a white heat, as if he had seized a writing-tablet and let off steam before his anger subsided:

> 'Tis better to be vile than vile esteemed
> When not to be receives reproach of being,
> And the just pleasure lost which is so deemed
> Not by our feeling, but by others' seeing.

For why should others' false adulterate eyes
Give salutation to my sportive blood?
Or on my frailties why are frailer spies
Which in their wills count bad what I think good?
No! I AM THAT I AM—*and they that level*
At my abuses reckon up their own.
I may be straight though they themselves be bevel,
By their rank thoughts my deeds must not be shown—
  Unless this general evil they maintain:
  All men are bad and in their badness reign. —

The poem has to do with undefined acts of the poet's—
"my deeds," "my abuses," "my frailties"—and with unnamed observers who condemned as vile what they saw.
They communicated their judgement to him: the poet says
he received the "reproach of being" vile. Yet from his
point of view, the events were not evil ("so deemed / *Not
by our* feeling," "what *I* think good"). Eye images abound,
indicating that the viewers misinterpreted or misunder-
stood what they *saw*—"others' seeing," "false adulterate
eyes," "frailer spies." Two phrases suggest a sexual nature
for the incidents—"my sportive blood" and "wills" ("in
their wills count bad what I think good"). In the language
of the day "will" could mean sexual desire or the sexual
organs. At the same time the poet states that, whatever the
incidents were—and it is anyone's guess—they were inno-
cent. He says it might have been better if he *had* been vile,
since he lost "the just pleasure" inferred from their seeing,
but not matched by his feeling. What angers him is their
assumption of moral superiority, and of the right to judge
and condemn. He says he is "straight" (is this the first use
of this word in the modern sense?) and they are aslant or

31

crooked ("bevel"). Their thoughts are rank and corrupt, and his deeds are not to be evaluated by such false adulterate eyes as theirs: he is what he is.

In the first line, the biting sound of the *b*'s conveys the poet's repressed anger. Reciting this sonnet aloud increases one's appreciation of its technical excellence: "better" and "be" must be stressed, the latter doubly so. It is interesting that in the first quatrain the poet uses the less personal pronoun, *"our* feeling," changing rapidly to *"my* sportive blood" as his anger mounts up to the explosion of "No!" in line 9. Mackail described[37] the first six words of the line as "almost appalling in their superb brevity and concentrated insight; beside them even the pride of Milton dwindles and grows pale: for here Shakespeare, for one single revealing moment, speaks . . . as though he were God himself"—the reference being, of course, to Exodus, III, 14.* This strikes me as too high-flown a reading; in its context, this marvellous line is the proud assertion not of godlike superiority but of a poet's humanity and integrity.

In view of the questions *we* still ask, it would not be surprising if some of Shakespeare's contemporaries wondered what was going on. This we can deduce from two examples of the period's gossip. The first is that dull and enigmatic, but in its day widely read, poem, *Willobie His Avisa,* entered in September 1594. It was frowned on by the authorities; its third edition was listed in the Stationers' Register for burning in 1599, but it was spared and went into six editions by 1635.† A fairly long work of seventy-three cantos, interspersed with prose passages, it tells the

---

* "And God said unto Moses, I AM THAT I AM . . ."
† *Willobie His Avisa, 1594,* edited by G. B. Harrison, Bodley Head Quartos, 1926, p. 185.

story of a married woman, Avisa, who is unsuccessfully pursued by a number of suitors, including a young man identified as "H.W." He appeals "unto his familiar friend, W.S., who not long before had tried the courtesy of the like passion and was now newly recovered from the like infection." The suspicion that the initials stand for William Shakespeare and Henry Wriothesley is strengthened by this allusion to *The Rape of Lucrece,* which had been published only a few months earlier:

> *Yet Tarquin plucked his glistering grape,*
> *And Shakespeare paints poor Lucrece' rape.*

The use of theatre parlance and an emphasis on differences in age between H.W. and W.S. are evident in this passage: "He would see whether another could play his part better than himself, and in viewing afar off the course of this loving comedy, he [W.S.] determined to see whether it would sort to a happier end for this new actor [H.W.] than it did for the old player [W.S.]." In canto 47, W.S. speaks in near-doggerel verse:

> *She is no saint, she is no nun,*
> *I think in time she may be won.* *

In the end Avisa is not won, but the book seems to glance at the amorous intrigues of a rising poet and his aristocratic young patron, to whom he had just dedicated *The Rape of Lucrece.*

The second, unrelated, gossipy item is the insinuation buried in Thomas Nashe's description of Southampton as "a lover and cherisher . . . . of the *lovers of poets.*" This

---

* The author seems to have been familiar with *Titus Andronicus,* published as a quarto in 1594: "She is a woman, therefore may be wooed, / She is a woman, therefore may be won." (II, i, 83–4.)

appeared in 1593, in the aborted dedication to the first edition of *The Unfortunate Traveller*—which was removed from subsequent printings (see page 204).

The love portrayed in the sonnets is not only complex and paradoxical but betrays its transitory and impermanent character as the story progresses, by reason of the fact that the poet's repeated assurances of eternal devotion apparently meet with little or no response from the young man. (Did our poet find him to be not sufficiently attentive? So the duplicated couplets in sonnets 36 and 96 would seem to indicate.) W. H. Auden's summary of the events in Q is no exaggeration: "The story of an agonized struggle by Shakespeare to preserve the glory of the vision he had been granted in a relationship, lasting three years, with a person who seemed intent by his actions upon covering this vision with dirt." Though the poet acknowledges "the injuries that to myself I do" (88.11), he blames himself rather than the young man for the change in their relations. In sonnet 87 he compares himself to a somnambulist who is awakening from sleep:

The cause of this fair gift [of love] in me is wanting,
And so my patent back again is swerving.
Thyself thou gav'st, thy own worth then not knowing,
Or me to whom thou gav'st it else mistaking,
So thy great gift, upon misprision growing,
Comes home again, on better judgement making.
　　Thus have I had thee as a dream doth flatter:
　　In sleep a King, but waking no such matter.

In the end he resignedly admits (92) that

I see a better state to me belongs
Than that which on thy humour doth depend.

The Sequence of the Sonnets

"Can we assume," Peter Quennell has asked, "that the poet's intention was to compose an autobiographical narrative?" Judging by the table of contents that follows, the answer is certainly not. On the contrary, we must conclude that the author's intention was much simpler: to compose a sonnet-sequence honouring his patron. He apparently felt it his duty to do so; in sonnet 26 he uses the word "duty" three times.

For an overall view of the sonnets as printed in Q, and to help verify the placement and sequence of particular poems, I have grouped them for convenience in twelve arbitrary parts, to each of which I have given obvious labels. *Linked sonnets,* whose frequency may come as a surprise, are indicated by the boxes round their numbers. In footnotes I have tagged individual poems, or clusters of poems, for topical or special reasons.

I THE "MARRIAGE" SONNETS

1   *From fairest creatures we desire increase*
2   *When forty winters shall besiege thy brow*

35

3   *Look in thy glass and tell the face thou viewest*
4   *Unthrifty loveliness why dost thou spend*
5   *Those hours that with gentle work did frame*
6   *Then let not winter's ragged hand deface*
7   *Lo, in the orient when the gracious light*
8   *Music to hear, why hearest thou music sadly?*
9   *Is it for fear to wet a widow's eye*
10   *For shame deny that thou bear'st love to any**
11   *As fast as thou shalt wane, so fast thou growest*
12   *When I do count the clock that tells the Time*
13   *O that you were yourself, but love, you are†*
14   *Not from the stars do I my judgement pluck*
15   *When I consider everything that grows*
16   *But wherefore do not you a mightier way*
17   *Who will believe my verse in time to come*

II FIRST LOVE POEMS

18   *Shall I compare thee to a summer's day?*
19   *Devouring Time, blunt thou the lion's paws*
20   *A woman's face with Nature's own hand painted***
21   *So is it not with me as with that Muse*
22   *My glass shall not persuade me I am old*
23   *As an imperfect actor on the stage*
24   *Mine eye hath played the painter and hath stelled*
25   *Let those who are in favour with their stars*
26   *Lord of my love, to whom in vassalage††*

* The first "I."
† Declaration of love.
** "Master-Mistress" sonnet.
†† *Lucrece* dedication paraphrased.

27	*Weary with toil, I haste me to my bed**
28	*How can I then return in happy plight*

III   "MY OUTCAST STATE"

29	*When in disgrace with Fortune and men's eyes*
30	*When to the sessions of sweet silent thought†*
31	*Thy bosom is endeared with all hearts*
32	*If thou survive my well-contented day*

33	*Full many a glorious morning have I seen***
34	*Why didst thou promise such a beauteous day*
35	*No more be grieved at that which thou hast done*
36	*Let me confess that we two must be twain*
37	*As a decrepit father takes delight*
38	*How can my Muse want subject to invent*
39	*O how thy worth with manners may I sing*

IV   DOUBLE BETRAYAL

40	*Take all my loves, my love, yea take them all††*
41	*Those pretty wrongs that liberty commits*
42	*That thou hast her it is not all my grief*
43	*When most I wink then do mine eyes best see*
44	*If the dull substance of my flesh were thought°*
45	*The other two, slight air and purging fire,*

* "Toil" duo.
† "Death" trio.
** "Guilt" quartet.
†† "Stolen mistress" trio.
° "Elements" duo.

46 *Mine eye and heart are at a mortal war**
47 *Betwixt mine eye and heart a league is took*
48 *How careful was I when I took my way*
49 *Against that time, if ever that time come*
50 *How heavy do I journey on the way†*
51 *Thus can my love excuse the slow offense*
52 *So am I as the rich whose blessèd key***

V   "WHO ARE YOU?" SERIES

53 *What is your substance, whereof are you made*
54 *O how much more doth beauty beauteous seem††*
55 *Not marble nor the gilded monuments*
56 *Sweet love, renew thy force, be it not said*
57 *Being your slave, what should I do but tend°*
58 *That god forbid that made me first your slave*
59 *If there be nothing new but that which is*
60 *Like as the waves make towards the pebbled shore*
61 *Is it thy will, thy image should keep open°°*
62 *Sin of self-love possesseth all mine eye*
63 *Against my love shall be as I am now*
64 *When I have seen by Time's fell hand defaced*
65 *Since brass, nor stone, nor earth, nor boundless sea*
66 *Tired with all these, for restful death I cry*
67 *Ah, wherefore with infection should he live*

* "Eye and heart" duo.
† "Horseback" duo.
** "Carcanet" sonnet.
†† "Scent" sonnet.
° "Patron" duo.
°° "Sleepless" sonnet.

|68| *Thus is his cheek the map of days outworn*
|69| *Those parts of thee that the world's eye doth view*
|70| *That thou art blamed shall not be thy defect**

VI   THE OLDER TO THE YOUNGER

|71| *No longer mourn for me when I am dead*
|72| *O lest the world should task you to recite*

|73| *That time of year thou mayest in me behold*
|74| *But be contented. When that fell arrest*
75 *So are you to my thoughts as food to life†*
76 *Why is my verse so barren of new pride*
77 *Thy glass will show thee how thy beauties wear***

VII   THE RIVAL POETS
(SEE PAGE 184)

|78| *So oft have I invoked thee for my Muse*
|79| *Whilst I alone did call upon thy aid*
|80| *O how I faint when I of you do write*
81 *Or I shall live your epitaph to make*
|82| *I grant thou wert not married to my Muse*
|83| *I never saw that you did painting need*
|84| *Who is it that says most? Which can say more*
|85| *My tongue-tied Muse in manners holds her still*
|86| *Was it the proud full sail of his great verse*

* "These last [days] so bad" quintet.
† "Starved for a look."
** "Schoolmaster" sonnet.

39

VIII   DEPARTURE

87 *Farewell, thou art too dear for my possessing*
88 *When thou shalt be disposed to set me light*
89 *Say that thou didst forsake me for some fault*
90 *Then hate me when thou wilt. If ever, now*

91 *Some glory in their birth, some in their skill**
92 *But do thy worst to steal thyself away*
93 *So shall I live, supposing thou art true*
94 *They that have power to hurt and will do none*
95 *How sweet and lovely dost thou make the shame*
96 *Some say thy fault is youth, some wantonness*

IX   RETURN

97 *How like a winter hath my absence been*
98 *From you have I been absent in the spring*
99 *The forward violet thus did I chide:*
100 *Where art thou, Muse, that thou forget'st so long†*
101 *O truant Muse, what shall be thy amends*
102 *My love is strengthened, though more weak in
     seeming*
103 *Alack, what poverty my Muse brings forth*
104 *To me, fair friend, you never can be old****
105 *Let not my love be called idolatry*
106 *When in the chronicle of wasted time*

* Sextet on faults.
† "Muse" duo.
** "Ay, ay, ay!"

40

107 *Not mine own fears nor the prophetic soul**
108 *What's in the brain that ink may character*

X "VULGAR SCANDAL" (ROBERT GREENE)
QUARTET

109 *O never say that I was false of heart*
110 *Alas, 'tis true I have gone here and there*
111 *O for my sake do you with Fortune chide*
112 *Your love and pity doth the impression fill†*

XI "I AM THAT I AM"

113 *Since I left you, mine eye is in my mind*
114 *Or whether doth my mind, being crowned with you*
115 *Those lines that I before have writ do lie*
116 *Let me not to the marriage of true minds*
117 *Accuse me thus: that I have scanted all*
118 *Like as to make our appetites more keen***
119 *What potions have I drunk of Siren tears*
120 *That you were once unkind befriends me now*
121 *'Tis better to be vile than vile esteemed††*
122 *Thy gift, thy tables, are within my brain*
123 *No, Time, thou shalt not boast that I do change*
124 *If my dear love were but the child of state*
125 *Were it aught to me I bore the canopy*
126 *O thou, my lovely boy, who in thy power* (ENVOI)

* "Mortal Moon" sonnet.
† "O'er-greene" sonnet.
** "Benefit of ill" trio.
†† "Angry" sonnet.

41

XII THE RAVEN-HAIRED MISTRESS
(SEE PAGE 173)

127   *In the old age, black was not counted fair*
128   *How oft when thou, my music, music play'st*
129   *The expense of spirit in a waste of shame**
130   *My Mistress' eyes are nothing like the sun*
131   *Thou art as tyrannous, so as thou art,*
132   *Thine eyes I love and they, as pitying me*
133   *Beshrew that heart that makes my heart to groan*
134   *So now I have confessed that he is thine*

135   *Whoever hath her wish, thou hast thy Will†*
136   *If thy soul check thee that I come so near*
137   *Thou blind fool, Love, what dost thou to mine eyes*
138   *When my love swears that she is made of truth***
139   *O call not me to justify the wrong*
140   *Be wise as thou art cruel, do not press*
141   *In faith I do not love thee with mine eyes*
142   *Love is my sin, and thy dear virtue hate*
143   *Lo, as a careful housewife runs to catch*
144   *Two loves I have, of comfort and despair***
145   *Those lips that Love's own hand did make††*
146   *Poor soul, the centre of my sinful earth*
147   *My love is as a fever, longing still*
148   *O me, what eyes hath Love put in my head*
149   *Canst thou, O cruel, say I love thee not*

* "Lust in action."
† "Will" duo.
** From *The Passionate Pilgrim*.
†† "Hate away" sonnet.

150 *O from what power hast thou this powerful might**
151 *Love is too young to know what conscience is*
152 *In loving thee thou know'st I am forsworn*

THE "BATH" SONNETS
(SEE PAGE 182)

153 *Cupid laid by his brand and fell asleep*
154 *The little Love-god lying once asleep*

"A LOVER'S COMPLAINT"
(SEE PAGE 210)

In carrying out the self-imposed task of a steady production of sonnets, without intending to compose an autobiographical narrative, our poet inevitably on occasion writes about himself. Such a sonnet—and it is one of the best—is 29:

When in disgrace with Fortune and men's eyes,
I all alone beweep my outcast state,
And trouble deaf heaven with my bootless cries,
And look upon myself and curse my fate,
Wishing me like to one more rich in hope,
Featured like him, like him with friends possessed,
Desiring this man's art and that man's scope,
With what I most enjoy contented least;

* "Gross" sonnets.

43

Yet in these thoughts myself almost despising,
Haply I think on thee . . .

While it is not untrue to say, as one critic does,[38] that the "Christian distinction between material and spiritual well-being functions as a hyperbolic metaphor" in this sonnet, how remote this seems from the sonnet's real essence. If Wordsworth's lines "With this key / Shakespeare unlocked his heart" apply to any of the sonnets (and they apply only to a few), they surely apply to this *cri du coeur.* Shakespeare even confesses that he wishes he were better looking ("Featured like him"). He considers his state in life, as playwright and actor, "outcast." He curses fate for the role it has assigned him; he is least contented with the gifts he most possesses; he envies another's art and desires another's scope; he sees himself "in disgrace" under "men's eyes"; he almost despises himself. Is all this a mere "metaphor" invented to justify the sonnet's resolution? Only a cynic who rejects the possibility of poetic sincerity could believe that.

 George Kittredge, who subscribed to the antibiographical fallacy, put the case this way: "A sonnet must either be patently artificial (and then it is bad) or good (and then it sounds like autobiography). There is no escape: a good sonnet appears to be a confession." Perhaps for a good reason: it may in fact be one. The sonnet's strength and credibility may derive from this reality: it *rings true.* Kittredge points out that the soliloquies of Hamlet, Macbeth, and even Iago are "sincere," and he goes on to ask: "What warrant have we for assuming other than a dramatic sincerity in the sonnets?"[39] We have an excellent warrant, the form the poet has chosen to use. Professor

Kittredge confuses two different media, as if dramatic representation and a lyric poem are similar or comparable means of expression. C. J. Sisson, as we shall discuss, commits the same mistake; his sound strictures against misinterpreting Shakespeare the playwright are wrongly applied to Shakespeare the sonneteer.

The writing of poems is an art and artifice, and their production in the quantity required for a sonnet-sequence is a test of the poet's ability to find original themes and fresh figures and metaphors. In Q our poet ranges from such grand themes as Immortality and Time to as homely an image as a housewife running after a chicken (143). Ordinary occupations like travelling in the rain (34), riding his horse (50–51), experiencing sleepless nights (27), and unusual ones like performing (or imagining himself in) the role of canopy-bearer at a public ceremony (125) provide imagery and thematic material, even as do the law, astronomy, the four elements, botany, architecture, medicine, the social order, and so on. The one indispensable book on this aspect of the sonnets is Blair Leishman's brilliant study of Shakespeare's themes; it explores thematic parallels with and affinities to those used by Horace, Ovid, Petrarch, Tasso, Ronsard, Sidney, Spenser, Daniel, Drayton, and others. He shows, for example, that in developing a theme already touched on in sonnets 15 and 16, Shakespeare in 19 uses a phrase, "Devouring Time," which was "almost certainly suggested" by Ovid's *"Tempus edax rerum"* in *Metamorphoses,* XV, 234. Leishman's critical superiority is proved for me not by his erudition, which is impressive, but when he ranks the autobiographical sonnet 29 among Shakespeare's "very finest."[40]

45

In calculating that the sonnets average out, over three years, to one a week, I am not suggesting that this was in fact Shakespeare's rate of composition. All writers know that creation is sporadic, and inspiration erratic. One of the few things we know about Shakespeare (from his fellows) is that he wrote rapidly. My guess is that the linked sonnets were probably written at single sittings, or within relatively short periods of time, but we cannot *know*. When our poet mentions an unproductive period of silence, as in 83, it seems to be accompanied by feelings of guilt:

> *This silence for my sin you did impute,*
> *Which shall be most my glory, being dumb,*
> *For I impair not beauty, being mute* . . .

Poets were *expected* to produce poems regularly. This was another convention of the Petrarchan tradition, and a good reason for doubting that Q's term of composition went very much beyond the three years alluded to in sonnet 104.

The Antibiographical Fallacy

In fact, I sometimes think only autobiography is literature.
VIRGINIA WOOLF

While it is true that there are numerous parallels in other Renaissance poems—Italian, French, and English—to the attitudes and language of many of the sonnets in Q, it is also true that a poet, even while borrowing poetic conventions, can be sincere. It was a Renaissance convention that every poet had to have a patron, a relationship that is defined in the work of the Italian poet Giovanni della Casa (1503–56) as very one-sided: the poet must submit to the insults and moods of the patron; he must demean himself, praising the other's virtues, overlooking his faults, and so on.[41] Shakespeare, in Q, follows this convention exactly: he acknowledges his duty to the patron, refers to his "vassalage," and to himself as "servant" and "slave," endures the patron's variable moods ("That you were once unkind . . ."), admits his own failings and unworthiness, and converts his patron's sins into graces.

One of the proofs that the sonnets were written early in Shakespeare's career is their display of vulnerability, as in the series on the rival poets. If Shakespeare had been absolutely sure of his position, it is unlikely that sonnets 78–86 would have been written. The poet of the sonnets is not the established writer, the man who became, in Auden's phrase, our Top Bard. Rather, it is Shakespeare at the beginning of his professional life in London, as a writer and actor. Players were classified by law as vagabonds if they lacked the protection of a nobleman. The statute of 1572 defined the vulnerable professions as "all fencers, bear-wardens, common players . . . All jugglers, peddlers, tinkers, petty chapmen [and] common players . . . shall be deemed rogues, vagabonds, and sturdy beggars." In a later statute, the initial punishment was that the culprit be "stripped naked from the middle upwards and shall be openly whipped until his or her body be bloody." The penalty, after three convictions, was death.

Nor was Shakespeare a university man, with a degree to classify him as a gentleman, nor did the university men active in the theatre let him forget it, especially Robert Greene, Master of Arts. It was inevitable that Shakespeare, after he had become a shareholder in his acting company in 1594 and had attained financial security, should have used the only means available to him of erasing the "brand" (his own word) of player, by re-applying through his father successfully for a grant of arms. He still had to suffer the derision of Ben Jonson (honorary M.A. from both universities), who in *Every Man Out of His Humour* ridiculed Shakespeare's motto, *"Non sanz droit,"* as "Not without mustard."*

The sonnets that contain the most deeply felt statements of self-reproach are concerned with acting and the theatre:

Alas, 'tis true I have gone here and there,
And made myself a motley to the view,
Gored mine own thoughts, sold cheap what is most
    dear . . .   (110)

The guilty goddess [Fortune] of my harmful deeds
That did not better for my life provide
Than public means which public manners breeds.
Thence comes it that my name receives a brand . . .
                                       (111)

* *Sogliardo:* "In faith, I thank God I can write myself gentleman now. Here's my patent, it cost me thirty pound by this breath." *Puntarvalo:* "Let the word be, 'Not without mustard.' Your crest is very rare, sir." (EOH, III, i, 201–47, first acted in 1599 with Shakespeare not in the cast.)

and these are followed by an extremely interesting and grateful sonnet (112) to his patron:

> *Your love and pity doth the impression fill*
> *Which vulgar scandal stamped upon my brow,*
> *For what care I who calls me well or ill,*
> *So you o'er-greene my bad, my good allow?*
> *You are my all-the-world, and I must strive*
> *To know my shames and praises from your tongue,*
> *None else to me, nor I to none alive,*
> *That my steelèd sense or changes right or wrong.*
> *In so profound abysm I throw all care*
> *Of others' voices that my adder's sense*
> *To critic and to flatterer stoppèd are:*
> *Mark how with my neglect I do dispense.*
> > *You are so strongly in my purpose bred*
> > *That all the world besides, methinks, are dead.*

A perceptive scholar, Edgar I. Fripp, suggested in 1938 that this sonnet was written in 1592.[42] Fripp concluded that the otherwise unused word, "o'er-greene," alluded to Robert Greene's attack on Shakespeare as "an upstart crow" who "is in his own conceit the only Shake-scene in a country." This scandal and insult (one of the first allusions in print to Shakespeare) were apologized for, several months later, by the publisher (and later playwright) Henry Chettle. Chettle had printed Greene's attack, and Greene was now dead. Shakespeare and others (including perhaps his patron) had complained to the publisher, who hastened to make honourable amends in a quickly published pamphlet, *Kind-Heart's Dream*. In the preface Chettle calls Shakespeare's demeanour "civil," describes him as "excellent in the quality he professes" (acting), and reveals that "divers of worship" (gentlemen or noblemen) have "reported his [Shakespeare's] uprightness of dealing, which argues his honesty, and his facetious [polished] grace in writing. . . ." An unusual, detailed, and generous apology. Sonnet 112 seems to be the work of a youngish poet in its admission that something in him *is* bad—in 1592 Shakespeare was twenty-eight—and in its carefree posture and pretence that he doesn't mind what he is called so long as his patron supports him. The fact is, he minded enough to remonstrate with Chettle.

Those who interpret literally Shakespeare's references in Q to his "tanned antiquity," and other self-proclaimed signs of aging, as evidence that he was old when he wrote the sonnets forget that the pretence of premature aging was another convention inherited from the Petrarchan tradition.

I consider that all the sonnets, save one,* belong to the early 1590s, when Shakespeare was still in his twenties (he turned thirty in April 1594). It was a time, as Colette said in one of her greatest remarks,[43] when "Shakespeare worked without knowing that he would become Shakespeare."

Certain critics rule out biographical considerations altogether, and insist on viewing the sonnets solely as literary efforts. Stephen Booth's edition of the sonnets (1977) belongs to this severe school. His book of 578 pages, containing subtle and erudite readings of many of the sonnets, reduces the perplexing question of pederasty to two humorous sentences: "HOMOSEXUALITY. William

* See page 191.

Shakespeare was almost certainly homosexual, bisexual, or heterosexual. The sonnets provide no evidence on the matter."[44] The author then refers the reader to a note, in which he says, reproachfully, "Most commentators have been concerned with finding out what Shakespeare was talking about, what the occasion of the sonnets was, rather than with the literary experience the poems evoke in us and/or evoked in a Renaissance reader."[45]

Finding out what a Renaissance reader felt—assuming it to be possible—is by such a standard more desirable than finding out what Shakespeare was talking about. The absurd limitations of this approach were wittily exposed by John Berryman: "One thing critics not themselves writers of poetry occasionally forget is that poetry is composed by actual human beings, and tracts of it are very closely about them. When Shakespeare wrote, 'Two loves I have,' reader, he was *not kidding.*"[46] E. K. Chambers admitted that he was more "inclined to look upon the unity of Shakespeare's sonnets, written over three or more years, *as an autobiographical one,* following the ups and downs of an emotional relationship, than as a planned attempt to develop a preconceived dramatic design."

Kenneth Muir, author of an excellent and recently published study, *Shakespeare's Sonnets* (1979), disarmingly admits reversing the biographical position he had taken in an earlier book.[47] It is curious that, after abjuring the biographical approach, Muir invariably refers to the young man of the sonnets as "Mr. W.H." Shakespeare never used this designation in his poems; it is an interpolation by Thomas Thorpe, the publisher, in his cryptic dedication "To the only begetter." We can only guess whom he meant by "Mr. W.H."; Thorpe may even have been mistaken. Since these initials were not written by the poet, isn't it improper and incorrect to employ them for the young man? Muir now argues that "even though there were probably events in Shakespeare's life which resembled in some respects those treated in the Sonnets, we cannot assume that any of the poems records an actual event." If this attitude is commendable, it is equally commendable to maintain that we cannot therefore assume the opposite—that no poem in Q records an actual event. The truth is that we cannot assume anything. To eschew the biographical approach in favour of the antibiographical, in the hope of obtaining a purer or more accurate literary understanding of the sonnets, is an illusion.

No one can deny the truth of Northrop Frye's contention that the "experience of love and the writing of love poetry do not necessarily have any direct connection."[48] Yet to say they have no *necessary* connection does not mean that it is impossible for them to have a connection. To maintain that poems, a product of the prosodic gifts, imagination, and verbal resources of an author (craftsmanship), cannot have any connection with actual events in his life (biography) is as fallacious as maintaining that they must have a connection.

One of the best statements on the dangers and pitfalls of biographical interpretation is C. J. Sisson's "The Mythical Sorrows of Shakespeare." After pointing out the error of confusing what Shakespeare "felt" with the emotions of the characters in his plays, Sisson dissects four major fallacies—that "dramatists write tragedies when their mood is tragic, and comedies when they are feeling pleased with life"; that "the actual evolution of Shakespeare's life must be read into his poetic and dramatic work"; that "Shakespeare was so far a child of his own age that he faithfully reflected its spirit in his literary work"; and finally, that the spirit of his age was "heroic and optimistic under Queen Elizabeth" and after the Essex troubles devolved "into disillusionment and pessimism" under James I. Sisson is scathing in his attack on "the precarious heights of intuitive certainty, from which there is no appeal." Yet within the lecture he makes his own biographical deduction concerning *Titus Andronicus,* the early Senecan play long denied a secure place in the canon by critics who considered it a collaborative work, unworthy of Shakespeare. Sisson states:

> *Titus Andronicus* is a vastly important play. . . . It really is proof that the player Shakespeare was already setting up claims to be considered as a poet-dramatist, essaying the Senecan manner that Sidney prescribed. This is no private discovery. Shakespeare was widely enough known before 1600 as a poet of promise and achievement, in his printed poems, in his stage-plays, and in his sonnets circulated among his friends in manuscript. His career, seen as a whole, and in its true light, is as much the career of a poet and artist as that of a purveyor for the stage.[49]

This is legitimate biographical interpretation, proof that the second of Sisson's four fallacies requires a slight emendation by his own reasoning—i.e., the actual evolution of Shakespeare's life can (not "must") be read into his work, but only when real *evidence* points to it.

In rightly condemning "imaginative biography," it is unfortunate that Sisson fails to make distinctions between the diverse nature of work like the plays and narrative poems and that of the short lyrics or sonnets. For example, he ridicules Arthur von Schlegel, the brother of Friedrich, for asserting in 1792 that Shakespeare's sonnets "describe quite obviously real situations and moods of the poet," and especially "the shame of his life as a player." It is certainly unwarranted to assume that Shakespeare was disgusted with life because Hamlet was so disgusted; here Sisson is on solid ground. But when Shakespeare uses a sonnet to tell us that "my name receives a brand" because Fortune "did not better for my life provide / Than public means which public manners breeds" (sonnet 111), is it unwarranted to conclude that at this moment in his life he is ashamed of his profession? Only if you believe that poets absolutely never write sonnets about themselves. Adherence to such an absurd belief constitutes the antibiographical fallacy.

"I am not maintaining that Shakespeare's mistress—*if he had one*—did not seduce his friend."[50] This is one of Kenneth Muir's statements, and the italics are mine. Would a critic be likely to write such a sentence about the poems of Catullus, to question whether in fact the poet had a mistress? He might question whether Lesbia was in fact her name, or Clodia, or whether her identity can be determined, but the poems of Catullus convince the reader that Lesbia-Clodia-Mistress is not fictitious. Shakespeare's poems have convinced me that he had a mistress, and that she had dark eyes and black hair. I do not know whether in life she was Emilia Bassano Lanier (nor does A. L. Rowse prove she was; see page 179), or Lucy Negro née Lucy Morgan, as Anthony Burgess and others suggest. Her identity really makes very little difference to our knowledge of most of the poems. The identity of the young man is quite another matter, because, if it can be determined, it would throw great light on the date of the poems' composition, on puzzling textual questions, and on matters of poetic sincerity and truth, and would thus increase enormously our understanding and appreciation of the sonnets.

One of the arguments of this book is that the young man is, as many have long thought, Henry Wriothesley, the third Earl of Southampton. Having concluded that the sonnets are early work, I did not on that account accept the corollary that the young man in the poems is therefore Southampton. I have reached this conclusion on the soundest basis possible—the evidence Shakespeare himself provides. I happen to wish the identity of the young man were different. In the sense that I do not find Southampton likable, I am not a Southamptonite. Several of his contemporaries, including the Queen, the dowager Countess of Southampton ("My son never was kind to me"), and Lady Bridget Manners, had negative opinions of him in his own time. I find him coldhearted, selfish, spoiled, and, as sonnet 94 states, one of those

> *Who, moving others, are themselves as stone,*
> *Unmovèd, cold . . .*

But it matters greatly to our understanding of the sonnets that Shakespeare was a Southamptonite, as the next pages demonstrate.

THE PATRON

The warrant I have of your honourable disposition . . .
SHAKESPEARE TO SOUTHAMPTON, 1594

Two Letters and One Sonnet

SHAKESPEARE left proof that he was a Southamptonite in two letters and in sonnet 26, a poetic paraphrase of the second letter.

On the occasion of the tercentenary celebration of the First Folio in 1923, at a service in the church of St. Mary Aldermanbury (the London parish of John Heminge and Henry Condell, the Folio overseers), the Archbishop of Canterbury stated: "There exists no single letter of Shakespeare's, not one recorded conversation, no character of him drawn with any fullness by a contemporary."[1] This expresses a widely held view, and one that is two-thirds accurate, but what the prelate says about the nonexistence of letters happens not to be true. There exist two letters written and signed by Shakespeare, and every student of the poet has read them. He published them fairly early in his career, as dedications to *Venus and Adonis* and *The Rape of Lucrece.* They have been widely reproduced, but because they are so familiar as dedications, their character as letters has been forgotten or ignored. Yet letters they are, in a literal and formal sense—with addresses, a salutation ("Right Honourable"), main texts, closings ("Your

59

Lordship's in all duty" and "Your Honour's in all duty");
and with the writer's full signature at the end (only the
final page of Shakespeare's will, of the handful of extant
documents, contains this kind of signature). In addition,
the letters can be dated with reasonably close accuracy at
18 April 1593 and 9 May 1594, the dates on which the
books in which they appear were registered.

The importance of these letters cannot be exaggerated.
They are the double foundations on which our knowledge
rests that Shakespeare had a patron, that the patron was
the third Earl of Southampton, and that the period of his
patronage was the early 1590s. Amidst the flood of con-
tradictory and confusing theories, it is reassuring to have
their Gibraltar-like solidity. Despite this knowledge,
Stephen Booth recently wrote: "The 'evidence' for Southampton includes . . . Shakespeare's dedication of *Venus
and Adonis* and *Lucrece* to him."[2] The inverted commas
are intended to denigrate the dedications as evidence. If
the poet's own letters are not evidence, the word evidence
has no meaning.*

The word "duty," which Shakespeare uses six times—
thrice in the letters and thrice in sonnet 26—provides
additional proof of the author-patron relationship. This
word appears, for instance, in John Stowe's dedication to
the Earl of Leicester of his *Summary English Chronicles*
(1565): "I . . . offer to your honour this my simple
work, in token *of my bounden duty.*" To the same patron,
John Florio dedicates *First Fruits* (1578): "I give them

---

* In fairness, Stephen Booth also even-handedly listed the First Folio
dedication by Shakespeare's fellows as "evidence" (in inverted commas)
for Pembroke. But two letters written and signed by Shakespeare belong
to a different order of evidence than a bid for financial help written by
others.

to you as a token of the zealous affection and *dutiful love* I bear unto your honour." Florio in another dedication (*Second Fruits,* 1591) writes: "I could not find my employment more agreeable to my power, or better seeming *my duty,* than this. . . ." In his letter of 1593, the word "duty" comes just before Shakespeare's signature:

> *To the Right Honourable Henry Wriothesley,*
> *Earl of Southampton, and Baron of Titchfield.*

RIGHT HONOURABLE,

I know not how I shall offend in dedicating my unpolished lines to your lordship, nor how the world will censure me for choosing so strong a prop to support so weak a burden. Only if your honour seem but pleased, I account myself highly praised, and vow to take advantage of all idle hours, till I have honoured you with some graver labour. But if the first heir of my invention prove deformed, I shall be sorry it had so noble a godfather: and never after ear so barren a land for fear it yield me still so bad a harvest. I leave it to your honourable survey, and your honour to your heart's content, which I wish may always answer your own wish, and the world's hopeful expectation.

> *Your honour's in all duty,*
> WILLIAM SHAKESPEARE.

In the second and shorter letter the word "duty" appears twice, in the penultimate sentence and again just before the signature. There is no salutation, almost as though it might delay the utterance of the bold noun which opens the letter.

TO THE RIGHT
HONOVRABLE, HENRY
VVriothesley, Earle of Southhampton,
and Baron of Titchfield.

HE loue I dedicate to your Lordship is without end: wherof this Pamphlet without beginning is but a superfluous Moity. The warrant I haue of your Honourable disposition, not the worth of my vntutord Lines makes it assured of acceptance. VVhat I haue done is yours, what I haue to doe is yours, being part in all I haue, deuoted yours. VVere my worth greater, my duety would shew greater, meane time, as it is, it is bound to your Lordship; To whom I wish long life still lengthned with all happinesse.

Your Lordships in all duety.

William Shakespeare.

26

Lord of my loue, to whome in vassalage
Thy merrit hath my dutie strongly knit;
To thee I send this written ambassage
To witnesse duty, not to shew my wit.
Duty so great, which wit so poore as mine
May make seeme bare, in wanting words to shew it;
But that I hope some good conceipt of thine
In thy soules thought (all naked) will bestow it:
Til whatsoeuer star that guides my mouing,
Points on me gratiously with faire aspect,
And puts apparrell on my tottered louing,
To show me worthy of their sweet respect,
　　Then may I dare to boast how I doe loue thee,
　　Til then, not show my head where thou maist proue me

The letter (1594) and the sonnet (26) compared

To the Right Honourable, Henry Wriothesley,
Earl of Southampton and Baron of Titchfield.

The love I dedicate to your Lordship is without end, whereof this pamphlet without beginning is but a superfluous moiety. The warrant I have of your honourable disposition, not the worth of my un-tutored lines, makes it assured of acceptance. What I have done is yours, what I have to do is yours, being part in all I have devoted yours. Were my worth greater, my duty would show greater. Mean-time, as it is, it is bound to your lordship, to whom I wish long life still lengthened with all happiness.

> *Your lordship's in all duty,*
> WILLIAM SHAKESPEARE.

"Between the dedications there is a significant contrast," writes Peter Quennell, adding that Shakespeare is "no longer modest and tentative, and adopts the tone of a de-voted friend." It is the use of the word "love" that makes all the difference.

The final link in the chain that binds the sonnets and the dedications is sonnet 26, in which "duty" also appears three times:

Lord of my love, to whom in vassalage
Thy merit hath my duty *strongly knit,*
To thee I send this written ambassage,
To witness duty, *not to show my wit.*
Duty *so great, which wit so poor as mine*
May make seem bare, in wanting words to show it,
But that I hope some good conceit of thine
In thy soul's thought, all naked, will bestow it;

Till whatsoever star that guides my moving
Points on me graciously with fair aspect,
And puts apparel on my tattered loving
To show me worthy of thy sweet respect.
   Then may I dare to boast how I do love thee:
   Till then not show my head where thou mayst prove me.

Note "The love I dedicate to your Lordship" as compared to "Lord of my love"; "my untutored lines" and "wit so poor as mine"; "were my worth greater" and "worthy of thy sweet respect"; the double use of "duty" in the dedication and its triple use in the poem. Sonnet 26 is a private and more personal expression of what the dedication of 1594 states in equally explicit words: "The love I dedicate to your lordship is without end. . . . What I have done is yours, what I have to do is yours." No other dedication in Elizabethan literature equals these simple, sincere, dignified, and convincing words. What was the man like to whom they were addressed?

Southampton's Lives

In examining Southampton's fifty-one years, one sees that in a sense he had two distinct lives. The first began with his birth on 6 October 1573, and appeared to have ended when he was condemned to death, went to the Tower to await execution, and was confined there for two long years and four months, until his second and happier life began.

He was twenty-seven when he received the death sentence for high treason, together with the Earl of Essex, on 19 February 1601. On that day they were led to the Tower, preceded by axe-blades pointed towards them, signifying death. Six days later, Essex was beheaded. The night before the execution, Shakespeare and his fellows, the Chamberlain's Men, were required to enact a play before the Queen at Whitehall. The title of the play is not on record, nor of course the cast. One month later, "as late as March 25th, spectators came to Tower Hill," according to G. P. V. Akrigg, the best biographer of the Earl, "drawn by a rumour that Southampton was to be executed there that day."[3] The spectators were disappointed. The fact that Southampton's life was spared was probably due to the efforts of his friend Sir Robert Cecil, the Queen's Principal Secretary. Southampton had cleared Cecil of the dangerous charge, recklessly made by Essex at their trial, that in the presence of both earls Cecil had uttered treason by asserting that the Spanish Infanta had a right to succeed Elizabeth on the throne of England.

Southampton's sentence was commuted to life imprisonment and he was attainted, losing his earldom and his estates and becoming plain Henry Wriothesley (pronounced Rizley). The aging Queen's decline in health after the death of Essex, and her growing melancholy, were remarked by everyone. Each day that passed in the Tower raised Southampton's hopes. In great secrecy Cecil, meantime, was doing all he could to ensure a peaceful transition to James of Scotland, who in this period wrote a letter expressing his concern for "poor Southampton,

who lives in hardest case."⁴ But after two years Elizabeth
still held on, while "thick and palpable clouds of darkness
. . . overshadowed this land," in the words of the translators of the King James Bible, so that it could "hardly be
known who was to direct the unsettled state."⁵

The young ex-Earl's "confined doom" lasted four
months longer. The Queen's death on 24 March 1603
finally ensured his return to the living: during this long
period in prison, official documents called him "the late
Earl." He later commissioned an artist (apparently John
de Critz) to paint him as he was in the Tower, with
the dates of his incarceration and release under the motto
In vinculis invictus (unconquered, though in chains). In
April, when the royal pardon of James I freed him from
the Tower, his second life (which was to last twenty-one
years) may be said to have begun. On his release Southampton was twenty-nine, some seven months short of his
thirtieth birthday. (This is roughly parallel to Shakespeare's age when, almost ten years earlier, he had completed the series of sonnets addressed to Southampton;
and six years were yet to pass before Thorpe published the
poems as Q.)

Southampton was one of the chief beneficiaries of
Elizabeth's death; the new King granted him a series of
generous favours: his earldom was restored at his original
date of precedence; he was installed as a Knight of the
Garter, an honour Elizabeth had always denied him; he
was appointed Captain of the Isle of Wight; and he was
rehabilitated financially by a grant of the monopoly of
sweet wines, which had been a chief source of Essex's
wealth. The King soon appointed him to the Privy Council, and after the peace with Spain, he became a grandee.

Several poets, including Samuel Daniel and John Davies of Hereford, wrote of Southampton's restoration in their verses, and not the smallest honour the Earl received was the "Mortal Moon" poem we know as sonnet 107 (see page 191). In a royal warrant dated 17 May 1603, Shakespeare, Burbage, Heminge, Condell, and their fellow-players—together with Lawrence Fletcher, apparently a Scots actor—were named actor-servants of James I, and their company was henceforth known as the King's Men. Southampton probably had a hand in the players' elevation to the status of royal servants and Grooms of the Chamber, with their red liveries.* They were also much more in demand; in the last four years of Elizabeth's reign they had performed at court only fourteen times, as against forty-one times in the first four years under James I.

Boy in Armour

A look at Southampton's origins and early career helps to shed light on the poet-patron relationship, since it is Southampton's youthful years that form the main background of the sonnets in Q. The earldom that Southampton inherited in 1581 had its beginnings in the reign of Henry VIII, when Thomas Wriothesley, his grand-

---

* Four yards of red cloth were issued by the Master of the Great Wardrobe so that they could join the King's procession through London on 15 March 1604.

father, rose rapidly among the Tudor *arrivistes*. Educated at Cambridge and later at Gray's Inn, Wriothesley shrewdly put himself forward as a protégé of Thomas Cromwell and developed into one of the most efficient, ruthless, and loathed politicians of the day. After the Reformation, he made his fortune by assisting Cromwell in the spoliation of the English monasteries. In 1538 he and his men entered Winchester Cathedral at three o'clock in the morning and demolished the shrine of St. Swithin. He also looted and destroyed nearby Hyde Abbey, after he had been given a sixty-eight-year lease to the land. He levelled the abbey, obliterating the tomb of Alfred the Great, and sold the carvings, tiles, and other stonework for a profit. In the wake of Cromwell's downfall and beheading in 1540, the new knight, Sir Thomas, became one of the King's two Secretaries of State, and joined the Privy Council with a warrant to keep forty gentlemen and yeomen with his livery. Four years later, he was created Baron of Titchfield. After serving as Keeper of the Seal, he was promoted in the spring of 1544 to the full dignity of Lord Chancellor. In 1545 he was made a Knight of the Garter, and in 1547 he wept as he reported the death of Henry VIII to Parliament. He then became an earl under suspicious circumstances: at the coronation of Edward VI, the governors of the boy King announced that Henry on his death-bed had confided to Secretary Paget a list of new promotions in the peerage, one of which created Thomas Wriothesley the first Earl of Southampton, with estates to finance his new status. Three years later the earl died, leaving a son and five daughters.

The widowed Countess of Southampton, who was a

devout Catholic, raised Henry, the second earl, still a minor, in the old faith under Queen Mary. Several years after Elizabeth I's accession, when the earl was nineteen, the Queen demanded his presence at court. He complied, but remained loyal to the old religion. Titchfield became a Catholic center and an asylum for recusants. In 1565 he married Mary Browne, the thirteen-year-old daughter of Viscount Montague of Cowdray. In 1571 the conspiracy that was created by the plans of the Duke of Norfolk, the premier peer of England and a Catholic, to marry Mary of Scotland put many recusants, including the second Earl of Southampton, under the shadow of treason. In October of that year, he was packed off to the Tower, from which he was not released until May 1573, a year after Norfolk's execution. The third Earl of Southampton, Shakespeare's patron, was apparently conceived in the Tower, since he was born at Cowdray on 6 October 1573.

Shakespeare's third sonnet says of Southampton,

> *Thou art thy mother's glass, and she in thee*
> *Calls back the lovely April of her prime.*

Their mirror-images become apparent by setting her wedding portrait beside the Hilliard miniature of her son in youth (pages 70–1). History provides our first glimpse of him in 1580 as a child of six, during a sad domestic crisis, when his mother and father were estranged and she used the boy as a go-between. Her husband had accused her of intimacy with "a common person," one of their servants, which she vehemently denied in a letter to her father, protesting her total innocence: "That your lordship shall be witness of my desire to win my lord [her husband] by all such means as resteth in me, I have sent you what I

Mother: the Countess of Southampton at the time of her marriage

Son: the third Earl of Southampton at 20

sent him by my little boy. But his heart was too great to
bestow the reading of it, coming from me. . . . . But good
my lord, procure so soon as conveniently you may some
end to my misery, for I am tired with this life." Not only
did her letter go unread by her husband, but little Lord
Harry was retained by him and not allowed to see his
mother again while the father lived. Nineteen months
later, on 4 October 1581, two days before the son reached
the age of eight, the father died and Henry Wriothesley
became the third Earl of Southampton.

A marble statue of him as a child, dressed in a suit
of armour, adorns the Southampton tomb at Titchfield
Church; he kneels on a cushion at a prie-dieu with his
hands in prayer, facing his mother in the same pose; because the sculptor has them filling equal heights, he appears, at eight, to be as tall as she. This sculpture was reproduced for the first time in the pioneer biography of
Southampton by Charlotte Carmichael Stopes.[6]

As a minor and an important child of state, the new
Earl came under the protection and direction of William
Cecil, Lord Burghley, Master of the Wards and Lord
Treasurer of England, the most powerful person in the
realm next to Queen Elizabeth. It was considered crucial
that the new Earl be weaned away from Catholic influ-
ences at Titchfield, and he was sent to live in London under Burghley's eye at Cecil House, on the north side of
the Strand. There he and several other noble wards followed a strict daily curriculum. Another ward was Robert
Devereux, who had preceded Southampton under Burghley's care by five years, having become the second Earl
of Essex at age ten. Seven years older than Southampton,
Essex completed his studies at Cambridge in 1581. By

1585, when at nineteen he accompanied his stepfather, the Earl of Leicester, on the campaign in the Low Countries and distinguished himself at Zutphen, he had become the boy's idol. Southampton's choice of Essex as his closest friend, who later, in a literal, military sense, became his general, meant that Essex also became his fate. After Leicester's death in 1588, Essex began to take his place at court as the Queen's favourite.

In 1585, Southampton at age twelve was himself ready to enter St. John's College, Cambridge. Extant from this period are two Latin essays in his boyish hand, one of which declares that every man "burns with a boundless lust for fame."[7] Late in 1587 a spectacular new play was put on by the Admiral's Men. Its language marked a significant new advance in verse for the theatre, and possessed a more stirring quality than anything hitherto heard on the London stage:

> *Our souls, whose faculties can comprehend*
> *The wondrous architecture of the world*
> *And measure every wandering planet's course,*
> *Still climbing after knowledge infinite*
> *And always moving as the restless spheres,*
> *Will us to wear ourselves and never rest*
> *Until we reach the ripest fruit of all,*
> *That perfect bliss and sole felicity,*
> *The sweet fruition of an earthly crown.*

The blank verse of Christopher Marlowe's *Tamburlaine the Great* had a powerful effect on the young countryman from Stratford, who at twenty-three may have been an apprentice actor during these "lost years." Whether the young Earl was allowed to see Marlowe's play we do not

73

know, but he probably knew that its author had recently left Cambridge (M.A., July 1587). The decisive victory over the Spanish Armada the following summer, a turning point in England's history, doubtless made the fourteen-year-old Earl regret that he was too young to don armour seriously and join the fight. (He was not too young in 1588 for Burghley to have him admitted to Gray's Inn, as his grandfather had been.) The great naval victory inspired renewed interest in the writing and acting of plays dealing with history: Shakespeare's first play on record, listed by Henslowe as *Harry the Sixth*, opened in March 1592.

On 6 June 1589 Southampton took his M.A. at Cambridge after a public oral. In October Burghley noted in his diary, "Southampton erat aetatis 16 annorum."[8] The young Earl, at sixteen, was approaching marriageable years, and already Burghley had a prospective wife waiting in the wings to whom he considered Southampton to be engaged. She was his granddaughter, the Lady Elizabeth Vere, age fifteen, daughter of the Earl of Oxford.

The Marriage Crisis

When in the summer of 1590 Burghley heard rumours of other marriage plans for his ward, he was incensed and the Southamptons became alarmed. The first sign of trouble turns up in the letter that Sir Thomas Stanhope, a friend of the Countess, wrote to Burghley in July. Stanhope was anxious to scotch the rumour that "I sought to have the Earl of Southampton in marriage to my daughter," and after denying this unequivocally, he describes the situation in the Southampton household as he sees it. The date is 15 July 1590:

> And my lord, I confess that talking with the Countess of Southampton thereof she told me you had spoken to her in that behalf. I replied she should do well to take hold of it, for I knew not where my lord her son should be better bestowed. Herself could tell what a stay you would be to him and his . . . She answered I said well, and so she thought, and would in good faith do her best in the cause, "but," saith she, "I do not find a disposition in my son to be tied as yet. What will be hereafter, time shall try and no want shall be found on my behalf."[9]

Burghley apparently could not understand why any normal young man would refuse such an eligible and advantageous match as one with his grandchild. He did not realize that this young man had no wish to marry anyone as yet. Burghley then consulted with the youth's maternal grandfather. Viscount Montague reported to the Lord Treasurer on 19 September 1590, after the boy and his mother had visited him at Cowdray: "First, my daughter affirms upon her faith and honour that she is not acquainted with any alteration of her son's mind from this your grandchild. And we have laid abroad unto him both the commodities and hindrances likely to grow unto him by change. . . . To our particular speech [we received] this general answer, that your lordship was this last winter well pleased to yield unto him a further respite of one year, to ensure resolution in respect of his young years."[10] Old Montague ended by assuring Burghley that he had warned his grandson the year was almost up, but the young Earl "was content that I should impart the same to your lordship."

From a youth of seventeen, such resolution against parental and court pressures is impressive. Burghley, as Master of the Wards, had a powerful weapon in the statute governing marriages of the Queen's wards: "If an heir, of what age soever he be, will not marry at the request of his lord, he shall not be compelled thereunto; but when he cometh to full age he shall give to his lord and shall pay him as much as any would have given for the marriage."[11] The Southamptons, Montagues, and their kin were aware that, in case of default, it was Burghley who would decide the amount of the fine. The animus of the powerful Lord Treasurer must have been unsettling.

During the period of his wardship, which would end only when he came of age in October 1594, Southampton was wholly dependent on Burghley for funds for the up-keep and maintenance of his property. This carefully worded but somewhat frantic letter to Burghley's secretary, Michael Hicks, pleading with him to use his influence with the Lord Treasurer, throws light on the young Earl's situation:

> Mr. Hicks, Whereas I am given to understand that my manor house at Beaulieu, with divers parcels of my inheritance there, are like to fall in great decay and danger to be lost through want of means to supply the charge of the reparations during my wardship, I would heartily request you to move my Lord Treas-

urer, according to the note I do send, to yield me his honourable favour in taking such course as shall seem best unto his wisdom whereby the said charges and reparations may be supplied. In doing whereof I shall rest most bound to his Lordship, and will be ready to requite your courtesy in what I may. From my lodging in the Strand this 26th of June 1592,

Your loving friend
H. SOUTHAMPTON[12]

The necessity for this indirect approach indicates that the Lord Treasurer had turned a deaf ear to his young ward's appeals and was determined to teach him an ugly lesson. Somewhat earlier, in 1591, Southampton had received another sign of displeasure from the same quarter. It arrived in the form of a Latin poem, "Narcissus." G. P. V. Akrigg, the first biographer to appreciate the poem's significance, discovered in 1968 that its author, John Clapham, was also one of Burghley's secretaries. The poem's unflattering theme—how a handsome young Englishman (the scene is not Greece but a "blessed island," ruled by a Virgin Queen) perished from self-love—and its pointed dedication were double affronts to Southampton. The subtitle, "Short and Moral Description of Youthful Love, and Especially Self-Love," also has a barb. Clapham's dedication to Southampton contains a subtle insult that turns on the word *"virtutis,"* meaning not virtue but manliness. The Latin reads "virtutis atque honoris incrementum multosque annos foelices exoptat"—John Clapham wishes Southampton *"increase of manliness* and honour and many happy years."[13] That the most powerful officer of the Queen acquiesced in, if not abetted, this literary attack on

77

one of her wards must have been a grave source of worry for the young Earl's family.

As 1591 drew to a close, the eighteen-year-old Earl of Southampton was still unmarried. Less than three years remained until his coming of age on 6 October 1594. No doubt the members of his family, especially his mother, hoped he could be persuaded to end this crisis, marry Lady Elizabeth Vere, and beget an heir. It is against this background, in 1592, that the first seventeen poems in Q, the "Marriage" sonnets, were apparently written.

Differing speculations have been advanced by Southampton's biographers about his first meeting with Shakespeare. Charlotte Stopes: "He [Southampton] felt he must have a private talk with this 'man from Stratford' and took him home with him to supper."[14] Akrigg: "If the present writer must add his own guess . . . he would suggest a backstage meeting in a London Playhouse sometime in 1591–2."[15] Others believe they met through the Countess, who commissioned the "Marriage" sonnets in line with her promise to Sir Thomas Stanhope that "no want will be found on my behalf" to bring about the engagement. J. Dover Wilson thinks that Shakespeare, as a former schoolmaster, might have first come into contact with Southampton in the capacity of a tutor: "The earl had one tutor in residence with him, John Florio, the translator of Montaigne, whose influence upon Shakespeare has been remarked by many critics; and if the dramatist acted as Florio's colleague for some months, his interest in the great French humanist would be explained."[16]

We cannot know how Shakespeare and Southampton met; the important fact is that Shakespeare acquired a rich and highly placed patron. Sonnet 104 reveals how the poet felt when he first laid eyes on the young man. The first seventeen sonnets show our poet's progress from indifference to infatuation. His earliest play on record opened on 3 March 1592 to unusual success. Philip Henslowe's *Diary* is the source of the first recorded information about Shakespeare's public life: the takings for the première of *Harry the Sixth,* according to the diary, were the largest for a single performance recorded up to that time—£3 16s. 8d. The play was repeated on March 7, 11, 16, 28, April 5, 13, 21, May 4, 7, 14, 19, 25, and June 12 and 19.[17] Its enormous popularity was also recorded by Thomas Nashe in *Pierce Pennilesse His Supplication to the Devil,* entered on 8 August 1592, with his comment on the most effective scene in the play, the death of Sir John Talbot: "How it would have joyed brave Talbot, the terror of the French, to think that after he had lain two hundred years in his tomb, he should triumph again on the stage, and have his bones new embalmed with the tears *of ten thousand spectators at least (at several times)* who, in the tragedian that represents his person, imagine they behold him fresh bleeding." Nashe's estimate of the size of the audience for the fifteen performances may not be greatly exaggerated. We know the play's run ended in June, when a riot of apprentices caused the Privy Council to order all playing in London to cease. Alleyn then took the company on tour. Soon after, the plague broke out in London, and the theatres remained closed. For a poet whose livelihood was acting, this hiatus provided an ideal time in which to make a bid for reputation with a major work. *Venus and Adonis* was apparently written in this period; it was published in April 1593.

The previous autumn, Queen Elizabeth had paid a visit

in state to Oxford, and young Southampton was among
those in attendance. When the university published a Latin
poem by John Sandford, chaplain of Magdalen, memorial-
izing the royal visit, it revealed that—even allowing for
official flattery—his contemporaries acknowledged Southampton's exceptional beauty at this stage of his life. He
would turn nineteen the next month. This is the passage
from Sandford's poem, captioned "Comes Southamp-
toniae":

> Post hunc insequitur clara de stirpe Dynasta
> Iure suo dives South-Hamptonia magnum
> Vendicat heroem: quo non formosior alter
> Affuit, aut docta iuvenis praestantior arte,
> Ora licet tenera vix dum lanugine vernent.

"After him [i.e., Essex], there follows a lord of noble line
that the rich [district of] Southampton claims as a great
leader in his own right. No other youth present was more
handsome, nor more distinguished in the arts of learning,
though his lip as yet scarcely blooms with tender down."[18]

The following May a rumour circulated at court that
Southampton was to be created a Knight of the Garter, as
his grandfather had been. Though he was nominated (by
Essex perhaps) for the honour, the Queen did not grant it;
perhaps Burghley, who was still waiting for the young Earl
to marry his granddaughter, advised a delay.

In the spring of 1594 Shakespeare published his "graver
labour," *The Rape of Lucrece*, with an open declaration in
his dedicatory letter to Southampton: "The love I dedicate
to your lordship is without end." The poem was well received, and reprinted seven times before 1640.

In October, when the young Earl came of age, Burghley's control ended, but not his revenge. He had kept his grandchild single as long as Southampton was his ward; in January 1595, he gave Lady Elizabeth Vere in marriage to the Earl of Derby. It had been estimated that at full age Southampton's income would amount to somewhat less than four thousand pounds annually—an impressive sum in that era. But Burghley levied a staggering fine of five thousand pounds "of present money"—that is, to be paid immediately—on his former ward for refusing to marry his grandchild. In addition, the Earl had to pay a large fee to the crown for the legal transfer of his lands back to him. Thus the marriage crisis ended in heavy financial punishment for Southampton.

Though the first seventeen sonnets, by means of which Shakespeare and Southampton became friends, had failed to change the young Earl's mind about marriage, they changed Shakespeare's life.

One Thousand Pounds

Nicholas Rowe published the following story in 1709: "He [Shakespeare] had the honour to meet with many great and uncommon marks of favour and friendship from the Earl of Southampton. . . . . There is one instance so singular in the magnificence of this patron of Shakespeare's that if I had not been assured that the story was handed down by Sir William Davenant, who was probably very well acquainted with his affairs, I should not have ventured to have inserted that my Lord Southampton, at one time, gave him a thousand pounds to go through with a purchase which he heard he had a mind to."[19]

Most scholars think that the figure of one thousand pounds (worth more than twenty thousand pounds today) is a mistake for one hundred pounds. It may be. Certainly Rowe was aware of the relative size of the figure, for he adds, ironically, "A bounty very great, and very rare at any time, and *almost* [my italics] equal to that profuse generosity the present age has shown to French dancers and Italian eunuchs." (He was doubtless referring to the castrato Signor Nicolino, the professional name of Nicolo Grimaldi, who in 1708 made a sensational appearance in a Scarlatti opera, was praised by Richard Steele in *The Spectator,* and lavished with gifts, including "a most singular and priceless jewel" from the Queen.)[20]

The figure of one thousand pounds, as William Empson has pointed out in his essay on sonnet 94, recurs again and again in the Prince Hal–Falstaff relationship. In *1 Henry IV* the hostess tells the prince of Falstaff's claim that "you ought [owed] him a thousand pound." Hal confronts Falstaff: "Sirrah, do I owe you a thousand pound?" and Falstaff replies, "A thousand pound, Hal? A million. Thy love is worth a million: thou owest me thy love." In the rejection scene at the end of *2 Henry IV,* after Falstaff hails the newly crowned Henry V as "My king! My Jove! I speak to thee, my heart!" he is answered with the brutal words, "I know thee not, old man. Fall to thy prayers. / How ill white hairs become a fool and jester," followed by twenty-four lines of further denunciation. When the King finally moves on, the first words that Falstaff can bring himself to utter are, "Master Shallow, I owe you a thousand pound." Empson admits in his essay, "I cannot help fancying an obscure connection between this sum and the thousand pounds which, we are told, Southampton once gave Shakespeare, to go through with a purchase that he had a mind to."[21] J. Dover Wilson has linked this gift of Southampton's with the formation in 1594 of the Lord Chamberlain's company of players, of which Shakespeare became a founding member, together with Burbage, Heminge, Augustine Phillips, and others.[22] It is possible that Southampton contributed Shakespeare's share of the capital required to set up the new company. Whatever the figure may have been, and we shall probably never know, no one seems to dispute the fact that Southampton was a generous patron.

The truth is that Southampton gave Shakespeare a much more important gift than one thousand pounds. "It is certainly true," writes E. K. Chambers, "that when the plague was over he [Shakespeare] began a series of plays with Italian settings, which were something of a new departure in English drama . . . that he seems to have been remarkably successful in giving a local colouring and atmosphere to these; and even that he shows familiarity with some minute points of local [Italian] topography."[23] Whether Shakespeare travelled to Italy with Southampton, we do not know. Whether Southampton's Italian tutor, John Florio, helped Shakespeare while he was writing *The Taming of the Shrew, Two Gentlemen of Verona, Romeo and Juliet,* and *The Merchant of Venice,* as he later was known to help Ben Jonson with the Italian aspects of *Volpone,* we do not know. We do know that Shakespeare's previous plays—the four English histories (the *Henry VI* trilogy and *Richard III*); the Senecan melodrama, *Titus Andronicus;* and the Plautine *Comedy of Errors*—are quite different from the Italianate plays that immediately follow. The latter move into a different world, in contrast with the royal tableaux of the histories—a brilliant social world seen from the inside. For example, in one of the Italian plays, *The Taming of the Shrew,* which scholars date in the early 1590s, there is a humourous induction scene in which a practical joke is played on Christopher Sly: when he awakens from his drunken stupor, he is to be treated as a nobleman. The directions given to the pranksters by "A Lord" are remarkably vivid and detailed:

Carry him gently to my fairest chamber
And hang it round with all my wanton pictures.
Balm his foul head in warm distilled waters
And burn sweet wood to make the lodging sweet.
Procure me music ready when he wakes,
To make a dulcet and a heavenly sound;
And if he chance to speak, be ready straight
And with a low submissive reverence
Say, 'What is it your Honour will command?'
Let one attend him with a silver basin
Full of rose-water and bestrewed with flowers;
Another bear the ewer, the third a diaper,
And say, 'Will it please your Lordship cool your hands?'
Some one be ready with a costly suit,
And ask him what apparel he will wear . . .
Another tell him of his hounds and horse . . .

The playwright seems to be familiar with the life-style of a wealthy and aristocratic household. All the nonsense expended on proving that the plays of Shakespeare were not written by the actor from Stratford but by an aristo-crat—the Earl of Oxford, the Viscount St. Albans (Francis

Bacon), and so on—may in some measure have been generated by what the genius from rural England learned from his Southampton connection.

The Queen's Displeasure

It was rumoured during one period in 1595 that the Earl of Southampton would replace Essex as Queen Elizabeth's favourite, but this appears to have been an illusion. Perhaps the Queen intended this pretence of favouring the handsome young courtier as a signal to Essex, whose displays of bad temper and petulance were causing annoyance. Rowland Whyte, the well-informed court gossip, reported that "my Lord of Southampton is a careful waiter [courtier] here and *sede vacante* [Essex being away] doth receive favours at Her Majesty's hands; all this without breach of amity between [the two earls]."[24] But a few weeks later, Whyte was telling a different story: "My Lord of Southampton offering to help the Queen to her horse, was refused, and is gone from Court."[25] As with her refusal to make him a Knight of the Garter in 1593, Elizabeth from this point on clearly demonstrated that he was in her bad graces. It may have had to do with his relations with Mistress Elizabeth Vernon, an attractive woman of his own age, whose mother was Essex's aunt. Financially dependent on Essex, through whom she had secured the post of maid of honour to Queen Elizabeth, Elizabeth Vernon was almost penniless and could bring Southampton no dowry in his present difficult financial situation. In September 1595, Whyte noted: "My Lord of Southampton doth with too much familiarity court the fair Mistress Vernon."[26] The young Earl seemed to have learned nothing from the fall into disgrace of Sir Walter Ralegh, for seducing Elizabeth Throgmorton, also one of the Queen's maids. In July 1596 Southampton failed to obtain the Queen's permission to join Essex in one of his great military victories, the capture of the Spanish naval base at Cádiz.

Southampton's desire to achieve fame as a soldier was inordinate, and in the summer of 1597, Essex, named commander-in-chief of a new naval expedition against the Spanish treasure fleet (each year it sailed from Havana carrying gold and silver from Philip II's mines in America), succeeded in having Southampton appointed commander of the *Garland*. The naval action in the Azores lasted from late summer to early autumn, but the Spanish ships eluded Essex and he failed to capture the booty. However, Southampton distinguished himself by capturing and sinking a Spanish frigate: he had finally tasted military fame. On his return, he found his finances to be in a critical state, with many pressing debts, and he began to sell some property. He sought the help of his friend, hunchbacked Robert Cecil, Burghley's son, who as Principal Secretary was preparing to leave on a mission to Henri IV's court at the Louvre; he asked Cecil's aid in obtaining permission to reside in France. By living quietly abroad for a while, Southampton thought he could cut costs and perhaps recoup his fortune.

An unfortunate contretemps then occurred in the royal Presence Chamber, involving an interrupted card-game and some hair-pulling. One of Rowland Whyte's gossipy newsletters provides the colourful details. Late one night, after the Queen had gone to bed, three card-players remained in the Presence Chamber—Sir Walter Ralegh, once again at court; the Earl of Southampton; and a Mr. Parker—who were waging bets at the game of primero. The squire on duty, Ambrose Willoughby, "desired them to give over," since the Queen had retired, but they ignored him and went on playing. He spoke to them again, warning that, if they did not leave, he would call in the guard and order the playing-board to be pulled down, "which Sir Walter Ralegh seeing, put up his money and went his ways." Parker followed, but Willoughby again had to order Southampton from the Presence Chamber. Shortly thereafter, "between the tennis-court wall and the garden," the Earl "took exceptions at him [Willoughby] and . . . struck him, and Willoughby pulled off some of his locks." Southampton's very long hair—he wore the left locks in front, over his heart—made it easy for Willoughby to do this. The Queen's reaction next day was humiliating for Southampton: she gave Willoughby "thanks for what he did in the Presence, and told him he had done better if he had sent him [Southampton] to the porter's lodge, to see who durst have fetched him out."[27] She also forbade Southampton to present himself at court for a month.

The Chamberlain's Men make a brief appearance on the record at this point. Southampton and three others (Ralegh and Lords Cobham and Compton) honored Cecil, on the eve of his embassy to France, with "plays and banquets." We do not know what plays were performed, but it was Southampton who made the arrangements.

87

The Queen held back permission for Southampton to leave England until almost the last moment; it came on 6 February 1598, four days before Cecil was to sail. She gave the Earl leave to go abroad for two years with ten servants, six horses, and two hundred pounds. Rowland Whyte: "My Lord Southampton is much troubled by Her Majesty's strangest usage of him. Some body hath played unfriendly parts with him. Mr. Secretary [Cecil] hath procured him licence to travel. His fair mistress [Vernon] doth wash her fairest face with many tears."[28]

Southampton departed for France with Sir Robert Cecil, but his plans to live abroad and repair his finances were fated not to be. Six months later, in secrecy, he returned to England, having learned that Elizabeth Vernon was pregnant as a result of one of their meetings in February. In London, after consulting privately with the Earl of Essex, he married Elizabeth Vernon at a place unknown. In late August, he returned to Paris alone.

On 3 September, when the Queen learned of his secret marriage, she was enraged. Cecil wrote him as follows: "She knows that you came over very lately, and returned again very contemptuously; that you have also married one of her maids of honour without her privity, for which with other circumstances informed against you I find her grievously offended." Southampton was ordered to return to London at once, without coming to court, "until her pleasure be known."[29]

Meanwhile, the new Countess of Southampton was imprisoned in the Fleet, with Essex paying for her maintenance. Southampton stalled some weeks in Paris, but finally had to face the music. On his return at the beginning of November, he joined his wife in prison. Their daughter, born about a week later, was christened Penelope, in honor of Essex's sister, Lady Penelope Devereux Rich, the Stella of Sidney's poem.

Thus in 1598, six years after the "Marriage" sonnets were written, the poet's admonition to the young Earl to "make thee another self" was heeded—except that it was not a male heir, as the poems took for granted: "You had a father, let your son say so." (It was only after seven more years of misfortune, tribulation, condemnation, and rehabilitation that, on St. David's Day, 1605, his wife bore Southampton a son, christened James after his godfather, James I.)

Meantime, Elizabeth allowed the truant parents to cool their heels in the Fleet for a month, after which, with the help of Essex, they were freed. In December Southampton was elated when Essex, who was to be the new viceroy of Ireland and commander-in-chief of the largest army Elizabeth ever sent outside the borders of England, asked him to serve as his second in command, as General of the Horse. The young Earl's immediate acceptance was premature; Essex had not received his formal commission and, after all that had happened, still did not understand the character of his monarch.

When she saw him at Richmond, Elizabeth told Essex that Southampton was not to have *any* command in the army. She was still as angry at him for the seduction of, and secret marriage to, her maid of honour as she had earlier been at Sir Walter Ralegh for the same reason. In spite of this obvious fact, Essex, seeking to comfort the greatly disappointed Southampton, fatuously wrote him that nevertheless, once the commission was formalized, he

(Essex) would have the right to name his own officers anyway, and "then if she quarrel with me [as if she would not!], her wrong is the greater and my standing upon it will appear more just."[30] Essex was clearly headed for disaster, and did not seem to realize that the Queen intended to remain sovereign: she would not refrain from interference in military affairs or give him the free hand he needed for military success. When he asked that a place on the Council of Ireland be given to his stepfather, Sir Christopher Blount, a distinguished veteran of many campaigns whom he had named marshal of the army, she refused. In anger, Essex said he would not in that case use Blount's services at all. The Queen sternly repeated that (a) Blount would remain a marshal; (b) she would certainly not have him as a councillor. Essex had got himself in a trap; he began to regret having accepted the Irish command, describing it as "mere banishment and proscription to the crudest of all islands,"[31] and foolishly continued to follow his collision course. In Dublin on 15 April 1599, Essex received the sword of state, which put his commission in effect, and at once he appointed Southampton General of the Horse.

His plan of military operations, presented to the Queen and the Privy Council, was to track down the leader of the rebellion, Hugh O'Neill, the Earl of Tyrone, in Ulster, crush his forces, and restore order in the rest of Ireland. A neat, simple plan, impossible of execution. Before news of Essex's disastrous failure began to reach England in the late summer, Shakespeare had written this brave passage in his 1599 play, *Henry V,* the words being spoken by a Chorus in the prologue to the fifth act:

Were now the General of our gracious Empress,
As in good time he may, from Ireland coming,
Bringing rebellion broachèd on his sword,
How many would the peaceful city quit
To welcome him!

In June, while Essex was bogged down with his troubles, the Privy Council on orders of the Queen sent him a devastating letter, just the kind to drive a general-in-the-field mad. The letter reads as if she herself had dictated it, which in essence she had, and the ministers' final apology reveals their distaste for the job:

> Her Majesty having of late received certain knowledge that your Lordship hath constituted the Earl of Southampton General of the Horse in Her Majesty's army under your charge, with which she is much displeased, hath given us commandment to signify her mind in that behalf, and to let your Lordship understand that she thinketh it strange, and taketh it offensively, that you would appoint his Lordship to that place and office, considering that Her Majesty did not only deny it, when she was here moved by your Lordship to that purpose, but gave you an express prohibition to the contrary, that he should not be appointed thereunto.

Essex was further told he must dismiss Southampton as General of the Horse and appoint someone else in his place. The basis of the Queen's objection to Southampton was then made clear: she considered it "a very unseasonable time to confer upon him any so great place, having so lately given her cause of offence towards him," i.e., his secret marriage. The ministers' closing words, "having discharged our duties, we are sorry for the occasion. The Court at Greenwich, 1599, June 10,"[32] probably held small comfort for Essex.

In Ireland, Southampton had shown exceptional bravery and devotion as a fighter for his general. While the Queen's orders were on their way, both men had been involved in a fierce skirmish at Arklow on the Irish east coast (vividly described by G. P. V. Akrigg, who visited the scene of action). Essex, with only eighty foot soldiers, was attacked by several hundred Irish troops. Southampton from his position on the beach, with the sea on his right, found that a bog lay between his small force and the woods that protected the attackers. Realizing Essex's peril, in desperation he ordered his twenty-four horsemen to charge across the bog, and this unexpected attack on their flank made the Irish temporarily withdraw to the woods. After he had returned to firmer ground, Southampton saw that three horsemen were caught in the mire, and he charged again to save them from capture and death. One of the three—and they were all wounded—was Robert Vernon, a relative of his wife's, who was caught beneath his fallen horse. Reinforcements then arrived from Arklow and the Irish broke off the engagement. Essex and Southampton were soon back in Dublin, where they were greeted by the letter of dismissal.

Incredibly, Essex wrote the Privy Council on 11 July asking that the dismissal be revoked. He had one sound argument—but it was not likely to move the Queen—that "if it pleased Her Majesty that I should execute it [his commission], I must work with my own instruments"— that is, he must have a free hand. It was much too late for this argument, and his resentment made him go far beyond the limits of tact, diplomacy, and good sense with this passionate outburst: "Was it treason in my Lord of Southampton to marry my poor kinswoman, that neither long imprisonment, nor no punishment besides, that hath been usual in like cases, can satisfy or appease? *Or will no kind of punishment be fit for him but that which punisheth not him, but me, this army, and poor country of Ireland?*"[33]

When the Queen was shown these words, she answered at once in her own hand: "For the matter of Southampton, it is strange to us that his continuance or displacing should work so great an alteration in yourself (valuing our commandments as you ought) or in the disposition of our army, where all the commanders cannot be ignorant that we not only not allowed of your desire for him, but expressly forbid it." After showing her contempt for Southampton as "such a one whose counsel can be of little, and experience of less, use," she expressed astonishment that Essex should "dare thus to value your own pleasing in things unnecessary, and think by private arguments to carry for your own glory a matter wherein our pleasure to the contrary is made notorious."[34] She was also angered by Essex's argument that Southampton's dismissal would discourage other gentlemen volunteers. The upshot was that Essex had to dismiss his friend as General of the Horse—but he refused to appoint anyone else; the post was abolished. Southampton took it all in good spirit and went on serving as a volunteer officer under Essex.

Thoughts of retribution against his enemies at court who were plotting his downfall (with considerable help from him) were already in Essex's mind. In August he met secretly at Dublin Castle with Sir Christopher Blount, who was wounded, and the Earl of Southampton, as the latter testified in 1601 at their trial, and told them of his plan to land with an army at Wales and march on London. "To which project," Southampton swore, "I answered that I held it altogether unfit."[35] When Sir Christopher Blount said that he, too, could not agree to it, Essex put the plan aside.

Perhaps to goad him into action against O'Neill in the north, Elizabeth had notified Essex that "until the northern action be tried" she was refusing him permission to return to England for consultation. Essex marched north from Dublin on 28 August, even though eighteen colonels and captains, including Southampton, had signed a letter protesting the sorry condition and unfitness of the army of two hundred horsemen and twenty-seven hundred foot soldiers. While encamping at Louth, Essex received a message that O'Neill wished to meet him for a parley and replied that he would meet only on a battlefield. There was a skirmish next morning, but both sides held back, and Essex turned his army south towards Kells. One of O'Neill's lieutenants then overtook Essex, telling him that the Irish commander desired the Queen's mercy and begged Essex to meet him at the ford of Bellaclynthe, in the river Lagan. When Essex accepted, his fate was sealed.

Southampton, who was ordered to keep everyone out of earshot of the parley, testified later that he had heard nothing of what the two men said. But others said they had heard them discussing treason—that is, what would happen in case of the Queen's death. Essex agreed to a truce with O'Neill, and sent a captain-messenger over to England with the news. When the Queen learned on 16 September of the meeting and truce, she sent the captain back next

day with a furious reply, commanding Essex not to issue a
pardon to O'Neill or enter into any terms with him until
she had seen all of it in writing and had given Essex her
warrant to proceed. His dramatic response is well known.
Despite her orders to the contrary, he rushed back to London with a small group, including Southampton, with
such speed that he reached the city within ten days. At this
time the court was at Nonesuch in Surrey, and that morning Essex rode alone straight to the palace, arrived bespat-
tered with mud, broke into the Queen's bedchamber un-
announced, fell at her feet, and kissed her hands. " 'Tis
much wondered at here," wrote Rowland Whyte, "that he
went so boldly to Her Majesty's presence, she not being
ready, and he so full of dirt and mire that his very face was
full of it."[36]

The Queen greeted him pleasantly, though she was not
yet attired or prepared to see anyone. Perhaps she secretly
feared him. Essex was happy at his reception, but later in
the day, Elizabeth ordered him confined to his quarters.
It was the last time she ever saw him. He was then ban-
ished from court and in June 1600 brought before the
Privy Council and publicly censured.

Meantime, Southampton stayed in London. It was reported at this time that "my Lord Southampton and Lord
Rutland come not to the Court; the one doth but very
seldom; they pass the time in London merely in going to
plays every day"[37]—including no doubt the new Shakespeare play at the Globe that autumn, *Julius Caesar*.

In October 1600, the Queen delivered a great financial
blow to Essex, refusing to renew the grant of a tax on
sweet wines, which for many years she had allowed him as
the most important source of his income. Since he had

mortgaged all his private estate to help cover his expenses in the war in Ireland, this gesture of the Queen's was fatal. In great depression, he listened to his followers, many of them men of desperate fortunes, and the Council became suspicious of his actions. On 7 February 1601, at the request of Essex's friends and before a large and enthusiastic audience of his followers, the Chamberlain's Men reluctantly, only on payment of a bonus, put on Shakespeare's *Richard II,* the play of regicide. After Essex's death, William Lambarde reported that Queen Elizabeth said to him, "*I* am Richard II, know ye not that?"[38] That night Essex was summoned to the court to explain his conduct; he refused to go, declaring it was a plot to murder him. The abortive rebellion took place next day: Essex fully expected that Londoners would rise and join him, but no one stirred, except a handful of his own men. On 19 February Essex and Southampton were tried for high treason in Westminster Hall and condemned to death. The first life of Henry Wriothesley had reached its end.

His later life is of little concern to our story, though the book known as Q was published in 1609 and he may have used his great position to help suppress it. There is not much on record to connect him to Shakespeare in this period, except for a small but significant incident in 1605 that is related on page 148. Shakespeare did not remember Southampton in his will, as he did his fellow-players, but perhaps this is due to the fact that in 1616 Southampton was a wealthy grandee whose days as Shakespeare's patron had long been over. When the players published the First Folio in 1623, they chose to dedicate it to the Earls of Pembroke and Montgomery. This does not mean that Shakespeare would have necessarily chosen to honour the same men if he himself had overseen the appearance of his plays in book form; *they* were not remembered in his will, either.

In the next year, the Earl of Southampton, having been called to the wars again as commander of one of the four English regiments aiding the Dutch alliance, took along as captain his nineteen-year-old son, Lord James. While they were abroad, the son contracted fever and died on 5 November. Five days later, before he had completed the sad journey homeward with the body of his son, the father died of the same fever. His younger son, Lord Thomas, became the fourth Earl of Southampton.

Shakespeare's Angel

One fact that emerges from the life of Southampton is how small a part Shakespeare seems to have played in it, in comparison to the crucial role the Earl played in his life. Considering the enormous differences in their stations at their first meeting—Shakespeare was a mere player and apprentice writer in 1591–92—this was to be expected, and it would have been unthinkable to their contemporaries that Southampton would be chiefly known to history *because of* Shakespeare. Another fact that emerges is how settled and productive Southampton's life became under James I, in contrast to the discontented and frustrating Elizabethan years.

It is the early years—from Southampton's late teens until his coming of age at the end of 1594, the years of the composition of the sonnets and, for the poet at least, of their closest relationship—that are the crucial ones. The available evidence does not flatter the Earl. William Empson describes "the miniature of him at nineteen, vain and resentful to the point of mania, the snarling at his Mum when she remarried in his own interests, the incapacity to treat the Queen as anything but a rival," this together with his participation in the Essex rebellion and his "unexpected ability to plead for his life without shame when the plan failed—it all makes him," Empson concludes, "an impressive monster, and one feels Shakespeare was brave to be able to love him."[39]

In one sonnet ("Two loves I have, of comfort and despair") Shakespeare calls Southampton an angel. Though he did not use it in the sense of modern theatre parlance, the word is also applicable to Southampton as one who put up the money. In this sense, Southampton was the sole angel in Shakespeare's career. There is another meaning of angel in Elizabethan slang, where the word is corrupted into ingle (from the German, *engel*), meaning a catamite. For example, Thomas Middleton's play *Blurt, Master Constable* has the line "Jove's own ingle, Ganymede,"[40] and Jonson in *Poetaster* asks, "What! Shall I have my son a stager now? An ingle for players?"[41] John Florio defined the Italian noun *catamito* as "a Ganymede, an ingle" and the verb *zanzerare* as "to ingle boys, to play wantonly with boys against nature."[42] Though it is obvious from his biography that Southampton was heterosexual, a number of references to him in his youth—dating back to "Narcissus" (1591), the Burghley-inspired poem by John Clapham—have homosexual implications. The most direct is in Thomas Nashe's *Pierce Pennilesse* (1592), where Southampton, under the guise of Amyntas, is called the "matchless image of honour and magnificent rewarder of virtue, Jove's eagle-borne Ganymede, thrice-noble Amyntas."[43] As the citations show, Ganymede was also Elizabethan slang for homosexual.

Lady Bridget Manners's description of Southampton in the summer of 1594 (just before the Earl turned twenty-one) is interesting as showing how someone of his own age and class judged him as a youth. When asked whether she would choose one of the young lords, Southampton or Bedford, for a husband, rather than an older suitor, Lord Wharton, a widower with four children, she said she preferred the older man because the other two "be so young and fantastical, and would be so carried away, that if anything should come to your Ladyship [her widowed mother] but good, being her [Bridget's] only stay, she doubteth their carriage of themselves, seeing some experience of the like in this place [the court]."[44] She gave no details of their behaviour at court that led to her conclusion.

Finally, there was the poison-pen letter (first published in bowdlerized form in Mrs. Stopes's biography) that an informer sent to Sir Robert Cecil at the time of the Essex-Southampton trial. Intended as an attack on a Captain Pearse Edmonds, an officer under the Earl of Essex, it alleged that Edmonds had had a homosexual relationship with Southampton during the expedition in Ireland, when the Earl had been months away from his wife: "He [Edmonds] was a Corporal-general of the Horse in Ireland under the Earl of Southampton. He eat and drank at his table and lay in his tent. The Earl of Southampton gave him a horse, which Edmonds refused a 100 marks for him. The Earl of Southampton would cull and hug him in his arms and play wantonly with him."[45] The Oxford English Dictionary defines cull as "to fondle," and cites *The Jewel of Joy* (1594): "To kiss and cull him as his dear darling." The word also occurs in Thomas Nashe's *Lenten Stuffe* (1599): "Hug it, ingle it, kiss it, cull it, now thou hast it." Of course an informer's allegation, made while Southampton was an attainted prisoner under sentence of death, is not the most reliable evidence. Cecil apparently ignored it, though the letter remains among the family's papers today. All one can conclude is that suspicions of homosexuality, especially in his younger years, hovered around Southampton. But as William Empson wrote in 1963, "English troops, I think, would say this about Southampton on no more evidence than the way he did his hair."[46]

The likeliest reason for Shakespeare's good fortune in finding the patron he very much needed in 1591–92 was Southampton's determination to live in the style of the Essex-Sidney circle. The members of that glittering coterie were in turn heirs of the traditions established by the Earl of Leicester, chief patron of literature in the earlier years of Elizabeth's reign. The word "generosity" derives from *generosus,* one of noble birth, and the ideal Renaissance nobleman was expected to be bountiful; he earned special kudos as a patron of the arts, especially the art of poetry. Southampton deserves high marks for emulating this ideal. It is also to his credit that he was far from money-grubbing and could act against his own financial interests in matters of principle. His behaviour during the marriage crisis, when acceptance of Burghley's choice of a bride would have been prudent and advantageous, is such an example. His refusal was perhaps an aristocratic way of saying, "No matter what it costs me, I will not be ruled by this man." (Burghley's ideas on money and gentility were the opposite of his ward's; one precept he wrote down for his son was the cynical and realistic definition, "Gentility is but ancient riches.")

Southampton spent money lavishly—on his clothes and personal adornments, to judge from his many portraits; on games and pastimes, including cards (in Paris he lost three thousand crowns in one day to the Marshal Biron); on betting (an old and doubtless exaggerated ballad[47] tells the story of his bet of "seven good thousand pound" that he could outleap the others in a sports match); and on his retinue of retainers (at his trial, he modestly revealed that, on the morning of the Essex uprising, "I had not above ten or twelve men attending me, which was but my usual company"[48]).

His personal extravagances, however, were fairly well matched by his benefactions. He purchased the entire library of the Puritan divine William Crashaw, father of the poet, in order to endow his college, St. John's. He contributed generously to the setting up of the Bodleian Library. He supported a grammar school at Newport, on the Isle of Wight, of which he was captain. Akrigg lists thirty-three books bearing dedications to Southampton during his lifetime; while it is not certain how many of their authors (like Thomas Nashe) were unrewarded, this shows that his contemporaries regarded the Earl as most generous.

In 1596 John Florio wrote of Southampton: "But as to

me, and many more [an allusion to Shakespeare among others], the glorious and gracious sunshine of your Honour hath infused light and life."[49] No poet could expect more, even from an angel.

THE PEDANT

*Florio was no uncouth schoolmaster. Pedantic
and precious he might be, but in the courtly,
not the grammar-school vein.*

FRANCES YATES

An Italian Englishman

As the opening words of an English-Italian conversation manual, this long sentence (only partially quoted) might strike a modern reader as inappropriate and overexcited:

> In this stirring time and pregnant prime of invention, when every bramble is fruitful, when every mole-hill hath cast off the winter's mourning garment, and when every man is busy working to feed his own fancies . . . with eclogues, songs, and sonnets, in pitiful verse and miserable prose, and most for a fashion: is not love a wag that makes men so wanton?[1]

Yet it conveys perfectly the buzzing literary climate of the spring of 1591, when John Florio wrote it. It also announces the new "fashion" of sonnet-writing. This seems to have been the moment when the actor William Shakespeare, twenty-seven, began a new career as playwright; his first history play, the trilogy of *Henry VI,* was produced a year later. The paths of Florio and Shakespeare apparently crossed in the Southampton household in the early 1590s. Florio, eleven years older than Shakespeare, outlived the poet by eight years. He seems to have known most of the leading writers of the Elizabethan and Jacobean eras, and to have been involved with several of them. His first wife was the sister of the poet Samuel Daniel, an important early influence on the poems of Shakespeare.

There is no evidence, except for the debatable "Phaeton" sonnet (to be discussed), that Shakespeare and Florio were more than accidental colleagues, or that their chance association under the aegis of the Earl of Southampton was for more than a limited time. Yet the crossing of their separate paths is pertinent to the story of Q in three ways —helping to date the sonnets; dating the sonnet-play, *Love's Labour's Lost;* and providing a possible link with Thomas Thorpe, the publisher of Q.

John Florio was born in London in 1553. His father, Michael Angelo Florio, had been born in Italy "of a father and mother baptized as papists," whose forebears, in his own words, were Jews: "my ancestors were Hebrews before baptism."[2] Michael as a youth entered a Franciscan friary, but left the order to become a Protestant follower of Socinus. He was imprisoned in Rome by the Inquisition for more than two years, escaped, and fled to France. After his arrival in England, he was appointed with the help of Archbishop Cranmer as preacher of a church of Italian refugees in London, where he became involved in a scandal with an unnamed Englishwoman. The trouble seems to have been solved when he married her, and apparently their offspring was John Florio. The father then became a tutor in classical and Romance languages at court, his pupils being young Edward VI, Lady Jane Grey, and Henry Herbert, Earl of Pembroke. On the accession of the Catholic Queen Mary in 1554, he quit England and took his infant son and English wife to Switzerland. Understandably, he never returned to Italy; nor is there any record of the son setting foot there, though he is usually called "an Italian" in the documents of the time.

By 1576 John Florio had returned to London, where two years later he published his *First Fruits,* an Italian-language handbook, under the patronage of the Earl of Leicester. In 1581 he matriculated at Magdalen, then the Puritan college at Oxford, where he was also language tutor to Emmanuel Barnes, brother of the poet Barnabe and son of the Bishop of Durham.

Called both Giovanni and John, Florio preferred the latter designation and usually signed himself "Resolute John Florio." Like his father, he moved in the highest court circles as a language tutor; the prestige of the Italian language in England was at its apogee. He tells us he had frequent occasion to be in the presence of Queen Elizabeth, whom he admired particularly for her mastery of languages. In his own words, he often had "the good hap and comfort to see that no Ambassador or stranger [foreigner] hath audience with Her Majesty but in his native tongue; and none hath answer but in the same, or in the common tongues of Greek or Latin by her sacred lips pronounced."[3] His portrait of Elizabeth as a lover of music and of Italy appears in this colloquy:

La Regina, tien Musici?	Hath the Queen musicians?
Signor si, affai, ma sono quasi tutti Italiani.	Yea sir many, but they are almost all Italians.
Amelagli Italiani?	Doth she love Italians?
Signor si, benissimo.	Yea sir, very well.

Si dilettela di parlar con lore?	Delights she to speak with them?
Signor si, e parlar elegantissimamente.	Yea sir, and she speaketh very elegantly.[4]
Parlela assai lingue?	Doth she speak many languages?
Lei parla otto lingue. Lei parla Greco, Latino, Italiano, Franzese, Spagniolo, Scozese, Fiamengo e Inglese: tutto questo lingue parla benissimo e eloquentemente.	She speaketh eight languages. She speaketh Greek, Latin, Italian, French, Spanish, Scottish, Flemish, and English: all these tongues she speaketh very well and eloquent.[5]

Concerning the English attitude towards foreigners, a tender subject with Florio, there is this revealing exchange:

Che vi par la gente di Inghliterra, sono amorevoli?	What do you think of the people of England, are they loving?
Io vi diro la verita, la Nobilita e molto cortese, ma la plebe e tanto piu discortese, e specialmento verso i Forestieri, la qual cosa, mi dispiace.	I will tell you the truth, the Nobility is very courteous, but the common sort are rude and especially towards strangers, the which thing doth displease me.[6]

Florio suffered personally from the common citizen's suspicions and hatred of foreigners. In 1584 the French embassy on Butcher Row, off the Strand, was attacked by

a mob during the period when Florio worked as an aide to
the French ambassador, as tutor to the ambassador's young
daughter, and simultaneously as an English spy for Sir
Francis Walsingham. The ringleader of the raid was a
William Gryse, a clerk of Queen Elizabeth's stable, who
apparently felt it was his patriotic duty to cause as much
mischief and trouble as possible for the ambassador. Gryse,
building a house in the same street, rearranged the drains
of the embassy in a way "the which causeth such a stink in
all my lodgings," the ambassador complained, "that it is
not possible to abide in the house." Gryse also encouraged
citizens to "set upon us, saying he had authority so to do
for that he was the Queen's servant."[7]

1584 was one of the anxious years, before the Armada,
when France and Spain were in *rapprochement* and when
the French ambassador was known to be in communica-
tion in England with the imprisoned Mary of Scots—doubtless one of the reasons for Florio's being on the scene at
the embassy. On the night prior to the ambassador's complaint, Gryse arrived around midnight with a crowd, including ten men with swords and other weapons. They
threw stones, shot arrows out of crossbows, broke all the
windows of the embassy, and hurt two French boys, one
of whom lost an eye. The ambassador's wife, "sick in her
bed, being fearful and very timorous, hath doubled her
grief and disease." His daughter's "schoolmaster" (Florio)
was driven out of his chamber, and the crowd threatened
to "kill and beat [my men] as they go in the streets." The
ambassador sent this complaint in the person of John
Florio, "the bearer hereof, an Englishman, to represent
unto you the truth whether I have right or wrong."[8] Walsingham of course took immediate action, and Gryse and

his friends were imprisoned—only to be released, at the ambassador's diplomatic request, a few days later.

Florio the Puritan

John Florio's Puritan orientation, which could not have been sympathetic to Shakespeare, was not limited to religious doctrine and theology, though he remained a strong polemicist and staunch Protestant to the end of his life. It also comes out in his strictures against the excessive consumption of food and liquor by the Elizabethans, a topic he brings up again and again. He also disapproved of fine clothes, and even more of people dressing above their station, as in this colloquy:

La gente vanno bene vestiti?

Go the people well apparelled?

Benissimo, e con gran pompa. Un mechanico vuol esser mercante, un mercante vuol esser gentilhomo, il gentilhomo vuol esser Conte, il Conte Duca, il Duca Re, tanto che ogni uno cerca di superar laltro in superbia.

Very well, and with great pomp. A handycraftman will be a merchant, a merchant will be a gentleman, a gentleman will be a Lord, a Lord a Duke, a Duke a King: so that every one seeks to overcome another in pride.[9]

This exchange, between Giovanni and Henrico, is not at all complimentary to the English plays of 1591:

G. *E dopo descinare anderemo e veder qualche comedia.*

And then after dinner we will go see a play.

H. *In Inghliterra non recitano vere comedie.*

The plays that they play in England are not right comedies.

G. *E pur non fan altro che recitar tutto il giorno.*

Yet they do nothing else but play every day.

H. *Si, ma non sono vere comedie, ne vere tragedie.*

Yes, but they are neither right comedies, nor right tragedies.

G. *Come le nominereste voi dunque?*

How would you name them then?

H. *Rapresentationi d'historie, senza alcun decoro.*

Representations of histories, *without any decorum.*[10]

"Decorum" to Florio meant propriety and consistency in portrayals, justified by nature and drawn from classical models—rules that were, of course, violated daily on Elizabethan stages. This critical attitude recommended Florio to Ben Jonson, whose theory of humours is related to that of decorum; they later became close friends. Florio's brother-in-law Samuel Daniel wrote Senecan tragedies and also adhered to the classical mode in drama.

It must have been as apparent to Florio's contemporaries as to us that on occasion he adopted a patronizing tone about things English, as one looking down from a

higher cultural level. Of course the civilization of Italy
was years ahead of England in art, literature, science, trad-
ing, banking, games and sports, and, most notably, social
refinements. This comes out in the experiences of Giordano Bruno, the famous philosopher from Nola (years
later burned at the stake by the Inquisition in the Campo
dei Fiori, Rome). He was a friend of Florio's who resided
with him at the French embassy in the 1580s. Bruno's sen-
sibilities were deeply shocked at a London supper party
that he attended with Florio and recorded in detail in *La
Cena de le Ceneri* (1584). What appalled the fastidious
Italian was the barbarous ceremony of the loving-cup:
"The goblet or chalice passes around the table from hand
to hand. . . . After the host has detached his lips, leaving
a smear of grease, another drinks and leaves a crumb, another a bit of meat on the rim, another a hair from his
moustache or beard. . . . If one prefers not to drink because he lacks the stomach, he need merely touch the cup
to his mouth so that he too can deposit on it the morsels
from his lips."[11] This supper took place, not in a common
inn, but at the rich London house of their host, the elegant
courtier and poet Sir Fulke Greville. Bruno was also
astonished that Greville had failed to send a carriage to
the embassy to fetch him, as the custom had been in Paris,
his previous place of residence. As a result, he and Florio
arrived late, having had to walk the muddy streets after
truculent and suspicious Thames boatmen misdirected and
cheated them.

As for the English language itself, Florio answers the
question "What think you of this English tongue, tell me,
I pray you?" with a scathing reply, "It is a language that

will do you good in England, but past Dover, it is worth nothing."[12]

For years scholars followed Edmund Malone's view that because Florio, "like our poet, was particularly patronized by Lord Southampton," therefore Shakespeare "would not make the Italian an object of ridicule" in his play, for fear of offending his patron.[13] Later scholars, with the knowledge of Florio's role as a spy for Walsingham and Burghley, realized that Southampton was aware of Florio's having been insinuated into his household. The attitude of Southampton and Shakespeare to the language-tutor's mannerisms—if one equates them with the characters Navarre and Berowne in *Love's Labour's Lost*—appears to have been one of amusement, rather than ridicule, mixed with admiration for his solid learning. Navarre, the Southampton figure, answers Berowne's wistful inquiry whether any recreation is to be allowed in their self-imposed exile:

> *Ay, that there is. Our court you know is haunted*
> *With a refinèd traveller of Spain,*
> *A man in all the world's new fashion planted,*
> *That hath a mint of phrases in his brain;*
> *One who the music of his own vain tongue*
> *Doth ravish like enchanting harmony . . .*

Their fun-making is good-natured rather than malicious. Florio's characteristics are used partly in Holofernes, the schoolmaster, and partly in Armado of Spain, about whom Navarre concludes:

> *But I protest I love to hear him lie,*
> *And I will use him for my minstrelsy [diversion].*

In Southampton's Pay and Patronage

When Florio entered and left Southampton's service cannot be stated precisely. A reasonable conclusion from a knowledge of the circumstances and the few pieces of available evidence is that his service extended over a few years, perhaps from 1591 to early 1595, coinciding roughly with Shakespeare's closest association with Southampton. The first piece of evidence is Florio's dedication to *A World of Words,* published in 1598, after much delay for economic reasons, in which he praises the "most noble, most virtuous, and most honourable Earl of Southampton, in whose pay and patronage I have lived some years."[14] However, it is misleading to regard 1598 as a terminal date in calculating the term of service. *A World of Words* had already been registered on 2 March 1596, by Edward Blount, as "a most copious and exact dictionary in Italian and English made by John Florio, dedicated to the right honourable the Earl of Southampton."[15] This rare mention of a dedicatee in the register pushes back the date of the pay-and-patronage statement at least two years.

It is obvious that Florio's appointment as Southampton's Italian language-tutor was connected with Burghley's supervision of his ward, and it is likely that Florio left the Earl's service not long after 6 October 1594, perhaps late that year or early in 1595. As for a possible starting date, Florio would have been freed for any new assignment of

Burghley's following the French ambassador's departure from England in 1589.

In her book *Giovanni Florio,* Clara Longworth de Chambrun points out that two of the speakers in *Second Fruits* (1591) are Henry and John or, in the Italian column, Henrico and Giovanni; and that the former stands for Henry Wriothesley and the latter for John Florio. Frances Yates concludes that "the latter identification [by Chambrun] meets with some support from the fact that John, or Giovanni, quotes the proverb *Chi si contenta gode,* which is the motto on Florio's portrait."[16] Yates goes on to say, "It is Giovanni who looks on as the others play tennis, and Florio may here have been picturing himself in his relations to his elegant pupils. Tennis, primero, the theatre, love, and other topics touched on in *Second Fruits* probably do represent Southampton's taste." With admirable caution, she then adds, "On the whole, it must be said that there is no definite proof of Florio's having been with the earl before 1594."[17] On the contrary, there is no definite proof of Florio's being with him after 1594.

There is incontrovertible proof of Florio's presence in Southampton's household for one day only, 12 October 1594, six days after Burghley's wardship ended. Since Florio tells us he lived for "some years" under Southampton, the years of service must have antedated 1594. Florio, on the occasion in question, behaved as if he had been a longtime Southamptonite. The incident, preserved in court records and other documents, occurred during the celebration of the Earl's twenty-first birthday at Titchfield; it involved the drama and danger of harbouring two fugitives from justice, his close friends the Danvers brothers, Sirs Charles and Henry, who had fled to him for help.

From "A World of Words" (1611): John Florio at 58

Southampton's birthday was on a Sunday. Two days before, on Friday, 4 October, a murder had occurred under circumstances that remind one of *Romeo and Juliet.*

The feud between the Danvers and Long families, according to the colourful account by the fugitives' mother, Lady Elizabeth Danvers (noted for her beauty and Italian birth), had become unendurable. She said they had suffered such insults as having beer thrown "in the face of the principal officer of the said Sir John Danvers [her late husband]," with the beer-throwers saying, "in derision they had now dubbed [the officer] a knight also."[18] The feud had been further inflamed by the murder of a Danvers servant, and the brothers advanced on the fateful Friday "with their followers to the number of 17 or 18 persons in a most riotous manner." One account has Sir Charles Danvers being challenged to a duel by Harry Long, who gained an advantage and had his arm raised to kill, whereupon Sir Henry Danvers intervened to save his brother and killed Long "accidentally" with a dagger.

The mother testified that Long had been sending her son abusive letters "of such form as the heart of a man indeed had rather die than endure," and she quoted Long's threat that "wheresoever he met him [Sir Charles], he would untie his points [untruss his pants] and whip his etcetera with a rod, calling him ass, puppy, fool, and boy. . . . How the beginning of all this quarrel was the prosecuting of justice against thieves, harboured and maintained by the Longs, all the country knows." She concludes passionately: "And if a life notwithstanding must be answered with a life, what may be trulier said than that my son slew Long with a dagger, and they have been the cause of slaying my husband with dolour and grief. And

117

if Sir John Danvers were a worthier man, and his life of more worth than Harry Long's, so much odds the Longs have had already of our good name and house!"[19] It sounds more Italian than English, as she tells it.

The report of a coroner's jury corrects some details: the encounter actually took place in an inn where Harry Long and his brother were eating with friends; Sir Charles Danvers, after striking Long, turned to leave, but found the door locked; Long then drew his sword on Sir Charles, who was "dangerously wounded in seven several places,"[20] and to save his brother, Sir Henry shot Long. Thus it was a bullet, not a dagger, as the mother had thought, that caused death. The Danvers brothers fled to Whitley Lodge, owned by Southampton, less than two miles from Titchfield. If it had not been for the help of Southampton and his loyal household, the Danvers brothers could not have made good their escape to France. (When Southampton went to Paris with Sir Robert Cecil on his mission four years later, he had a reunion with the brothers at the court of Henri IV.)

One document of special interest lists thirteen "principal menservants of the Earl of Southampton, not yet examined" in the matter of the fugitive brothers, and among them is John Florio. After James Hunning, the Earl's steward; Francis Robinson, gentleman of the Earl's horse; and Payne, keeper of the Earl's wardrobe, there appear "the barber, Humphrey Drewell, who threatened Mr. Grose the Sheriff, and Signior Florio, an Italian, that did the like." On Saturday, 12 October, while the Danvers brothers were still in hiding, Lawrence Grose, sheriff of Southampton, was crossing on the Itchen-Southampton ferry in search of the fugitives, when two men on board, "one

Florio, an Italian, and one Humphrey Drewell, a servant of the Earl of Southampton, being in the said passage boat, threatened to cast Grose overboard, and said they would teach him to meddle with their fellows, with many other threatening words."[21] These two members of the Earl's staff do not sound like newcomers at Titchfield.

An interesting fact about Humphrey Drewell, the Figaro-like servant of Southampton, is that he was later knighted by Essex at Cádiz (the battle in which Southampton wanted to participate); apparently class lines in Elizabethan England were not insurmountable, at least in cases of military valour and good connections. Our last glimpse of the Southampton birthday crisis at Titchfield centers on a backstairs comic scene as played by Thomas Dredge, a stable-boy, and Humphrey Drewell. Dredge saw a bloodied velvet saddle that he recognized as the Danvers'. When he was ordered to saddle up seven horses for an unknown purpose, he realized something unusual was up and became excited. He started to blab to others, but Drewell took him aside and sternly asked why he was saying that Sir Henry Danvers was at Whitley Lodge when he had not actually seen him. Dredge explained about the bloodied saddle, whereupon Drewell "sware deeply by God's wounds and charged him upon pain of his life, not to speak any more of it, for that it was his lord's will and pleasure that the said Sir Henry Danvers should be there at Whitley Lodge."[22] We hear no more of John Florio in Southampton's service after this crisis.

In view of Southampton's culpability in arranging the escape, it is curious that the authorities took no action against him. Akrigg's theory is that the enormous damages levied by Burghley against the Earl at this juncture may have been partly a disguised fine, with the understanding that, if the Earl paid up immediately, the investigation into the brothers' escape would not go forward. One thing is certain: with Florio in Southampton's household during the wardship, Burghley knew everything.

The "Phaeton" Sonnet

In the front matter of *Second Fruits* there is a fine sonnet, signed "Phaeton," that is good enough to be Shakespeare's work. In studying the sonnets of this period, especially those of Sidney, Daniel, and Drayton, the English critic William Minto came to the conclusion that this poem was Shakespeare's. He presented a good case for his belief in *Characteristics of English Poets*. In Florio's book, the poem is given a full page by itself:

PHAETON TO HIS FRIEND FLORIO.

Sweet friend, whose name agrees with thy increase,
How fit a rival art thou of the spring!
For when each branch hath left his flourishing,
And green-locked summer's shady pleasures cease,
She makes the winter's storms repose in peace
And spends her franchise on each living thing:
The daisies sprout, the little birds do sing,
Herbs, gums, and plants do vaunt of their release.
So when that all our English wits lay dead
(Except the laurel that is evergreen),

Thou with thy fruits our barrenness o'erspread
And set thy flowery pleasance to be seen.
Such fruits, such flowerets of morality,
Were ne'er before brought out of Italy.

PHAETON.

"Those familiar with the commendatory verse of the period," Minto wrote, "will recognize at once its superiority. . . . Whereas most others strike us as making desperate efforts to find something to say, Phaeton seems to hit easily upon a fresh and fruitful idea. . . . There is a peculiar earnestness and simplicity in his tone. This is all the more noticeable because the main idea seems to have been suggested by one of the sonnets of Petrarch, which professes to have been sent with a present of flowers in the spring. There is no imitation beyond [this main thought]: and Phaeton follows it out in his own way."[23] Actually, Florio's preface is dated "The last of April, 1591," so that the poet's springtime tribute is most appropriate.

Minto also finds parallels between the sonnet's diction and that of the early plays, pointing out that "whose name agrees with thy increase" is echoed in Richard II's "O how that name befits my composition!" He overlooks a more obvious comparison in *The Rape of Lucrece:* "The little birds that tune their morning's joy" and "the little birds do sing" in line 7; and sonnet 12, in which "summer's green all girded up in sheaves" resembles "And greenlocked summer's shady pleasures cease." The variation of the Petrarchan rhyme-scheme used by Phaeton is not, of course, the rhyme scheme of the sonnets in Q.

The poet's use of the name Phaeton is worth exam-

121

ining. It occurs in Shakespeare's plays five times, all in early plays, twice in *3 Henry VI,* once each in *Two Gentlemen of Verona, Richard II,* and *Romeo and Juliet,* the most interesting perhaps being that in *Two Gentlemen:* "Why, Phaeton (for thou art Merops' son), wilt thou . . . with thy daring folly burn the world?" Phaeton, the symbol of a rash and presumptuous youth who almost burnt up the world by losing control of the sun-chariot lent him by Phoebus Apollo, is depicted in classic literature as a redhead. Interestingly, Shakespeare was a redhead. Professor M. H. Spielmann, an authority on the Stratford bust which was, of course, commissioned by the Shakespeare family, determined from his examination of the paint that the color of our poet's hair and beard was auburn. That is how the bust was painted originally, and after Edmund Malone caused it to be painted white in 1793, those colors were restored in the nineteenth century.[24] Minto explains Shakespeare's choice of the name Phaeton in terms of his defiance of the university wits: "When we remember how the player [Shakespeare] was jeered at by the University men for attempting the task of the learned (i.e., themselves), we see a characteristic meaning in 'Phaeton.' "[25] Greene's attack was not, of course, printed until the autumn of 1592, more than a year and a half after *Second Fruits,* but this would not have precluded earlier verbal or unpublished attacks on the "upstart."

Minto's conjecture that Shakespeare wrote the "Phaeton" sonnet is not, in the view of E. K. Chambers, "very convincing, although the sonnet has merit. And we are rather in the dark as to the possibilities of any association between Shakespeare and Florio as early as April 1591."[26]

Unfortunately, we are rather in the dark about most of Shakespeare's life. From a literary point of view, it is possible that the "Phaeton" sonnet is an early poem of Shakespeare's. From a scholarly point of view, it is clearly impossible to prove it. Assuming for a moment that it is Shakespeare's poem, three interesting facts would be added to our knowledge of the poet: the "Phaeton" poem would become his first work known to have appeared in print; his reference to the unofficial poet laureate, Sir Philip Sidney, would be added to the record ("Except the laurel that is evergreen"); and it would prove definitely that he knew Florio and Southampton in 1591.

Frances Yates wrote that "if one must hazard a guess as to the authorship of this poem, Samuel Daniel is the most obvious person."[27] However, Daniel left convincing evidence to controvert this suggestion, a laboured commendatory poem he later wrote for Florio's revised edition of *A World of Words*. This is three-fourths of the poem, which is too dull to quote in full:

To MY DEAR FRIEND AND BROTHER, M. JOHN
FLORIO, ONE OF THE GENTLEMEN OF HER
MAJESTY'S ROYAL PRIVY-CHAMBER

I stand not to give praise before the face
  Of this great work that doth itself commend,
But to congratulate the good and grace
  That England comes thereby to apprehend.
And in her name to thank your industry,
  Labourious Florio, who have so much wrought
To honour her in bringing Italy
  To speak her language, and to give her note

Of all the treasure that rich tongue contains.
  Wherein I cannot but admire your pains
In gathering up this universal store
  And furniture of words for every art
And skill of man: so that there seems no more
  Beyond this search that knowledge can impart.

[TEN LINES OMITTED]

And it were well, if in this season when
  They leave erecting churches, colleges,
And pious monuments, they would build men
  Who of their glory would be witnesses,
And what they do be theirs: as masons raise
  Works not for them but for their masters' praise.
For would they but be pleased to know how small
  A portion of that over-flowing waste
Which runs from them would turn the wheels and all
  The frame of wit, to make their glory last,
I think they would do something, but the stir
  Still about greatness gives it not the space
To look out from itself, or to confer
  Grace but by chance, and as men are in place.
But that concerns not me. It is enow
  I do applaud your work. Thus from my plow.

SAMUEL DANIEL.

It compares with the charming "Phaeton" sonnet as dross with gold. We may never know with certainty the identity of the talented author who in 1591 signed himself Phaeton but, if he continued as a poet, he probably enriched his country's literature.

Last Years

Florio worked with, helped publish, and became friends with many writers in the years following his departure from Southampton's service. A record of his special association with Ben Jonson is preserved in the poet's hand in a copy of *Volpone* that came into the collection of George III's books in the British Library: "To his loving father, and worthy freind [*sic*], Master John Florio: the aid of his Muses—Ben Jonson seals this testimony of freindship [*sic*] and love." The title-page bears the colophon "Printed for Thomas Thorppe [sic], 1607," the year in which Florio was fifty-four. Among Florio's other noted literary friends are Nicholas Breton, who dedicated *A Mad World, My Masters* to him in 1603; James Mabbe, the Spanish scholar and translator, who wrote a commendatory verse for the First Folio; Richard Hakluyt, author of the *Voyages,* who employed Florio as translator; and the melancholy Robert Burton, who appears with Florio as a character in William Vaughan's *Golden Fleece.*

In 1617, at age sixty-three, the widower Florio married his second wife, Rose Spicer. Queen Anne had made him a Groom of her Privy Chamber in 1604, which assured him a fixed income until her death in 1619. He then retired to Fulham, where, unfortunately, he lived in poverty until he died in 1624. His last will and testament makes sad reading. He left his daughter, Aurelia, the

BEN: IONSON

his

VOLPONE

or

THE FOXE.

—— *Simul & iucunda, & idonea dicere vitæ.*

Printed for *Thomas Thorppe.*
1607.

wedding-ring "wherewith I married her mother, being aggrieved at my very heart that by reason of my poverty I am not able to leave her anything else." The will indicates there was a financial dispute of some kind with his son-in-law, who "hath in his hands as a pawn a fair gold ring of mine, with thirteen fair table diamonds therein enchased, which cost Queen Anne, my gracious mistress, seven and forty pounds sterling." He left his library of 340 books to the Earl of Pembroke, as well as his unpublished manuscripts, asking Pembroke to see that "my dictionary and dialogues may be printed and the profit thereof accrue to my wife."[28] The Earl refused both the books and the manuscripts. Rose Florio died in 1626.

Florio's important bequest to the nation was not of course mentioned in his will—his great translation of Montaigne, "probably one of the most influential books ever published in this country," according to Yates.[29] We have no record of a connection between Florio and Shakespeare after the period of the sonnets, except a remote one—the traces of Florio's Montaigne that are to be found in *Hamlet*. This connection was pointed out by T. S. Eliot in his famous essay on the play: "We should like to know whether, and when, and after or at the same time as what personal experience, he [Shakespeare] read Montaigne, II, xii, *Apologie de Raimond Sebond.*"[30] The book of the play *Hamlet* was registered in 1602; the Bad Quarto was published in 1603, and the Good Quarto in 1604. Florio's translation of Montaigne, entered in 1600, was published in 1603.

These last years of Elizabeth's reign were by all reports very gloomy, especially the period following the abortive Essex-Southampton uprising on 8 February 1601. What a dramatic transformation had taken place in the ten years between 1591, which Florio called "this stirring time," and 1601, when "thick and palpable clouds of darkness" overshadowed England, according to the translators of the King James Bible, while the patron of John Florio and William Shakespeare suffered a confined doom in the Tower.

THE PLAY

*All books are full of love, with so many authors,
that it were labour lost to speak of love.*

JOHN FLORIO

"Jack Hath Not Jill"

THE REASON for introducing one of Shakespeare's plays into a book about his sonnets is that *Love's Labour's Lost* and the poems in Q are linked in significant ways. They were apparently written during the same period of time. This is evident from parallels between the language of the sonnets and that of the play; from the play's obsession with sonnets and sonnet-writing; from its private, even intimate, connections with Southampton; and from the generous use in the play of phrases and sentences from Florio's writings, starting with the play's title. The play and the poems cast light on each other.

The writing of sonnets, a preoccupation of the play's male characters, starts with Berowne's pretense of disliking the vogue, "Tush, none but minstrels like of sonneting," and ends with his confession: "By heaven, I do love, and it hath taught me to rhyme and be melancholy. . . . Well, she hath one o' my sonnets already." Four sonnets are recited in the play—Navarre's "So sweet a kiss the golden sun gives not"; Dumaine's "On a day, alack the day"; Longaville's "Did not the heavenly rhetoric of thine eye"; and Berowne's "If love make me forsworn, how shall I swear to love?" The contagion of sonnet-writing even affects Armado: "I am sure I shall turn sonnet! Devise, wit. Write, pen—for I am for whole volumes in folio!"

A climactic scene in Act IV has each of the men, thinking himself to be unobserved, come onstage reading his love poem, until each in turn is exposed. Berowne, the chief exposer, is the last to be caught. He then recites a magnificent hymn of praise for love, "From women's eyes this doctrine I derive," a line that paraphrases the ninth line of sonnet 14, "But from thine eyes my knowledge I derive."

Rosaline, Berowne's mistress, is black-eyed and raven-haired, like the woman of the sonnets. The dialogue repeatedly stresses her coloring. *Navarre:* "By heaven, thy love is black as ebony." *Berowne:* "Is ebony like her? O wood divine! / A wife of such wood were felicity." Shakespeare's dislike of the falsity of cosmetics and blond wigs is evident in these lines of Berowne:

> *O, if in black my lady's brows be decked,*
> *It mourns that painting and usurping hair*
> *Should ravish doters with a false aspect,*
> *And therefore is she born to make black fair*

just as it is in sonnet 68, the "False Hair" sonnet,

> *Before the golden tresses of the dead,*
> *The right of sepulchers, were shorn away*
> *To live a second life on second head,*
> *Ere beauty's dead fleece made another gay.*

The earliest critical view of *Love's Labour's Lost* was that it was Shakespeare's first play, and not a good one.

One of the early editors, Charles Gildon, wrote in 1710: "Since it is one of the worst of Shakespeare's plays—nay, I think I may say the very worst—I cannot but think it is his first."[1] Others began to conclude that it could not be Shakespeare's, until Dr. Johnson sternly rejected their assumptions: "In this play, which all the editors have concurred to censure and some have rejected as unworthy of our poet, it must be confessed that there are many passages mean, childish, and vulgar; and some which ought not to have been exhibited, as we are told they were, to a maiden Queen. But there are scattered through the whole many sparks of genius, nor is there any play that has more evident marks of the hand of Shakespeare."[2] One of the unexpectedly vulgar puns is delivered by Armado, boasting how intimate he is with the King of Navarre, who is pleased "sometime to lean upon my poor shoulder and with his royal finger, thus, dally with my excrement"—at this the other players freeze, until Armado adds: ". . . with my mustachio. But sweet heart, let that pass" (V, i, 110). One suspects that the maiden Queen was just as amused as her courtiers with this sort of humour as they were with the "greasy," joking talk between Boyet, Maria, and Costard at the end of the hunting-scene (IV, i, 131–40).

Love's Labour's Lost was the only play of Shakespeare's never performed during the Restoration, or in the eighteenth and early nineteenth centuries. Henry Irving considered it impossible to produce effectively. It is a comedy, but it does not end happily. As Berowne acknowledges in the final scene, "Our wooing doth not end like an old play: Jack hath not Jill . . ." Fortunately, in our time, the Old Vic Company, the Royal Shakespeare Festival, the New York Shakespeare Festival, and many other companies rescued it for the delight of theatregoers and proved that it can be produced brilliantly.

Love's Labour's Lost contains 2,785 lines, with more than twice as much rhyme (1,150 lines) as any other play except *A Midsummer Night's Dream* (798). It has nearly as much prose as the *Dream,* and less blank verse than any play except *Merry Wives.* Mark Van Doren perceived the fascination that the writing of *Love's Labour's Lost* must have exercised over its author: "The play is literary, but it is a delight to any listening ear," he wrote. "It is satire, but it has absorbed the best along with the worst of the manners which it satirizes. It is Shakespeare's most artificial work, but it ends with his most natural song."[3] Kittredge called this song of spring and winter, when daisies are pied and icicles hang by the wall "one of the best songs in the world."[4] *Love's Labour's Lost* is the only play about which we have critical testimony from one of the original players: in 1605 Richard Burbage told a knight who apparently never heard of it that "for wit and mirth *Love's Labour's Lost* will please her [Queen Anne] exceedingly."[5] Though it was not his first play to be published, it was the first to bear William Shakespeare's name on its title-page.

Usually Shakespeare is chary of topical allusions, but this play abounds in them. For the most part they are "in" jokes, obscure or inexplicable when detected (there are at least seven textual cruxes), and suggest that originally the play was written not for the general public but for a select or courtly audience. However, these unrecoverable allusions and strained puns do not lessen the dramatic effect; in performance, they hardly matter.

The story of *Love's Labour's Lost* seems to be original, and no source has been discovered for it, although Primaudaye's *The Academy,* translated into English in 1586, may have suggested the setting. Four young men resolve to abstain from the company of women for three years and to live as "fellow-scholars" in a celibate academy, except that four appealing young women arrive on the scene and make nonsense of their stern resolves. The pairing and grouping of this octet is almost choreographed, with formal and elegant movements, while their witty tongues seldom rest. For laughs and horseplay, the author has introduced a substructure of stock characters from Italian comedy—a braggart soldier or *capitano* (Armado), a witty boy or *zanni* (Moth), a schoolmaster or *pedante* (Holofernes), a parasite or *affamato* (Nathaniel), a clown or *pantalone* (Costard), and so on. The title-page of the 1598 quarto reveals that contemporaries regarded the play as "A Pleasant Conceited Comedy," that is to say, one full of fanciful, ingenious, and witty conceits. *Love's Labour's Lost* is, among other things, a play about playing with words. As Moth says, "They have been at a great feast of languages, and stolen the scraps." And Costard: "O, they have lived long on the alms-basket of words."

The play's date may be 1593–94. It contains allusions to the plague of 1592–93, to Henri IV's conversion in July 1593, and to Chapman's *The Shadow of Night* (1594). It is no coincidence that in 1592 three of Lyly's plays were published, giving Shakespeare a model for this kind of witty social comedy directed at a select audience. I believe the inspiration of *Love's Labour's Lost* is in some way connected with Greene's savaging of Shakespeare in

A
PLEASANT
Conceited Comedie
CALLED,
Loues labors loſt.

As it vvas preſented before her Highnes
this laſt Chriſtmas.

Newly corrected and augmented
By W. Shakeſpere.

Imprinted at London by *W.W.*
for *Cutbert Burby.*
1598.

Title-page of "Love's Labour's Lost," in revised quarto, 1598

September 1592. Our poet's need to prove himself capable of a learned comedy (since the thrust of Greene's slur was against his lack of a university education) would have been great. It is no accident that the play has so much rhyme and so little blank verse. Greene's taunt "[he] supposes he is as well able to bombast out a blank verse as the best of you" apparently hit its mark.

The most baffling crux is Armado's "some enigma, some riddle," also called the "envoy" (III, i, 90–93):

> *The Fox, the Ape, and the Humblebee*
> *Were still at odds, being but three,*
> *Until the Goose came out of door*
> *And stayed the odds by adding four.*

Frances Yates suggests a numerological background for these lines: "There is probably a memory of some jargon familiar to the 'School of Night' in this and other passages hinting at 'number.' "[6] For example, when Berowne's love for Rosaline is exposed, Dumaine says: "Now the *number* is *even*," and Berowne replies: "True, true, we are *four*." This is a plausible explanation, but no one has discovered precisely who are meant by the Fox, the Ape, the Humblebee, and the Goose. (Essex, at his trial for treason, cried out when Sir Walter Ralegh took the stand: "What boots it the Fox to testify?" "Goose" was a synonym for prostitute. As for the Ape, my guess is that Greene's characterization of Shakespeare as "one of those Apes" was not easily forgotten.) However, the meaning of these lines is unrecoverable. The allusions were probably understood only by a few. They were not intended to be meaningful to the general audience, then or now.

While it is a learned, rhyming, and literary play, at the

same time *Love's Labour's Lost* satirizes false learning and
literary pretension. Its deepest thrust is against affectation
and falseness *of any kind*—of language, as in euphuism;
of life-style, as in the artificial and celibate "academe"
doomed to failure from the start; of pedantry, as in the
mangled and undigested scraps of learning mouthed by
pompous Holofernes and obsequious Nathaniel; of status,
as in Armado's high social pretensions while he lacks a
clean shirt. Berowne's recantation at the end is itself a
dazzling display of style, even as he vows to reform that
style:

Taffeta phrases, silken terms precise,
Three-piled hyperboles, spruce affectation,
Figures pedantical; these summer-flies
Have blown me full of maggot ostentation.
I do forswear them, and I here protest
By this white glove—how white the hand, God knows!—
Henceforth my wooing mind shall be expressed
In russet yeas and honest kersey noes.   [V, ii, 406-13]

There are an astonishing number of parallels between
the language of the sonnets and that of the play. These
examples are a few of the most notable:

But from thine eyes my knowledge I derive   SON. 14
From women's eyes this doctrine I derive   LLL, IV.3.302

Devouring Time, blunt thou the lion's paws   SON. 19
When spite of cormorant devouring Time   LLL, I.1.9

I will not praise that purpose not to sell   SON. 21
To things of sale a seller's praise belongs   LLL, IV.3.240

. . . *my heart / Which in thy breast doth live*   SON. 22
Hence ever then my heart is in thy breast   LLL, V.2.890

I lose both twain   SON. 42
I remit both twain   LLL, V.2.459

. . . *the world-without-end hour*   SON. 57
. . . *a world-without-end bargain*   LLL, V.2.863

Therefore my mistress' brows are raven black,   SON. 127
Her eyes so suited, and they mourners seem
At such who, not born fair, no beauty lack,
Slandering creation with a false esteem.

O if in black my lady's brows be decked   LLL, IV.3.257F.
It mourns that painting and usurping hair
Should ravish doters with a false aspect,
And therefore is she born to make black fair.

Then will I swear beauty herself is black,   SON. 132
And all they foul that thy complexion lack.

That I may swear beauty doth lack . . .   LLL, IV.3.268–9
No face is fair that is not full so black.

Past cure I am, now reason is past care   SON. 147
Great reason, for past cure is still past care.   LLL, V.2.29

There are also two word-combinations, unusual for the period, that appear both in the sonnets and the play— "new-fired" and "new-fangled," the only other use for the latter being in *As You Like It*. But what evidence is there for connecting *Love's Labour's Lost* with the third Earl of Southampton?

A Sonnet-Play for Southampton

To the best of my knowledge, no one has hitherto shown that the opening words of the play are derived from the young Earl himself: "Let fame, that all hunt after in their lives . . ." The Southampton figure, Ferdinand, King of Navarre, not only opens the play with these words, but proceeds in heightened language reminiscent of Q to introduce two of the sonnets' main themes, "devouring Time" and Death:

> Let fame, that all hunt after in their lives,
> Live registered upon our brazen tombs
> And then grace us in the disgrace of death
> When, spite of cormorant devouring Time,
> Th' endeavour of this present breath may buy
> That honour which shall bate his scythe's keen edge
> And make us heirs of all eternity.

The first line states the theme of an essay Southampton wrote for Lord Burghley as an undergraduate at St. John's, in the summer of 1586. As Akrigg has pointed out, without making a connection with this play, Southampton "became decidedly eloquent when declaring how every man 'burns with a certain boundless lust for fame.' "[7] Although the fair copy of this Latin essay now rests in the archives of the Cecil Papers, the young essayist, in author-like fashion, no doubt kept his own copy, which a few years later gave Shakespeare his opening line. "The opening speech of the king on the immortality of fame," wrote Walter Pater in 1895, "on the triumph of fame over death, and the nobler parts of Berowne display something of the monumental style of Shakespeare's sonnets, and are not without their conceits of thought and expression. This connection of *Love's Labour's Lost* with Shakespeare's poems is further enforced by the actual insertion in it of three sonnets and a faultless song."[8]

Another connection with Southampton is the reappearance in the play of the curious locution "both twain," borrowed from the sonnet about Southampton's robbery of Shakespeare's mistress; it occurs nowhere else in Shakespeare's writing. The bitter line in sonnet 42 reads:

Both find each other, and I lose both twain.

In the play the phrase is repeated by Berowne. The masked ladies have swapped their jewels, in order to trick the men into mistaking their identities, and this causes Berowne to court the Princess and Navarre to woo Rosaline. After the hoax is exposed, the Princess asks Berowne ironically, "What! Will you have me, or your pearl again?" and he replies rather sharply, "Neither of either. I remit both twain." Perhaps the only other person who might have appreciated this allusion to the sonnet was Southampton; perhaps the author alone got wry amusement from it. It is as "in" an allusion as one can conceive, but there it is.

Another Southampton connection involves Sir Philip Sidney's posthumous work of criticism, *An Apology for Poetry,* written around 1581 but not published until 1595, which would have been accessible to Southampton, as well as to his poet, through Essex. That it provided Shakespeare with a source of inspiration for his comedy is confirmed by the following passage:

> I speak to this purpose, that all the end of the comical part be not upon such scornful matters as stirreth laughter only, but mixed with it that delightful teaching which is the end of poetry. . . . For what is it to make folks gape at a wretched beggar and a beggarly clown? . . . But rather a busy loving Courtier, and a heartless threatening Thraso; a selfwise-seeming Schoolmaster; an awry-transformed Traveller; these if we saw walk in stage names, which we play naturally, therein were delightful laughter, and teaching delightfulness.[9]

Shakespeare not only took Sidney's advice literally, in inventing his characters, but had schoolmaster Holofernes describe the braggart soldier and traveller from Spain (Armado) in the first scene of Act V in these words: "His humour is lofty, his discourse peremptory, his tongue filed, his eye ambitious, his gait majestical, and his general behaviour vain, ridiculous, and Thrasonical." This concatenation indicates that Shakespeare was influenced in part by *An Apology for Poetry*.

There is a final connection with Southampton in the curious ending of *Love's Labour's Lost,* where Jack hath not Jill. The situation in the play, the "little academe" of unmarried men, is consonant with Southampton's status during the critical years 1593–94, when he was still resisting Lord Burghley's pressure to marry his grandchild. For the playwright under these circumstances to have ended his play with the traditional climax of marriage might not have pleased his patron. How did he solve the problem? He arranged a sudden entrance for Marcade, announcing the death of the King of France, whose daughter must now depart with her ladies. Richard David has called this ending "one of the greatest *coups de théâtre* in Shakespeare, and it brings, after the whirlwind of fooling that has preceded it, the still small voice of sincerity and actuality."[10] It not only works perfectly as theatre, but Shakespeare's genius tops it off with the song that "in some mysterious way," according to Alfred Harbage, puts the world in perspective. The female quartet then gives the four men "a twelvemonth and a day" of grace, a convenient year of mourning for the dead King, before their marriages can be possible. This conforms with Southampton's desire, as reported to Burghley by Viscount Montague, for a "further respite of one year, to ensure resolution in respect of his young years."

As for John Florio, while it would be inaccurate to say that he is literally a character in the play, his contributions of language and of his profession of schoolmaster to at least one of the characters, Holofernes, and his influence on the play's composition are evident in several ways, starting with the play's title.

The Florio Connections

In his "Discourses upon Music and Love" in *First Fruits*, John Florio concludes: "We need not speak so much of

143

love, all books are full of love with so many authors, that it were *labour lost to speak of love.*" These humourless lines not only gave Shakespeare a comical title for his play, but a light suddenly breaks when we find Florio in his next dialogue, a "Discourse upon Lust," proving pedantically and anticlimactically that "Lust was the cause that Troy was ruinated . . . Sodom and Gomorrah were destroyed, and . . . Holofernes fell in love with Judith." The name Shakespeare chose for the pedant in *Love's Labour's Lost* is Holofernes.

Without citing these coincidences, William Warburton flatly asserted in 1747 that "by *Holofernes* is designed a particular character, a pedant and schoolmaster of our author's time, one John Florio, a teacher of the Italian tongue in London, who has given us a small dictionary of that language under the title *A World of Words.*"[11] But an impressive pair of authorities, Samuel Johnson and Edmund Malone, rejected this identification of Holofernes for different reasons. Dr. Johnson had another candidate and said that "notwithstanding the plausibility of Dr. Warburton's conjecture," he (Johnson) "considered the character of Holofernes as borrowed from Rombus of Sir Philip Sidney,"[12] in the masque *The Lady of May.* Malone argued that Holofernes could not be Florio because Shakespeare "would not make the Italian an object of ridicule" while they were both under Southampton's patronage.[13] For a long time this double rejection of Florio seemed much too weighty to be challenged, but in recent years it has been overturned.

First, Malone's argument collapsed when it was finally understood that Lord Burghley, during his wardship, had installed Florio in Southampton's household as a spy. The

Essex-Southampton circle was much too sophisticated to have been unaware of this. In the play there even seems to be an oblique reference to Florio's double-dealing. In the masque of the Worthies in Act V, Holofernes is baited mercilessly as he thrice repeats the phrase "Judas I am." Unless a deep private animus were at work, it would seem excessive for the others, including Berowne, to jeer at him and call him Judas Iscariot, when he is acting the part of Judas Maccabæus.

Second, not until this century was the unpopular Bishop Warburton's "conjecture" about Holofernes reexamined as belonging perhaps to an early verbal tradition about the Italian tutor and the play. "To state with such confidence that Florio was Holofernes seems an extraordinary assertion for anyone, even an eighteenth-century editor, to have made entirely out of his own imagination," Frances Yates concluded in her book, the most detailed and knowledgeable study of *Love's Labour's Lost*. Florio's presence in the play can no longer be "dismissed with Olympian scorn."[14]

There is additional evidence of Florio's presence, in that Holofernes quotes an Italian proverb from *First Fruits* (which Florio repeated in *Second Fruits*): "Venetia, Venetia, / Chi non ti vede, non ti pretia (Venice, Venice, who sees thee not, praises thee not)." There is also Holofernes' habit of stringing out a series of synonyms, as Florio does in his dictionary: ". . . hangeth like a jewel in the ear of caelo, the sky, the welkin, the heaven; and anon falleth like a crab on the face of terra, the soil, the land, the earth." And I note an echo of Florio's unintentionally funny scenes of price-haggling in *First Fruits,* as in this colloquy about the cost of a pair of gloves: "You shall give me half a crown." "It is too much, certain." "Not so, sir." "I will give you two shillings." "It is too little, sir." "It is enough, certain." "Well, take them."[15] In the play, this has a parallel in the clown's colloquy. Costard: "Remuneration? O that's the Latin word for three farthings. . . . 'What's the price of this inkle?' 'One penny.' 'No, I'll give you a remuneration.' . . . I will never buy and sell out of this word" (III, i, 138–42).

It would be foolish to insist that Florio is the *exclusive* source for Holofernes, or that the character is a "portrait" of Florio. Shakespeare was an imaginative artist, and Holofernes is a dramatic creation, a comic triumph with a character and persona of his own who will continue to amuse audiences as long as plays are performed—and who would, of course, do so if Florio's existence were unknown to us. There is proof in the 1598 quarto that in Shakespeare's mind Holofernes was already a stage type before our poet gave him a name. This is revealed in the stage directions, which list him in a few places as "Pedant," just as Armado is similarly listed as "Braggart." It is a tribute to Shakespeare's humanity that, despite the rough treatment accorded Holofernes, the schoolmaster delivers an effective reproof to the merciless courtiers: "This is not generous, not gentle, not humble." Armado also recovers from similar humiliation in his defense of Hector: "Sweet chucks, beat not the bones of the buried. When he breathed, he was a man."

There may be other sources for Holofernes besides Florio, and whether Sidney's Rombus is one of them any reader of *The Lady of May* can decide; the only resemblance I can find is that they are both pedants. In one sense, Dr. Johnson was right in detecting the influence of Sidney in this play, though he does not cite *An Apology for Poetry.*

My interest in Florio's connections with *Love's Labour's Lost* is limited to what his presence therein reveals about the play's date of composition and that of the sonnets. The ups and downs of the critical status of the play over the centuries demonstrate the vagaries of Shakespearean criticism. What was once considered his "worst play" is in our time regarded as his first comic work of real genius. Its artificiality and its preposterous accents of Elizabethan literary pedantry are, at the end, transcended by the extraordinary simplicity and reality of this winter song:

> *When all aloud the wind doth blow*
>   *And coughing drowns the parson's saw,*
> *And birds sit brooding in the snow,*
>   *And Marian's nose looks red and raw,*
> *When roasted crabs hiss in the bowl,*
> *Then nightly sings the staring owl,*
>   *Tu-who,*
> *Tu-whit, tu-who: a merry note,*
> *While greasy Joan doth keel the pot.*

"They Have Revived an Old One"

Notwithstanding Gerald Eades Bentley's claim that "the only *facts* so far established [about the Earl of Southampton as the poet's patron] are Shakespeare's dedication of two long poems to him in 1593 and 1594,"[16] there is another interesting fact about his patron for which documentary evidence exists. In January 1605 Southampton presented a revival of *Love's Labour's Lost* in his house for the entertainment of Queen Anne. There are three documents establishing the facts, the first being a letter from Sir Walter Cope to Southampton's old friend Robert Cecil, now Lord Cranborne, with whom the Earl was apparently sharing the responsibility for the Queen's revels during the holiday season. "I have sent, and been all morning hunting," wrote Sir Walter, "for players, jugglers, and such kind of creatures, but find them hard to find. Wherefore, leaving notes for them to seek me, Burbage is come, and says there is no new play that the Queen hath not seen, but they have revived an old one, called *Love's Labour* [*sic*] *Lost,* which for wit and mirth he says will please her exceedingly. And this is appointed to be played *tomorrow night* [my italics] at my Lord of Southampton's, unless you send a writ to remove the corpus cum causa to your house in Strand. Burbage is my messenger, ready attending your pleasure."[17]

Cranborne could have responded to his friend Southampton's courtesy in only one way. In view of the Earl's arrangements—"this is appointed to be played tomorrow night"—the new lord was not likely to misunderstand Cope's joking advice (or was it Southampton's?) to "send a writ," particularly when the Earl outranked him.

The second document is a letter dated 15 January 1605, which Dudley Carleton wrote to John Chamberlain: "It seems we shall have Christmas all the year. . . . The last night's revels were kept at my Lord of Cranborne's, where the Queen with the D[uke] of Holst[ein] and a great part of the Court were feasted, and *the like two nights before* [my italics] at my Lord of Southampton's."[18] This letter pinpoints the Southampton dates as 12 and 13 January, with the former perhaps more likely for the presentation of the play. The third document is an entry in the Revels Account of a performance by His Majesty's players, early in January, of *Love's Labour's Lost.*[19] E. K. Chambers believes it got entered there, although it was not paid for by the Treasurer of the Chamber, because in view of the Queen's presence the Revels officer was in attendance.[20] It is also conceivable (though we do not know) that John Florio, as a Groom of the Queen's Privy Chamber, may have attended for the same reason. If so, and if he recognized himself in Holofernes, Resolute John probably was not amused.

This revival for the Queen seems to have given the play a new lease on life. A 1631 title-page shows that, after the players had acquired the Blackfriars, it was performed there. The reasons for Southampton's decision to revive *Love's Labour's Lost* during the Queen's revels in the second year of the new reign may have been nostalgic or sentimental ones, or simply his good taste; we can only guess. But his revival of the sonnet-play after Elizabeth's death establishes this fact: Southampton's interest and delight in Shakespeare's work was very much alive in 1605.

In reviewing the many interconnections we have so far considered, they can be recapitulated as follows: Sonnet 26, a paraphrase of the 1594 dedicatory letter, connects Shakespeare's sonnets with Southampton. The sonnets are connected with *Love's Labour's Lost* by the recurrence in the play of phrases from the sonnets; by Rosaline, the raven-haired "wanton" with whom Berowne is in love; and by the play's four sonnets and its obsession with sonnet-writing. Southampton is connected to the play by the opening line; by the character of Navarre, the unmarried nobleman who "hath not Jill" at the play's close, and whose bachelorhood is given the respite of "a twelvemonth and a day." Florio is connected to Southampton by his "pay and patronage" statement, and by his deportment when the Danvers brothers sought refuge in the household. Florio is connected to *Love's Labour's Lost* by the play's title; by the character of the pedant, Holofernes, and perhaps that of Armado; and by citations from and references to his published work.

All these incidents and coincidences, including the 1605 revival of the play, were over and done with long before Q was published in 1609. If one were to diagram these interconnections, the pattern would be circular: Shakespeare—Southampton—Sonnets—*Love's Labour's Lost*—Florio—Southampton—Shakespeare. There is no direct connection between Shakespeare and Florio, unless the "Phaeton" sonnet could be proved to be Shakespeare's. As for Florio's connection with Thomas Thorpe, we shall now review the career of the publisher of Q.

THE PUBLISHER

So this your poor friend though he have found much of you, yet doth still follow you for as much more.

THORPE TO FLORIO, *1610*

The Former Bookseller

THOUGH WE SHALL probably never know exactly how the sonnets reached print, we do know a few facts about their publisher. Thomas Thorpe had three distinctions: literary taste, insufficient capital, and a penchant for writing elaborate dedications. A single dedication has assured him a permanent place in literary history, the famous and baffling pattern of words in Q: "To the only begetter of these ensuing sonnets . . ."

Thorpe was born in 1569 or 1570 in Barnet, Middlesex, the son of an innkeeper. An autodidact who devoted his whole life to the book trade, he started at fourteen as an apprentice to a reputable stationer, Richard Watkins. By 1594 he had achieved the "freedom" of the Stationers' Company, the right to publish books on his own. For a time he had a bookstore, The Tiger's Head, at St. Paul's Churchyard; his younger brother, Richard, was a bookseller in Chester.[1] It was not until 1600, when he had reached thirty, that Thorpe possessed sufficient financial means to make his debut as a publisher.

Edward Blount, the friend of Marlowe who had published the unfinished *Hero and Leander* two years earlier,

helped Thorpe acquire the rights to the first book of Marlowe's translation of Lucan's *Pharsalia*. When Thorpe
issued the book in 1600, he wrote a dedication in the
form of a letter to Blount, recounting in ironic terms his
lack of success in obtaining a rich patron, a theme which
seemed to haunt him. The letter starts with a pun on his
friend's name, as well as a publishing pun on the word
"sheets," meaning both the pages of a book and the
shroud of a ghost in the Churchyard—that is, St. Paul's,
the book center:

To his Kind and True Friend:
EDWARD BLUNT [*sic*]

Blount: I purpose to be blunt with you, and out of
my dullness to encounter you with a *Dedication* in
memory of that pure elemental wit, *Christopher
Marlowe,* whose ghost or *Genius* is to be seen walk
the Churchyard in (at the least) three or four sheets.
Methinks you should presently look wild now, and
grow humourously frantique upon the taste of it.

Well, lest you should, let me tell you. This spirit
was sometimes a familiar of your own, *Lucan's first
book translated,* which (in regard of your old right
in it) I have raised in the circle of your Patronage.
But stay now, Edward, (if I mistake not) you are to
accommodate yourself with some few instructions
touching the property of a Patron that you are not
yet possessed of, and to study them for your better
grace as our Gallants do fashion.

First, you must be proud and think you have merit
enough in you, though you are ne'er so empty. Then

when I bring you the book take Physic, and keep
state, assign me a time by your man to come again,
and afore the day be sure to have changed your
lodging. In the meantime, sleep little and sweat with
the invention of some pitiful dry jest or two which
you may happen to utter, with some little (or not at
all) marking of your friends when you have found
a place for them to come in at: or if by chance
something has dropped from you worth the taking
up, weary all that come to you with the often repetition of it; censure scornfully enough, and something
like a traveller; commend nothing lest you discredit
your (that which you would seem to have) judgement. These things, if you can mould yourself to
them, *Ned,* I make no question but they will not become you. One special virtue in our Patrons of these
days I have promised myself you shall fit excellently,
which is to give nothing. Yes, thy love I will chal-
lenge as my peculiar Object both in this, and (I
hope) many more succeeding offices: Farewell, I
affect not the world should measure my thoughts to
thee by a scale of this Nature: Leave to think good
of me when I fall from thee.

> *Thine in all rites of perfect friendship,*
> THOM. THORPE

The connection between Thorpe and Florio seems to
date from late in 1608 or early in 1609. John Healey's
translation of Joseph Hall's satiric work in Latin prose,
Mundus Alter et Idem, was entered by Thorpe on 18 January 1609, three months before he entered Q. *The Dis-*

covery of a New World, as Healey rendered the Latin title, is dedicated to William Herbert, the third Earl of Pembroke, whose patronage of the work had been procured by Florio. (Florio's father, Michael Angelo Florio, had in his day been patronized by the Earl's father.) Frances Yates has detected Florio's influence in the tone of Healey's prefatory letter to Hall: "Let the whole world of fleering critics traduce me or no, it skills not whether. Both I am armed for, one I look for, neither I care for. Thus from him that ever will be yours. Resolute J.R."[2] Yates remarks on the "combative strain" of these words, and adds: "How strange that Healey should sign himself with Florio's own battle-cry of 'Resolute'!"[3] She also suspects Florio's hand in the translation itself; one passage describing the obesity of the women of Eat-allia (Pamphagonia) says: "The German *fraus* do prettily well in imitation of these fusty-lugs," but in Hall's Latin the fat women are Italian.

One year later, when Thorpe published another Healey translation, this time from the Greek, *Epictetus His Manual,* his dedication to John Florio reveals the latter's role in having obtained Pembroke's "impregnable protection" for the previous book. Does it reveal more? Thorpe's second sentence after "Sir" is perhaps unintentionally informative:

To a true favourer
of forward spirits,
MAISTER JOHN FLORIO.

Sir, as distressed Sostratus spake to more fortunate Areius, to make him his mediator to Augustus, "The

learned love the learned, if they be rightly learned."
So this your poor friend though he have found much
of you, yet doth still follow you for as much more—
that as his Maecenas you would write to Augustus,
"Be as mindful of Horace as you would be of myself." For his apprentice's essay you procured (God
thank you) an impregnable protection. He now
prays the same Patron (most worthy of all praise)
for his journeyman's masterpiece. Yet as· Horace to
Vinnius for his verses to Augustus, *Ne studio nostri
pecces.* And though the land be the Lord's wherein
he most laboured, yet see a handful of fruits is fallen
to your share who first showed his workman-
ship. . . .

[THE OMITTED PASSAGE EXTOLS THE VIRTUES
OF EPICTETUS.]

He is more senseless than a stock that hath no good
sense of this Stoic. For the translation and translator,
to whom better recourse than one so travail'd in
translation; both pattern and patron of translators.
Artificers best judge of arts. Wise they must be that
judge the wise. But a short book would have no long
Epistle than a small Town a great gate. Wherefore,
as he desired, I have done: Who rest,

Yours in true hearted love,
TH. TH.

In calling himself "your poor friend," in comparing himself to "distressed Sostratus," in alluding to Florio as
"more fortunate Areius" (Florio was now a groom of

Queen Anne's privy chamber at an annual salary of one hundred pounds), Thorpe reveals that he was in need of money in 1610 and that apparently his publication of Q in the previous year had not been a financial success. It is intriguing to speculate whether the "much" that Thorpe "found of" Florio included the manuscript of Shakespeare's sonnets, in addition to resolute John's success in securing Pembroke's patronage for the Joseph Hall satire. Was Florio the procurer of Q? He was at least in a position to obtain copies of the sonnets when he and Shakespeare were under Southampton's patronage. It may even have been part of his job to pass on to Lord Burghley copies of poems addressed to his ward.

The answers, of course, remain speculative, but considering the coincidence of the dates, it seems remarkable that in the voluminous studies of the sonnets over the centuries no one has hitherto commented on the possible implication of the words of Thorpe's dedication to Florio in 1610.

A List of Distinction

Thomas Thorpe's publishing career lasted from 1600 to 1624, and he published forty books in all—relatively small in quantity, but notable for twenty-six books of enduring quality. In addition to Marlowe in 1600 and Shakespeare in 1609, he published four plays of Ben Jonson, including *Volpone* and *Sejanus;* three plays of

George Chapman; Healey's translations of Epictetus, Theophrastus, Augustine's *The City of God,* and Joseph Hall's satire; the anonymous play, *Histriomastix, or the Playwright Whipt,* usually attributed to John Marston; and *The Odcombian Banquet,* by the travelling Jacobean, Thomas Coryate.

Thorpe formed a brief partnership with William Aspley (a member of the syndicate that later launched the First Folio, and one of the two distributors of Q) for the publication of a few books, among them John Marston's *The Malcontent* in 1604 and *Eastward Ho* by Chapman, Jonson, and Marston in 1605. The latter play, which the authorities objected to as anti-Scots, landed the first two poets temporarily in prison.

Thorpe in 1604 published a curious eighteen-page booklet by Thomas Wright, entitled *A Succinct Philosophicall declaration of the nature of Clymactericall yeeres, occasioned by the death of Queen Elizabeth.* Its author was an interesting and, for those complicated times, unusual Catholic priest. Fr. Thomas Wright, whom Essex had defended to the Queen as "as good a subject as any she had," had been ordained a Jesuit. He was a member of the recusant Wright family of York; his younger brother, William, was also a Jesuit. After many years abroad in the Jesuit missions, he condemned the Spaniards, arguing that English Catholics were loyal subjects of their sovereign. The intercession of the Provincial, Fr. Persons, saved Wright from expulsion from the Society; he was released from his vows and in 1595, as a secular priest, returned openly to London, where he surrendered to Anthony Bacon, secretary of the Earl of Essex. He was the only Catholic priest that Southampton,

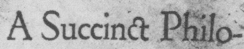

A Succinct Philo-
sophicall declaration of the nature
of *Clymactericall* yeeres, occasioned by the
death of Queene *Elizabeth*.
(·.·)

Written by T: W:
[Thomas Wright]

· LONDON
Printed for Thomas Thorpe , and are to be
sold in Paules Church-yard at the signe
of the Crane, by Walter Burre.
1 6 0 4.

A Thomas Thorpe title-page, 1604

at his trial for treason, acknowledged having known. Wright also had the distinction of being the apparent instrument of Ben Jonson's conversion to Catholicism around 1598.

The 1604 booklet about climacterical years, which was published separately by Thorpe, was also incorporated as a final chapter into Wright's major opus, *The Passions of the Mind.** This work of nearly four hundred pages, originally published in 1598, was revised and reissued in 1601 and in three editions thereafter. Apparently too expensive a project for Thorpe, it contains Wright's dedication to Southampton, recently released from the Tower, as well as one of Ben Jonson's rare sonnets, "To the Author." The conjunction of Thomas Thorpe, John Florio, and Ben Jonson occurs, at least visually, in the inscribed copy of *Volpone* in the British Library (see page 126).

Of all the books published by Thorpe, only two—a Chapman play and Healey's translation of Epictetus—had a second printing during Thorpe's lifetime. His good taste was rarely accompanied by good luck, and he never had enough cash. Things apparently looked up a bit in 1616, when he printed the second edition of Epictetus. The Earl of Pembroke's patronage, which had been unavailable for the earlier edition despite Thorpe's plea of financial distress, was finally obtained with Florio's help. It enabled Thorpe once more to indulge himself by writing a dedication to Pembroke, but the tone this time is obsequious to the point of embarrassing modern ears: "It may seem strange to Your Lordship out of what frenzy one of my

---

* *The Passions of the Mind* by Thomas Wright, reprinted from the 1604 edition by the University of Illinois Press, Urbana, 1971, with an excellent introduction by Thomas O. Sloan.

meanness hath presumed to commit this sacrilege," wrote
Thorpe.[4] (This reminds one of the Heminge and Condell
dedication to Pembroke and his brother Philip in the First
Folio: "We have justly observed no man to come near
Your Lordships but with a kind of religious address.")
Thorpe's dedication proudly displays the Earl's titles at
length. Yet some contend that the Thomas Thorpe who
wrote these words was, in his most famous dedication,
addressing the Earl as "Master W.H."

The chief reason for Thomas Thorpe being remembered today is, of course, Shakespeare's *Sonnets*. As a
member of the book trade, he had good reason in 1609
to think that he might have a best-seller on his hands.
Shakespeare's reputation and popularity were at their
height. Two poems, including one of the more sensational sonnets, "Two loves I have, of comfort and despair," revealing that one of the loves was a man and the
other a woman, had already appeared in several printings
of *A Passionate Pilgrim.* This alone might have been expected to create advance interest in and ensure the success
of the collected sonnets—"Never before Imprinted," as
Thorpe announced, not entirely accurately, in large type
on the cover. There are other signs that he anticipated
success: he had two booksellers, instead of the usual one,
stock his book—William Aspley, and John Wright,
"dwelling at Christ Church gate." Commercial euphoria
is also implicit in Thorpe's self-description, "the well-
wishing adventurer in setting forth."

Northrop Frye has characterized Thorpe's strange dedication as "one floundering and illiterate sentence . . .
no more likely to be an accurate statement of fact than
any other commercial plug."[5] Let us now examine it, in

the context in which it belongs, as the work not of our poet but of the publisher.

"*To the Only Begetter*"

The peculiar punctuation of the thirteen lines—as much as the ambiguity of the word "begetter"—makes a circular and unsolvable puzzle out of the strange concoction that Thorpe signed "T.T.":

TO . THE . ONLY . BEGETTER . OF .

THESE . INSUING . SONNETS .

M^r. W. H. ALL . HAPPINESS .

AND . THAT . ETERNITY .

PROMISED .

BY .

OUR . EVER-LIVING . POET .

WISHETH .

THE . WELL-WISHING .

ADVENTURER . IN .

SETTING .

FORTH .

T. T.

Thorpe gave more generous space to the dedication than to any single element in the book. It is preceded by one blank page and followed by another—the *only* blanks among the cramped eighty pages—while the sonnets run on, page after page, in annoyingly crowded fashion (see page 229). Its genesis may have been an accident, the result of a printing problem. (This is not unknown in book publishing; T. S. Eliot, for example, revealed that the American publisher of *The Waste Land* asked him to increase the number of pages of his slim book with the "bogus" notes—his adjective—that became permanently attached to the poem.[6]) If Q's dedication was, in fact, brought about by the kind of printer's problem familiar to those experienced in book production, it could have happened thus:

Following the paging of Q, Thorpe was informed by the printer that out of the nine eight-page and two four-page signatures making up the book, three blank pages remained. Did Thorpe wish to fill them up, and if so how? He had the option of putting a blank leaf (two sides) at the end, also leaving the title-page verso blank. He rejected this, perhaps because it would not be considered good publishing to display a slim quarto on the bookstalls with a blank back cover. There was another option: to make use of the three blanks in the front-matter. A table of contents? But the poems had no titles (which would also have prevented their use as back-matter). A prefatory note? The less said about an unauthorized book the better. A dedication? That would do it—a *brief* note about the begetter, in an interesting design, to be signed with the publisher's initials . . .

As for the meaning of the dedication, would not everyone agree that the following is a fair and accurate re-arrangement of the inverted words: "Thomas Thorpe, the well-wishing adventurer, in setting forth wishes to the only begetter of these ensuing sonnets, Master W.H., all happiness and that eternity promised by our ever-living poet"? No, everyone would not agree. This re-wording has been called wrong because it imposes punctuation (the commas around Master W.H. and after other words) that is not in the original.

In a letter to the *Times Literary Supplement* in 1973, Ivor R. W. Cook of Surrey claimed that the dedication was clearly *written by Master W.H.* Mr. Cook's version reads: "Mr. W.H. wishes all happiness and that eternity promised by our ever-living poet to the well-wishing adventurer on the occasion of his own departure."[7] He believes that in 1609 Shakespeare may have been an investor, or "adventurer," in the expedition to Virginia and the Somers Islands headed by Sir William Harvey (who is Master W.H. to Mr. Cook). It is Harvey, not Thorpe, who is wishing happiness "back upon" Shakespeare (presumably in the form of dividends).

In this version the first two lines constitute a dedication to Shakespeare—TO THE ONLY BEGETTER OF THESE ENSUING SONNETS—followed by a full stop (a slug of white space would have helped make this clearer), after which Master W.H. begins *his* good wishes. This ingenious interpretation at first seems tenable, at least grammatically, but it collapses when one realizes (1) that it inserts a nonexistent preposition, "to," in front of "the well-wishing adventurer" and (2) that it does not account for Thomas Thorpe's initialled signature. Perhaps we are being asked (Mr. Cook doesn't make this clear) to believe that Thorpe's initials apply only to the first two lines. In that case, Sir William (would he *call himself* Master W.H.?) inserted ten lines between the dedication to Shakespeare and the signature, T.T. No, this rendering won't do, and it was chosen from scores of others to illustrate the peculiar fact that there is *no* interpretation that does not have a flaw.

If a reader with no preconceived notions, willing to forget questions of identity, were to try to make sense of the dedication, he or she would inevitably reach the same conclusion as the earliest commentators—like sensible Edmund Malone—that the word "begetter" means inspirer. Unfortunately, there are three possible interpretations of the word:

"BEGETTER" MEANS CREATOR. The word refers to the one who wrote the sonnets, and therefore Q is dedicated by Thorpe to the author, William Shakespeare. According to this interpretation, Mr. W.H. is a misprint for Mr. W.S. Considering the number of incredible misprints in the history of book publishing, and in Q itself, this is entirely possible. (A humourous variant of this theory says that Mr. W.H. stands for Master William Himself.) One would be happy to accept this solution—anything to make sense of the puzzle!—but it doesn't work. The flaw is that Shakespeare, "our ever-living poet," cannot be both the dedicatee and the promiser of eternity to himself.

"BEGETTER" MEANS PROCURER. The word refers to the one who obtained the manuscript for Thorpe. A difficulty with this reading is that the dedication says "the *only* begetter." Why should anyone, wishing to acknowledge another's role as procurer of a manuscript, make such a fuss over the singularity of his role? Whether the procurer had help, or acted alone, is much too inconsequential to stress in this way. If begetter means procurer, "only" has a hollow ring—just as, if it means inspirer, it rings true. Another flaw is that this interpretation has Thorpe asserting that Shakespeare has promised happiness and eternity to the procurer of a manuscript that Shakespeare never intended for publication.

A favourite candidate as procurer is Sir William Harvey, Southampton's second stepfather. The young Earl's mother may well have commissioned the "Marriage" sonnets in the 1590s, when she was the widowed Countess of Southampton. But the Harvey theory assumes that the Countess, who was not on the best of terms with her son, got possession of and preserved copies of all the sonnets, including those to the dark mistress as well as to her son, not to forget "A Lover's Complaint." If she had kept all these poems, which seems unlikely, she could have left them to Harvey on her death in 1607. The dates and circumstances fit, and "Master W.H." may be correct for Sir William Harvey, but there are still grave flaws. Why should our ever-living poet wish Harvey "eternity" when Southampton bitterly opposed his mother's marriage to Harvey, obtaining Essex's support in delaying it? It has been suggested that, after the widower Harvey remarried in 1608, Thorpe was wishing him eternity in the form of heirs. But T.T.'s dedication clearly says that eternity or immortality is promised *by the existence of the poems themselves.* While the first poems do indeed argue that procreation is a guarantee of continuous life, the eternity promised throughout Q is immortal fame for the one who begot the poems, by causing them to be written. The theory of "begetter" as the procurer of the manuscript does not hold up.

"BEGETTER" MEANS INSPIRER. This is the most obvious and soundest theory; "begetter" means the man to whom the sonnets are addressed. It leaves us, however, with a different kind of flaw—four letters, "Mr. W.H." If the young man is the poet's "Lord of my love," the title Mr. (no matter whom the initials stand for) is absurd. Nor does this title fit the image that the sonnets themselves create of a high-born young man who is the "world's fresh ornament" and who has the position and power to wield "the strength of all thy state," and of whom Shakespeare says "thou with public kindness honour me."

If one accepts "begetter" as inspirer and yet cannot accept a mere mister (and neither Oscar Wilde's imaginary young actor Willie Hughes, nor Samuel Butler's ludicrous candidate, sea-cook William Hewes) as the subject of the poems, what sense can one make of the dedication? One can decide, like Northrop Frye, to ignore this curious interpolation in the front-matter of Q, which, after all, Shakespeare did not write. Or one can conclude that Thorpe may have been mistaken, or misinformed, about the identity of Mr. W.H. One can even surmise that Thorpe really knew who it was, and wanted to hint at it, without giving it away. William Empson wrote a letter in the same issue of the *Times Literary Supplement* as Mr. Cook, suggesting that Thomas Thorpe "wanted to set us guessing, and we are still at it."[8] In Empson's view, Thorpe's motive for writing so cryptic a dedication was that he "was trying to keep out of trouble," while at the same time attempting to create interest in a new book. The history of book publishing is strewn with examples of commercially motivated work by all the parties concerned in the production of books. I find Empson's conclusions convincing: Thorpe's odd dedication reads like something a book publisher with a commercial motive *and* a printing problem might, under the circumstances, produce.

Death in an Alms-Room

It appears that Thomas Thorpe neither kept out of trouble nor created sufficient interest in the book, and that he suffered a financial loss from the publication of Q, either from its suppression or its failure to sell. He ended his days in poverty. In 1635 he was admitted to an almsroom for indigents in the hospital at Ewelme, Oxfordshire. Since the Honor and Manor of Ewelme were part of the royal estates, and since the Stationers' Company had ample funds for the care of their own members, Thorpe's admission to a royal almshouse has puzzled scholars. A key to this puzzle is provided by an interesting book, *The Spanish Elizabethans: The English Exiles at the Court of Philip II* (1963), by Albert Loomie, which throws new light on Thomas Thorpe. In 1597 a legal inquiry was conducted in the Court of the Exchequer into reports of the recent death in Spain of Sir Francis Englefield, who had served as co-Master of the

Court of Wards under Henry VIII and later became a Catholic exile in Spain. One witness in court was Thomas Thorpe, "stationer," who testified that late in 1596 he had been in Spain where "by means of Father Persons he did lie in the said Francis Englefield's house in Madrid . . . by the space of three weeks after the death of the said Sir Francis." He also related that the steward had hoped to conceal the news of Englefield's death until all his master's pensions were paid and, "gathering all the keys of his said late master's lodgings and chests, did lock up everything in the same rooms." Thorpe also testified that Robert Persons, S. J., exiled provincial of the English Jesuit order, had gathered up Englefield's papers and correspondence and taken them to the Jesuit residence. All this would suggest that Thorpe was in the employ of the government as a spy, like his friend John Florio. If Thorpe were also a Catholic, it also suggests why he was Ben Jonson's publisher in his Catholic period, and Father Thomas Wright's publisher as well. Finally, it explains why, in his old age, he found asylum in the royal almshouse at Ewelme, where he died at age seventy. His death apparently removed a final barrier to the publication in 1640 of John Benson's pirated mélange of poems, including the patched-together, falsified, and bowdlerized sonnets, with their made-up titles.

T.T., a poor stationer with good taste, earned a niche for himself in literary history, as the author of an enigmatic dedication destined to become the most notorious red herring in English literature, and as the publisher of William Shakespeare's *Sonnets*.

THE POEMS II

Shakespeare worked without knowing that he
would become Shakespeare.

COLETTE

The Raven-Haired Mistress

T HE SONNETS that follow the first 126 poems deal mainly with a single subject: the poet's sexual obsession with a dark beauty whose eyes and hair are black. She is faithless to him and to her husband, and as an early sonnet (41) tells us, she seduced the young friend, the beautiful "thou" of these lines:

> *Beauteous thou art, therefore to be assailed,*
> *And, when a woman woos, what woman's son*
> *Will sourly leave her till she have prevailed?*

The poet calls his mistress "my plague," and insults her constantly and ingeniously. In sonnet 141, for example, he says she offends all five of his senses:

> *In faith I do not love thee with mine eyes*
> *For they in thee a thousand errors note. . . .*
> *Nor are mine ears with thy tongue's tune delighted,*
> *Nor tender feelings to base touches prone,*
> *Nor taste, nor smell desire to be invited*
> *To any sensual feast with thee alone.*

Yet he concludes that neither his wits nor his senses can dissuade his "foolish heart from serving thee." In sonnet 130 he ridicules her complexion, breath, voice, and gait:

I have seen roses damasked, red and white,
But no such roses see I in her cheeks,
And in some perfumes is there more delight
Than in the breath that from my mistress reeks.
I love to hear her speak, yet well I know
That music hath a far more pleasing sound.
I grant I never saw a goddess go:
My mistress when she walks treads on the ground.

"And yet, by heaven, I think my love," he continues, "as rare / As any she . . ."

One theory has it that, because the poems are so full of insults, he never showed them to her. Yet others saw them: they were so well circulated that two of them turned up in *The Passionate Pilgrim,* and Thomas Nashe apparently knew about them. It seems likely that in these circumstances they reached her, their prime subject.

If she did read them, she could not have been over-joyed at being called my female evil, thou usurer, the worser spirit (his friend being the better), liar, cheater, bad angel (his friend being the good angel), and an-chored in the bay where all men ride. Surely she was not pleased by his citing "thy foul faults," or by such epithets as despised, black in thy deeds, foresworn, black as hell, or by his admissions that "against myself [I] with thee partake," that "I love what others do abhor," and "all my best doth worship thy defect." His obsessive lust for her is such that, as he confesses, "I myself am mortgaged to thy will," the last word having three concurrent meanings

—Elizabethan slang for the sexual organ, a synonym for desire, the poet's nickname. In sonnet 135, "Whoever hath her wish, thou hast thy Will," there are thirteen "wills" in fourteen lines.

Undeniably many of the poems in this series are artificial word-games and exercises in wit. Wordsworth characterized the sonnets to the dark mistress as "abominably harsh, obscure, and worthless."[1] Yet among them are at least two sonnets, not addressed to her, that belong with Shakespeare's best poetry. The first is sonnet 129, "The expense of spirit in a waste of shame," extraordinary for its day and impressive any day. Sir Philip Sidney's fine sonnet on sexual desire may have provided inspiration:

Thou blind man's mark, thou fool's self-chosen snare,
Fond fancy's scum, and dregs of scattered thought,
Band of all evils, cradle of causeless care,
Thou web of will, whose end is never wrought—
Desire, desire! I have too dearly bought
With price of mangled mind thy worthless ware. . . . .

but our poet takes the theme of sexual passion a step further, and describes the tyranny of the sex act itself— "lust in action":

. . . and, till action, lust
Is perjured, murderous, bloody, full of blame,
Savage, extreme, rude, cruel, not to trust,
Enjoyed no sooner but despised straight,
Past reason hunted, and no sooner had
Past reason hated as a swallowed bait
On purpose laid to make the taker mad.
Mad in pursuit, and in possession so,
Had, having, and in quest to have, extreme;

A bliss in proof, and proved a very woe,
Before, a joy proposed; behind, a dream.
  All this the world well knows, yet none knows well
  To shun the heaven that leads men to this hell.

Bernard Shaw considered it "the most merciless passage in English literature."

The theme of the other great sonnet in this series, 146, is death. As with sonnet 129, the poet does not address the mistress, or the friend, or anyone other than himself:

Poor soul, the center of my sinful earth,
. . .* these rebel powers that thee array,
Why dost thou pine within and suffer dearth
Painting thy outward walls so costly gay?
Why so large cost, having so short a lease,
Dost thou upon thy fading mansion spend?
Shall worms, inheritors of this excess,
Eat up thy charge? Is this thy body's end?
Then, soul, live thou upon thy servant's loss,
And let that pine to aggravate thy store;
Buy terms divine in selling hours of dross:
Within be fed, without be rich no more,
  So shalt thou feed on Death, that feeds on men,
  And Death once dead, there's no more dying then.

"This sonnet contains more," George Santayana has written, "than a natural religious emotion inspired by a single event. It contains reflection. . . . A mind that habitually ran into such thoughts would be philosophically pious; it would be spiritual." It also clearly foreshadows the Shakespeare of *Hamlet*. It is sobering to think that, as far as we

* Perhaps "Fooled by."

can tell, the poet either did not want so great a poem as this published or was indifferent whether or not it was.

The twenty-six sonnets to the dark mistress seem to have been written in fairly random fashion and, not surprisingly, show little progression or development in their monotonous obsession with the theme of sex. As a result, they do not lack for rearrangers who insist on putting them in their "correct" order. J. Dover Wilson, for example, renumbers almost every poem from 127 to 154 according to his "conjectured order of writing"; mercifully, he does this in a table at the end of his edition, leaving the main text in the 1609 order. This veteran critic's reordering starts with 140 instead of 127, and follows with 139, 153, 154 (the "Bath" sonnets!), 130, 127, 144, and so on. He believed the reordering gives a different impression of the poet's attitude to his mistress, underlining the statement in sonnet 42 "I loved her dearly." I get this impression fully from the printed order, which makes as much sense as any other order: for example, with 127, "In the old age black was not counted fair," introducing the physical attraction of the mistress; with 133 and 134, a linked pair, in obviously correct sequence; with the two "will" sonnets following each other; and with the two "Bath" sonnets logically appended at the end. Unless one accepts the order as given, chaos is come again.

The earthiest sonnet in Q, one of the so-called "Gross" sonnets, which horrified so many Victorian and later critics,* is 151, "Love is too young to know what con-

* R. G. White, 1854: "It is impossible to admit that Shakespeare would, in his own person, address to *any* woman such gross *double entendres* as are contained in this sonnet." T. G. Tucker, 1924: "From the nature of the contents, [this sonnet] might well be let to die."

science is." Its soubriquet is derived from the words "my gross body's treason," and the sonnet presents as its central image the rise and fall of the poet's penis:

> *. . . flesh stays no farther reason*
> *But, rising at thy name, doth point out thee*
> *As his triumphant prize. Proud of this pride,*
> *He is contented thy poor drudge to be,*
> *To stand in thy affairs, fall by thy side.*
>   *No want of conscience hold it that I call*
> *Her "love" for whose dear love I rise and fall.*

"The sonnets addressed to the dark lady are concerned with that most humiliating of all erotic experiences, sexual infatuation," W. H. Auden has written. "No other poet, not even Catullus, has described the anguish, self-contempt, and rage produced by this unfortunate condition so well as Shakespeare in some of these sonnets."[2] As prime examples, Auden singles out two poems—141, "In faith I do not love thee with mine eyes," and the "Gross" sonnet quoted above.

What was the dark lady's name, at whose utterance our poet's passion could rise so triumphantly? He does not tell us in Q, but in *Love's Labour's Lost* and *Romeo and Juliet* he may have given clues. Both lovers, Berowne and Romeo, are infatuated with a mistress whose name is Rosaline. Berowne falls madly in love with Rosaline at first sight. This is his description of her appearance and, perhaps more important, her character:

> *A whitely wanton with a velvet brow,*
> *With two pitch balls stuck in her face for eyes.*
> *Aye, and by heaven one that will do the deed . . .*

At the start of *Romeo and Juliet,* Rosaline is the mistress with whom Romeo has long been in love, his "old desire." He goes to the Capulet ball hoping to find her there, and instead he and Juliet first set eyes on each other. It is interesting that the play's chief source, Arthur Brook's poem *The Tragical History of Romeus and Juliet,* includes the familiar names of the principals, the Montagues, the Capulets, Mercutio, Tybalt, and even the Nurse. But there is no name for the mistress, "Whose beauty, shape and comely grace did so his heart entrap" (Brook's version) before he met Juliet. Luigi Da Porta, whose Italian poem was Brook's source, also starts with Romeo in love with a "cruel mistress," unnamed, whom he follows to a fatal Cappeletti feast. Only Shakespeare gives her a name, which Romeo sees on the Capulet guest-list: "Rosaline." Of course, the use of this name by the poet in plays he is believed to have written in 1593–94 and 1594–95 does not prove that the dark lady of the sonnets was named Rosaline. Yet the coincidence of her nature, physical attributes, and the kind of infatuation she inspires suggest that the name Rosaline had a special significance for our poet.

However, A. L. Rowse still claims that his identification of the dark lady as Emilia is "unanswerable."* Unfortunately, his chain of evidence never makes a final link with Shakespeare. It is true that Mistress Emilia Bassano Lanier might be the dark mistress of the sonnets,

* A. L. Rowse devoted a full page (*Spectator,* 4 September 1982) to attacking my book's position on the dark lady: "Mr. Giroux has not enough knowledge of the period to know that of course it [a personal letter of Southampton's] would not survive." *Of course?* But his letter to his wife ("Sweet hart") after his arrest in 1601 survived.

but she also might not be. For any reasonable person, the case is not proved. The dates and the circumstances are right: Emilia was five years junior to our poet, she was half-Italian and musical, mistress for several years to the Lord Chamberlain Hunsdon, who, when she became pregnant, in 1592 married her off to Captain Alfonso Lanier, a court musician (or, as Simon Forman puts it, "she was for colour married to a minstrel"). Since Shakespeare was a leader of the Lord Chamberlain's Men, as their playwright, shareholder, and actor, there also existed every opportunity for Emilia to come into contact with our poet and Southampton. Awaiting the final piece of evidence, the link that would tie them all together, the reader is told by Rowse: "In regular Elizabethan fashion, he [Shakespeare] got a social superior, his patron, to write to the Lady he desired access to."[3] There are extant many letters of Southampton's, but the letter referred to has not been seen by Professor Rowse or anyone else. A few sentences later the imaginary letter is further metamorphosed into fact: "She had taken the opportunity of Southampton's writing to her on his poet's behalf to get hold of the young man."[4] This is not very much different from Charlotte Stopes telling us that "He [Southampton] felt he must have a private talk with this 'man from Stratford' and took him home with him to supper." Emilia Lanier is as good a guess for the dark mistress as any previously made, but that is all she is—an unproved guess.

Professor Rowse concludes: "It is now all quite clear. When one comes to think of it, who else, who more convincingly, would the Dark Lady have been?"[5] Well, any one of scores of Elizabethan women who had black eyes and hair, played the virginal, and brought their lovers to heel. She could have been a woman named Rosaline.

In view of Shakespeare's verbal treatment of his mistress, I find it somehow refreshing to note, amidst the flattery heaped on the high-born young patron, that harsh and blunt words are occasionally directed at him. Assuming he read all the poems, what did the youth think of "thou dost common grow" (69); "those errors that in thee are seen" (96); or sonnet 94, "They that have power to hurt and will do none," about whose ambivalence William Empson wrote such a dazzling analysis? Nor must we overlook the couplet previously cited: "I see a better state to me belongs / Than that which on thy humour doth depend" (92). Auden concluded that none of the sonnets was shown to the youth or mistress, but that they were written as a diary, for the poet's eyes alone, with no thought of a public. But this could not have been true of the "Marriage" sonnets, which would have made no sense unless they were shown to the youth, and I doubt that it is true of the others. Auden is right in one respect: *we* were not meant to see the sonnets.

The odd question, whether Shakespeare was lame, requires a mention, since it owes its existence to Q. In sonnet 37 he writes, "So I, made lame by Fortune's dearest spite," and in 89, "Speak of my lameness, and I straight will halt," that is, limp. This has provided enough evidence for the attribution of lameness, which may seem absurd, since Shakespeare was an actor. Yet the roles with which he is traditionally associated, like the ghost in *Hamlet* and old Adam in *As You Like It,* might have been possible for a lame actor. Most readers, including myself, prefer to regard "lame" and "lameness" as metaphors for his profession and state in life. In the absence of specific contrary proof, it is reasonable to accept the reassurance of the antiquarian John Aubrey, in *Brief Lives* (1681), that Shakespeare "was a nandsome well shap't man: very good company."

The "Bath" Sonnets

The two final poems, following the sonnets to the poet's mistress, are known as the "Bath" sonnets. They are unusual in only one respect: they say exactly the same thing in two sets of words, as Edmund Malone noticed in 1780. They recount a legend concerning the torch of love, the fiery brand of Eros / Cupid, which became the origin of hot springs when Diana's love-nymphs stole the torch and plunged it in water. These beneficial warm waters served as a remedy for love-sickness, "strange maladies" (venereal disease), and other such ailments of the "sad distempered guest" who visited the spas. Scholars have found a Greek source for the legend in an epigram of Marianus Scholasticus; a Latin source in an epigram of Regianus, who locates the curative springs at Baiae; and an Italian source in M. Statio Romano's verses *de l'acque di Baia.* It is not known whether Shakespeare had access to or used these or other sources.

Since the word "bath" occurs four times in the twenty-eight lines, the poems are believed by some to refer to Bath, the use of whose mineral waters dates from Roman and Saxon times. Other watering-places, such as the hot sulphur springs used by the Roman emperors at Baiae, could also account for the use of "bath," which is not capitalized in Q. A reference to Wells is perhaps as likely as one to Bath; the words, "a cool Well by" (capitalized this time), occur in line 9 of sonnet 154.

Shakespeare's description of Cupid as "the General of hot desire" in line 7 of 154 echoes his famous passage in *Love's Labour's Lost:*

> *This wimpled, whining, purblind, wayward boy,*
> *This senior-junior, giant-dwarf, Dan Cupid,*
> *Regent of love-rhymes, lord of folded arms,*
> *The anointed sovereign of sighs and groans,*
> *Liege of all loiterers and malcontents,*
> *Dread prince of plackets, king of codpieces,*
> *Sole imperator and great General*
> *Of trotting 'paritors. . . .*

and suggests a comparable date of composition.

It may be that the two poems were exercises in which the poet was proving to himself something on the order of "It *is* possible to compose two distinct sonnets, repeating only a few words, on a single theme." Edmund Malone: "The poet perhaps had not determined which [sonnet] he should prefer. He hardly could have intended to send them both into the world."[6] Perhaps not, but the world has them. Naturally they have been rejected by a few scholars as too trivial, unworthy of the Top Bard. Yet they have precisely the same credentials as the other sonnets.

The Rival Poets

A serious crisis, distressing to the poet, is recorded in Q in a series of eight sonnets. Continuous from 78 to 86, with one exception (sonnet 81 reverts to the Ovidian and Petrarchan theme of eternal fame for the friend), these poems record the poet's foreboding that "I be cast away." What disturbs him is the appearance on the scene of several rival poets who are bidding for, and in some cases apparently receiving, Southampton's favour:

> . . . *every alien pen hath got my use*
> *And under thee their poesy disperse.*

"Disperse" could mean either circulate in manuscript or publish, and we can now identify two rival poets with a poem in each category. The first, Thomas Nashe's erotic poem *The Choosing of Valentines,* begins and ends with sonnets to "Lord S." It was never printed in its day and was, so to speak, known only in *samizdat* form: a few manuscript copies have survived. The poem, whose setting is a brothel, is so pornographic that R. B. McKerrow excluded it from his edition of *The Works of Thomas Nashe* (1910), except for a limited subscriber's edition; it finally got into the 1958 reprint. In this poem Nashe's opening sonnet describes Southampton's beauty in superlative terms: the "fairest bud the red rose ever bore." It dates around May 1593, because these lines clearly refer to *Venus and Adonis,* and to Southampton's patronage of it:

> *Thus has my pen presumed to please my friend;*
> *Oh, mightst thou likewise please Apollo's eye!*
> *No, honour brooks no such impiety,*
> *Yet Ovid's wanton muse did not offend.*

Around the same time another rival poet, Barnabe Barnes, published his collection of poems, *Parthenophil and Parthenophe,* with a commendatory sonnet to Southampton. Barnes's book, entered on 10 May 1593, also appeared only a few weeks after *Venus and Adonis.* Shakespeare seems to allude to both rivals: in sonnet 82 the line "And their gross painting might be better used" could be read as his criticism of *The Choosing of Valentines;* similarly, he could be referring to both poets in the lines "The dedicated words which writers use / Of their fair subject . . ." Perhaps other poems were also dedicated to Southampton and circulated in manuscript; during this period of contagious sonnet-writing, there was busy traffic from one scrivener's shop to another. But none besides these has turned up.

Neither Nashe nor Barnes appears to be the rival who was chiefly feared, however. Nashe's poem is inferior as verse, if not as pornography, and sonnet 82 derides its "gross painting." Barnabe Barnes, as Mark Eccles has demonstrated,[7] was the more promising poet at this stage; his book is impressive if only for the variety of poetic forms it undertakes. Hyder Rollins is guilty of a rare lapse in dismissing Barnes with these words: "If Barnes—by 1598, as Eccles shows, a poisoner and jail-bird—actually was the rival, then Shakespeare could hardly have been serious in praising his verse."[8] Far from praising his rivals' verse, in the first sonnet (78) of this series, Shakespeare uses such scornful phrases as *"every* alien pen" and *"their poesy* disperse." Rollins's reference to Barnes's criminality is, critically speaking, irrelevant; Christopher Marlowe, Thomas Watson, George Chapman, and Ben Jonson were also "jail-birds," and three of them went to prison on charges of murder. Surely genius has been known to exist in bad characters. The fact is that Thomas Churchyard, a contemporary of Barnes, called him "Petrarch's scholar" and ranked him in his *Praise of Poetry* (1595) with Spenser and Daniel. "The allusion is interesting," according to Mark Eccles, a most impressive and underrated Shakespearean scholar, "as evidence that Barnes had a certain reputation at a time when Shakespeare was probably writing his sonnets." In the same essay, Eccles writes: "Whether or not Barnabe Barnes was that mysterious being, the Rival Poet, *it is clear that he was one of the rivals for Southampton's favour.*" That is all I would claim for both Barnes and Nashe.

It is only when Shakespeare speaks of "a worthier pen" and, in sonnet 80, of "a better spirit," that the superiority of a particular rival poet becomes clear. At this juncture Shakespeare acknowledges that he has been rendered tongue-tied; he mentions his own "dumb [i.e., not written] thoughts" (85). He regrets that "therefore have I slept in your report" (83), and the seriousness of the situation for him is now apparent. His opinion of the poetic gifts of his rival is so high that he denigrates his own talent, contrasting his rival's craft, which is "of tall building and of goodly pride," with "My saucy bark, inferior far to his."

The last line of sonnet 83 reveals that this rival has also succeeded in obtaining the friend as a patron: *"both your poets."* In the final poem of the series, he describes the rival's "great verse":

> *Was it the proud full sail of his great verse,*
> *Bound for the prize of all too precious you,*
> *That did ripe thoughts in my brain inhearse,*
> *Making their tomb the womb wherein they grew?*
> *Was it his spirit, by spirits taught to write*
> *Above a mortal pitch, that struck me dead?*
> *No, neither he, nor his compeers by night*
> *Giving him aid, my verse astonishèd.*
> *He, nor that affable familiar ghost*
> *Which nightly gulls him with intelligence,*
> *As victors, of my silence cannot boast;*
> *I was not sick of any fear from thence.*
> > *But when your countenance filled up his line,*
> > *Then lacked I matter, that enfeebled mine.*

In this sonnet the poet reverses the problem of rivalry: it was not, he says, fear of a supergifted rival that made me sick and unable to write; it was your (Southampton's) favourable response that did it. "But when your countenance filled up his line" means not only that the rival had made the Earl the subject of his poem (just as, in the guise of Adonis, he had been Shakespeare's) but that the rival had received assurance of the Earl's favour. It appeared to Shakespeare that he was going to "be cast away."

The one poet Shakespeare might have regarded as "great" and "a better spirit" than himself in 1592–93, and to whom he might have acknowledged himself to be "inferior," was Christopher Marlowe. *Hero and Leander,* which Marlowe was busy composing at Scadbury in Kent in the early months of 1593, is also the one poem Shakespeare might have thought superior to *Venus and Adonis*. Over eight hundred lines (the first two sestiads) had been completed and apparently shown to Southampton before Marlowe's death. There is no question that Southampton's countenance, in the character of Leander, filled up these flattering and homoerotic lines:

> *His body was as straight as Circe's wand,*
> *Jove might have sipped out nectar from his hand.*
> *Even as delicious meat is to his taste,*
> *So was his neck in touching, and surpassed*
> *The white of Pelops' shoulder. I could tell ye*
> *How smooth his breast was and how white his belly,*
> *And whose immortal fingers did imprint*
> *That heavenly path, with many a curious dint,*
> *That runs along his back; but my rude pen*
> *Can hardly blazon forth the loves of men,*
> *Much less of powerful gods; let it suffice*
> *That my slack muse sings of Leander's eyes. . . .*
> *Some swore he was a maid in man's attire,*
> *For in his looks were all that men desire. . . .*
> *It lies not in our power to love and hate,*
> *For will in us is overruled by fate. . . .*
> *When both deliberate, the love is slight;*
> *Who ever loved that loved not at first sight?*

A few years later, *Hero and Leander* rose again to the surface of Shakespeare's mind, when he came to write *As You Like It:* "Dead shepherd, now I find thy saw of might: / 'Who ever loved that loved not at first sight?' "

It is not surprising that Marlowe has often been put

forward as *the* rival poet. The first writer to do so was
Robert Cartwright, in 1859: "Marlowe is the man . . .
the familiar ghost, Mephistopheles. Marlowe was also just
the splendid and dissipated character to dazzle and lead
the young lord [Southampton] astray."[9] Cartwright was
joined in his opinion by Gerald Massey in 1869, by
A. Hall in 1884, by the German writers M. J. Wolff and
Hermann Conrad in 1903 and 1919, by D. J. Snider in
1922, and by Peter Alexander in 1939. In her biography
Christopher Marlowe (1927), Una M. Ellis-Fermor nominated the Mephistopheles of *Dr. Faustus* as Marlowe's
"familiar ghost," which A. L. Rowse repeated in 1963.

I agree with them that Marlowe is the man. He alone,
"bound for the prize of all too precious" Southampton's
favour, was gifted enough to have displaced Shakespeare,
and might have done so had he not been killed on 30 May
1593. The news that Marlowe had been stabbed by Ingram Frizer in a small room of the widow Eleanor Bull's
inn at Deptford, in a dispute over the payment of a food
and bar bill (or so the two shady "witnesses"—both of
them informers—said), must have come as a shock. Marlowe, like Shakespeare, was born in 1564; his career
started much earlier than our poet's, and he knew success
long before his late-starting fellow-playwright. It is worth
noting that Shakepeare's other reference to Marlowe,* in
As You Like It, is to the scene of his death: "When a
man's verses cannot be understood . . . it strikes a man
more dead than a great reckoning in a little room."

Professor Rowse concluded, correctly I think, that son-

---

* A. L. Rowse's statement that "Marlowe is the only contemporary
poet to whom Shakespeare ever referred" is wrong. A sonnet by Thomas
Watson, Marlowe's friend and (as Mark Eccles discovered) fellow-
prisoner in 1589, is quoted in *Much Ado,* I, i, 263.

net 86 was written after Marlowe's death. Unlike the previous sonnets in the series, it employs the past tense. Rowse was unfairly criticized because there are also two verbs in the present tense, "gulls" and "cannot boast." Altogether, the poem has seventeen verbs—twelve in the past tense, one infinitive, two participles, and two in the present tense. How can we account for the anomalies of "cannot boast" and "gulls"? Was the sonnet originally written in the present tense and changed after Marlowe's death? No, because three verbs in the past tense, "grew," "[did] inhearse," and "astonishèd," are parts of the rhyme-scheme. They are either examples of Q's misprints or slips of the pen. The tone of the poem, with its unrestrained praise, suggests it was inspired by the shock of the poet's death.

The identity of *the* rival poet cannot, of course, be proved in the conclusive way that the dedicatory letters together with sonnet 26 prove that Southampton was the patron and friend. However, what anyone who has ever worked with poets would find powerfully convincing are those words, "a better spirit" and "his great verse," applied by Shakespeare to *the* rival, while he calls his own gifts "inferior." To me it is grotesque to suppose he might be referring to George Chapman, perennial candidate for the role. One has only to read the last four sestiads of *Hero and Leander,* which Chapman completed, against Marlowe's lines. There are grounds for concluding that Shakespeare's lines (*Love's Labour's Lost,* II, i, 15–16), "Beauty is bought by *judgement* of the eye, / Not uttered by base sale of *chapmen's* tongues," constitute the poet's reply to Chapman's attack in *The Shadow of Night* on playwrights who "with affection to great men's fancies take upon them as killing censures as if they were *judgement's butchers"*—our poet, of course, being the son of a butcher-tanner-glover. It is highly unlikely that Shakespeare would call Chapman's verse great. Marlowe, as Cartwright first suggested, is the man.

The "Mortal Moon" Sonnet

Notwithstanding the fact that the sonnets as a whole belong to the first half of the 1590s, one sonnet was written in 1603, on the death of Queen Elizabeth. This so-called dating sonnet (107), which many scholars believed would determine the date of composition of all the sonnets, dates nothing but itself. The extraordinary circumstances of its composition account for its unique distinction. Turning up amidst the early sonnets, this late poem added greatly to the confusion about Q. Its date also confirms the psychological validity of identifying the patron, the Earl of Southampton, as the chief subject of the poems. This is the text:

> *Not mine own fears nor the prophetic soul*
> *Of the wide world dreaming on things to come*
> *Can yet the lease of my true love control,*
> *Supposed as forfeit to a confined doom.*
> *The mortal Moon hath her eclipse endured*
> *And the sad augurs mock their own presage.*
> *Incertainties now crown themselves assured*
> *And peace proclaims olives of endless age.*
> *Now with the drops of this most balmy time*

My love looks fresh, and Death to me subscribes,
Since spite of him I'll live in this poor rhyme,
While he insults o'er dull and speechless tribes.
And thou in this shall find thy monument,
When tyrants crests and tombs of brass are spent.

This sonnet could not have been written before 24 March 1603, the date of Queen Elizabeth's death, for a good reason: the word "tyrant" was risky to put on paper at any time during her reign, and mortally dangerous if coupled with a reference to her. It is generally agreed that "mortal Moon" refers to Elizabeth. The lunar metaphor for the Queen was made popular by Walter Ralegh; in his lost poem, which he read to Edmund Spenser in Ireland in 1589, Cynthia was portrayed as Ralegh's "mistress swaying the hopes and fears of the lover, as the Moon sways the ebb and flow of the tides." Only a fragment survives of the poem whose verse Spenser described as "the music of nightingales" but its characterization of the Queen as moon-goddess was imitated widely.

The strongest opponent of dating this sonnet in 1603, E. K. Chambers, acknowledged that the mortal Moon is Elizabeth. However, he was unable to imagine that an eclipse of the moon meant death because, he said, "it is not easy to think that to 'endure' an eclipse can mean to die."[10] Peter Quennell repeated this interpretation: "Much turns on the meaning of the word 'endured.' The 'mortal Moon' being Elizabeth herself—again and again, by Ralegh and others, she was deified as Cynthia the moon-goddess—the phrase must surely indicate not that her radiance had been at length eclipsed, but that she had passed through some crisis in her life and triumphantly emerged from it."[11]

Chambers's authority is so strong that for years I accepted this proscription of "endure" as unanswerable, until I found it demolished by one source superior to all others, the writing of Shakespeare himself. Astonishingly, it appears in one of the most famous passages—Edgar's lines in *King Lear* (V, ii, 9–11):

> *Men must endure*
> *Their going hence, even as their coming hither.*
> *Ripeness is all.*

Men must endure their deaths, even as their births; ripeness is all there is. "Endure" can of course mean survive, but the O.E.D. also defines it as "to suffer without resistance, to submit to, to undergo," and that is how Shakespeare uses the word in both places. By "The mortal Moon hath her eclipse endured," Shakespeare means that, as a mortal, the Queen has undergone death. *"Her* eclipse" instead of *"an* eclipse"—which would have been the more appropriate wording, if Peter Quennell's interpretation were correct—further emphasizes a permanent rather than a temporary state.

It is interesting that a few lines later in *King Lear* (a play believed to have been written in 1604–5 and known to have been performed at court in 1606), after the King and Cordelia have been captured, Lear tells his daughter they will be happy together in prison, far away from such depressing court news as "who loses and who wins, who's in, and who's out,"

> *. . . And we'll wear out,*
> *In a walled prison, packs and sects of great ones*
> *That ebb and flow by the Moon.* [*V, iii, 20–23*]

193

Again, these words could not have been written before the Queen's death. They are unmistakably a bitter allusion, not only to the late monarch, but to Southampton's two years and four months of imprisonment in 1601–3. Southampton, as a leading courtier under James I, might have heard these lines with very special interest.

On grounds of language alone, long before the problem of "endure" was eliminated, sonnet 107, alone among the poems in Q, seemed to be a late poem. There is nothing anywhere else in the sonnets like the mastery and freedom of the first quatrain:

> *Not mine own fears nor the prophetic soul*
> *Of the wide world dreaming on things to come*
> *Can yet the lease of my true love control,*
> *Supposed as forfeit to a confined doom.*

This single sentence, one marvellous breath, could only have been written by a poet in the fullness of his powers. Auden noted that these lines "foreshadow the freedom of his later verse"[12]—foreshadow, because Auden had concluded that the poems are essentially early work. And so they are, but sonnet 107 is the one exception, written long after the other poems in celebration of an event happy for patron and poet.

Other historical allusions in this sonnet place the poem solidly in 1603. Many of them have been pointed out by Garrett Mattingly, historian of this period and author of *The Armada.* He states that the era of peace referred to in line 8, "And peace proclaims olives of endless age," must date from the accession of James I, because England was continuously at war from 1595 to 1603—always with Spain and usually in Ireland: "It is rather to the peaceable union with the old enemy, Scotland, and to the apparently permanent relief from the danger of civil war that the phrase, 'olives of endless age' is to be applied. . . . Peace with Spain and union with Scotland . . . the two gifts which James proudly offered his first Parliament, may be dated from May 1603."[13]

Uncertainty over the succession and the danger of civil war, both of which were averted by the accession of James I, are memorialized by the translators of the King James Bible (1612) in these words: "For whereas it was the expectation of many, who wished not well unto our Sion, that upon the setting of that bright Occidental Star Queen Elizabeth . . . some thick and palpable clouds of darkness would so have overshadowed this land that men should have been in doubt which way they were to walk; and that it should hardly be known who was to direct the unsettled state."[14] The sad augurs of doom were mocked by the happy turn of events. Gervase Markham, in his reminiscences of James I, wrote that the King came "not with an olive branch in his hand, but with a whole forest of olives round about him."[15]

John Donne gives a vivid picture of the near-hysteria in London as Elizabeth's death approached, in his sermon on the accession of James I, describing the panic brought about by the prophets of doom, the "sad augurs" later mocked by their own predictions, as "every one of you in the City were running up and down like ants with eggs bigger than themselves, every man with his bags, to seek where to hide them safely."[16] C. J. Sisson confirms this picture: "King James, as welcome a king as England has ever known, actually saved England from people like Essex, from civil war, and brought peace and increased prosperity. His accession dispelled the dangerous shadow that hung over the death-bed of Elizabeth, assuring the succession of the throne firmly. . . . He solved the century-old problem of security from the North, and in his person created the United Kingdom. He made peace with Spain, and the whole country was freed of an incubus."[17]

In our poet's words, 1603 was the year in which

> *Incertainties now crown themselves assured,*
> *And peace proclaims olives of endless age.*
> *Now with the drops of this most balmy time*
> *My love looks fresh . . .*

At Southampton's trial, it had been remarked how youthful he still looked. On his release from the Tower in April 1603, he was in his twenty-ninth year; he would turn thirty in October. "The drops of this most balmy time" confirms the date of composition in another way: the spring of 1603 was a season of mild, warm rains. Contemporary eulogists, such as Gilbert Dugdale, likened these rains to the showers of clemency attending the progress of James I southward from Scotland.

"Tombs of brass," in the sonnet's final line, is not an allusion to Queen Elizabeth's tomb, made of marble and not completed until 1606, but to the events of 28 April 1603, when her body was borne through the crowded streets of London and placed in the chapel of Henry VII in Westminster Abbey. The Queen's coffin rested in the shadow of the great tomb of Henry and his wife, the most notable tomb of brass in England, by Torrigiani, while around the chapel the throngs of visitors would have seen commemorative crests.

If Shakespeare thought of Elizabeth I as a tyrant, he

Southampton at 29 in the Tower

would not, says Mattingly, "have been alone in that view, nor would that view have seemed strange to many conservative aristocrats if applied to all the Tudors. . . . The more closely one examines the events of the spring of 1603, as they were seen by Shakespeare's contemporaries, the more consistent do they appear with the language of sonnet 107, even in its slightest details. . . . Nor do the allusions in the sonnet seem appropriate to any other sequence of public events during Shakespeare's lifetime."[18]

Ever since an unidentified "J.R." first put forth the thesis in 1848, many leading scholars have maintained that 1603 is the date of sonnet 107, including Canon H. C. Beeching and J. Dover Wilson, both Pembrokeites; Sidney Lee, Mark Eccles, Alfred Harbage, and J. B. Leishman. G. P. V. Akrigg, while writing about the accession of James I in *Jacobean Pageant,* acknowledged that he had had "a sudden complete conviction that the sonnet belonged to 1603"; he has also revealed that G. B. Harrison, who had previously assigned the sonnet to 1596, revised the date to 1603, "when he came back to the sonnet after working on his *Jacobean Journal.*"[19] The date of composition is indeed one of the most difficult and crucial questions about the poems in Q.

The Date of Composition

"The question when the sonnets were written," wrote Hyder Edward Rollins in 1944, "is in many respects the most important of all the unanswerable questions they pose." The truth of this assertion is self-evident, though it may have been incautious of the fair-minded and meticulous editor of the New Variorum edition of the *Sonnets* not to have qualified his second adjective with "probably." The date of composition is far from undeterminable nor, as Rollins felt, is the answer forever destined to remain "an idle dream." One of the reasons is to be found in his very next words: "Evidence that at least some of the sonnets were written early in Shakespeare's literary career is reasonably sound; *but it does not necessarily apply to the entire collection.*"[20] In other words, some of the sonnets are early and some are late. This is true: sonnet 107 is quite late—1603—and all the others are early, but that is not, of course, what Rollins means. He means (at least in this sentence) that an unknown number are early, an unknown number are late, and it is idle to guess how many of each there are.

The mistaken assumption behind this concept is that Shakespeare's sonnets stretched over an extended period of composition—eight to ten years. It would indeed be idle to guess about dates if the premise that many of the sonnets are late were true. But this premise is wrong, as Rollins later, perhaps unconsciously, admits (page 207). As Shakespeare's fellow-players boasted, and as Ben Jonson complained, our poet wrote rapidly. It is absurd to think he continued writing sonnets for eighteen years, from 1591, when the fashion began, to 1609, when Q was published; or even to 1603—twelve years. He tells us in sonnet 104 that he had known the young man three years. If evidence is reasonably sound that some of the sonnets were written as early as 1592, then the *terminus ad quem* is three or so years later.

Another reason why it cannot be true that the sonnets are late is that Shakespeare is not likely to have continued to follow a literary fashion long after it was outmoded. Collections of love sonnets practically ceased in 1597, with the publication of Robert Tofte's *Laura.* The sonnet fashion, whose earlier background included the poems of Wyatt, Surrey, Watson, and others, was launched anew in 1591 with the publication of Sir Philip Sidney's *Astrophel and Stella,* the story of his passion for Essex's sister. This unauthorized book also contained some sonnets by Samuel Daniel. In 1592 there followed Daniel's *Delia* and Henry Constable's *Diana;* in 1593, Barnabe Barnes's *Parthenophil and Parthenophe,* Giles Fletcher's *Licia,* Thomas Lodge's *Phyllis,* and Thomas Watson's *The Tears of Fancy;* in 1594, Michael Drayton's *Idea's Mirrour;* and in 1595, Edmund Spenser's *Amoretti,* to name only the most famous. The historic fact is that, in one brief, dazzling era, Elizabethan poets wrote sonnet-cycles in concentrated periods of composition.

There are many reasons for concluding that the bulk of the sonnets in Q represent early work. For example, Rollins concedes that the vogue "ended *a decade or more before* Shakespeare's were published"[21]—that is, it was over by the time the first reference to Shakespeare's "sugared sonnets among his private friends" was published by Meres in 1598 and before *The Passionate Pilgrim* appeared in 1599.

AFTER 1594–95 SHAKESPEARE HAD NO NEED OF A PATRON. The relationship of the poet to the young man he addresses in the sonnets is that of a social inferior to a powerful patron. One of the disturbing elements in the sonnets is Shakespeare's use of self-abasing language to his supporter and protector. Where there is a patron, there is someone patronized. It is not likely that, after the widespread success of *Venus* and *Lucrece,* as well as the early plays, Shakespeare would continue to remain in a position of "vassalage" any longer than he had to. He had no reason to do so after he was established—apparently with his patron's help—as a shareholder in the Chamberlain's Men around 1594. (The single exception to early dating, the sonnet on the extraordinary occasion of his patron's release from prison in 1603, is not surprising; it is in keeping with everything we know of Shakespeare's character, including what Henry Chettle, who met him, described as his civil demeanour.)

"MY PUPIL PEN." These words occur in the opening group of poems—in sonnet 16, the second sonnet dealing with the theme of Time. They occur nowhere else in Shakespeare's work and are obviously significant. They tell us he is aware that his sonnets are the work of a beginner, just as the phrase "the first heir of my invention," in his dedicatory letter of 1593, confirms that *Venus and Adonis* is his first published book. "My pupil pen" comes after a reference to "your painted counterfeit"—that is, the portrait (perhaps the Hilliard miniature) of the young man—but, says the poet,

> . . . *this time's pencil, or my pupil pen,*
> *Neither in inward worth nor outward fair*
> *Can make you live yourself in eyes of men.*

Some critics committed to a later dating of the sonnets define "my pupil pen" as the writing implement of a mature writer who is willing to learn. This is desperate. Anyone acquainted with the profession of writing knows that while a rare author might reluctantly admit he is not omniscient, few would ever acknowledge the need of tutelage. Shakespeare's words mean what they say: "I'm a new writer, and I'm learning."

SONNETS 94 AND 142. The concluding words of sonnet 94 are "Lilies that fester smell far worse than weeds." This line also occurs in *Edward III* (II, i, 451), an anonymous play entered on 1 December 1595. ("Scarlet ornaments," another image used in the same act and scene of *Edward III,* also turns up in sonnet 142, line 6.) Scholars believe Shakespeare may have had a hand in writing some of the play's scenes, though no one believes he wrote the whole play. Whether he did or not, whether the playwright quoted the sonnet or the poet quoted the play, it matters (as far as dating the sonnets is concerned) not a whit. Finally, it takes time for a play to be written, produced, and become well enough known for a publisher to be able, or want, to publish it—probably at least a year, which could put *Edward III'*s composition in 1594. It is the early dating of these coincidences that matters.

SONNET 26. This sonnet is a poetic paraphrase of the dedicatory letter in *Lucrece,* which was registered on 9 May 1594. If sonnet 26 was intended to accompany the presentation copy of *Lucrece* in holograph, it would have had to be ready late in 1593 or in early 1594.

One year later Shakespeare was ready to acknowledge ("Then may I dare to boast how I do love thee") in public print, in that extraordinary dedication of *Lucrece* (see page 62), what he had written privately in sonnet 26. The date of the sonnet's composition may be the spring of 1593, and is certainly no later than the spring of 1594.

PARALLELS WITH OTHER EARLY WORK OF SHAKE-SPEARE. Two nineteenth-century scholars, Horace Davis in America and Hermann Conrad in Germany, independently made detailed studies of parallels between the language and imagery of the sonnets and those of Shakespeare's other poems and plays. Conrad's findings were published in 1884;[22] those of Davis, which remain in manuscript, were reported on in the teens of this century by other American scholars.[23] It is interesting that, while they found different numbers and examples of parallels, both Davis and Conrad agree on the same five Shakespearean works as leading the list: *Venus and Adonis* (Davis finds 64 parallels and Conrad 34), *Lucrece* (60 and 38), *Love's Labour's Lost* (49 and 36), *Romeo and Juliet* (48 and 47), and *Two Gentlemen of Verona* (35 and 31). The most impressive aspect of their discoveries is that all five works are *early* Shakespearean compositions: the two narrative poems, published in 1593 and 1594 respectively, were probably written or at least begun in 1592 and 1593; and scholars are generally agreed that the three plays date from the first half of the decade.

SONNET 25. Sir Walter Ralegh—after enjoying ten years (1582–91) as a favourite of Queen Elizabeth, as the recipient of grants, offices, and monopolies, an appoint-

ment as Captain of the Queen's Guard, and a lease of
Sherborne Castle through her favour—was, in February
1592, while waging a privateering expedition against
Spanish shipping, relieved of his command and recalled to
London to face disgrace. The cause, according to William
Camden, was Ralegh's seduction of one of the royal maids
of honour, Elizabeth Throgmorton, whom the Queen
forced him to marry. Ralegh was imprisoned in the Tower
in July 1592. This fall from honour and glory of a brilliant soldier, explorer, poet, and gallant courtier stands
behind these lines of sonnet 25:

> *Great princes' favourites their fair leaves spread*
> *But as the marigold at the sun's eye,*
> *And in themselves their pride lies buried,*
> *For at a frown they in their glory die.*
> *The painful warrior, famoused for might,*
> *After a thousand victories once foiled,*
> *Is from the book of honour rased quite,*
> *And all the rest forgot for which he toiled.*

The Essex-Southampton faction, which looked on Ralegh
as their chief rival at court, might well have gloried in his
fall, but despite his loyalty to his patron, Shakespeare was
too great a poet and human being not to give expression
to the irony and tragedy of this dramatic incident of 1592.
He might even have intended it as a warning to those still
in good standing with the Queen: if you're one of a great
prince's favourites, watch out.

THOMAS NASHE'S STRANGE REMARK. On 17 September
1593, six months after the publication of *Venus and
Adonis*, Thomas Nashe's picaresque novel *The Unfortu-*

nate Traveller: or, the Life of Jack Wilton was registered.
The first edition contains a rather long dedicatory letter to
the Earl of Southampton, who like Nashe had also studied
at St. John's, Cambridge. In his letter Nashe imitates
Shakespeare's dedication in *Venus and Adonis* ("these
unpolished leaves" compared to the latter's "my unpolished lines"; Nashe's blunt "If you set any price on
them, I hold my labour well satisfied" compared to "If
your honour seem but pleased, I account myself highly
praised"; Nashe's words at the beginning, "I know not
what," echoing Shakespeare's "I know not how," and so
on). The novel was a success, and before the end of the
year, a second edition was issued, from which, for some
unknown reason, the dedication was dropped. The obvious
conjecture has been that Southampton failed to respond to
Nashe's demand for payment, and Nashe therefore deleted
his dedication. I am sure this is true, but I have discovered
an additional and more significant reason for the Earl's
cold response.

In words that have puzzled me for years, Nashe's dedication describes Southampton's interest in poets: "A dear
lover and cherisher you are, as well of the lovers of poets
as of poets themselves. Among their sacred number I dare
not ascribe myself, though now and then I speak English."
A lover and cherisher *of the lovers of poets?* What a
strange way of putting it, unless he means people who are
having love-affairs with poets. Nashe's use of the plural
here resembles Shakespeare's plural dilution in the Ralegh
sonnet ("princes' favourites," instead of the specific and
more dangerous "prince's favourite"). Nashe does not say,
and could not possibly have meant, *poetry lovers*—aristocratic Southampton a lover and cherisher of such a mob?

Ingenious Nashe is actually saying, 'You, Southampton, are known to be the lover and cherisher of certain poets' lovers, as well as the lover and cherisher of the poets themselves.' Either some of those sugared sonnets in the hands of private friends—especially sonnets 40–42 and 133–34 —had already reached Nashe, or talk of them had reached him. He clearly suggests that the seduction of a particular poet's mistress by Southampton was literary gossip in certain circles in the autumn of 1593.

Did Nashe count on young Southampton's being amused by his cryptic sentence, which only the cognoscenti could decode? Did he mean to imply in the second sentence that on occasion, if need be, he could speak *plain* English? Not many months earlier, during the plague of 1592, Nashe had composed a great lyric, for which alone he deserves to be numbered in the sacred ranks:

> *Beauty is but a flower,*
> *Which wrinkles will devour.*
> *Brightness falls from the air,*
> *Queens have died young and fair,*
> *Dust hath closed Helen's eye.*
> *I am sick, I must die:*
> > *Lord, have mercy on us.*

Apparently young Juvenal received no gold from Southampton for his long, flattering, and indiscreet dedication. Nevertheless, we have reason to be grateful to Nashe for another clue to the sonnets' early fame and (in certain circles) notoriety.

SONNETS 110–12 AND "O'ER-GREENE." "Through three and a half centuries, up to the publication of Hyder Rollins' enormous variorum edition of the sonnets in 1944," John Berryman observed, "hardly anything was discovered about when they were written, and Rollins overlooked the shrewdest suggestion perhaps ever made, that of Fripp's about 'o'er-greene.' "[24] As previously pointed out, Edgar I. Fripp, whose investigations into Stratford records and Elizabethan documents are painstaking and reliable, suggested that "o'er-greene" is "a reply to *Shakescene*. It is a word coined for the purpose and never used again." Robert Greene's fusillade of insults aimed at Shakespeare (*upstart crow, an absolute Johannes factotum, the only Shake-scene in a country,* one of *those apes, rude grooms, buckram gentlemen, peasants,* and *painted monsters*) graced the bookstalls of St. Paul's Churchyard in September 1592. "Here," Berryman writes, "was a congeries of contempt and slander that might enter into the soul." The result was "the extremely bitter trio [of sonnets] 110–11–12." Their most probable date of composition is thus the autumn of 1592.

HYDER EDWARD ROLLINS: "Nobody has ever surpassed Shakespeare at following, while improving upon, current fashions. He must have been annoyed to find himself featured in 1609 as the author of an elaborate collection of old-style quatorzains that he had carefully hidden from the public gaze *at the very time when almost everybody else was reading or writing sonnets.*"[25] The only possible meaning of these words is that the date of the sonnets' composition is early. This conclusion by "the greatest authority on the *Sonnets* in this century" (the judgement is that of S. Schoenbaum[26]) is impressive and stimulating, coming after his earlier pronouncement that "a solution to the question when the sonnets were written has been and remains an idle dream." I readily agree with Professor Schoenbaum's estimate of Rollins. Only the greatest of scholars could safely make such an intuitive leap.

WIDOWHOOD. In the final line of sonnet 13 the use of the past tense in the phrase, "You *had* a father," indicates a state of widowhood—another proof of early composition. The Countess Southampton, the Earl's mother, ended her widowhood of more than twelve years when she married Sir Thomas Heneage on 2 May 1594. This puts the sonnet in 1593 or earlier.

EARLY EVENTS IN SOUTHAMPTON'S LIFE. One of the reasons why E. K. Chambers found the case for Southampton unconvincing was that, as he wrote, "If it were sound, one would expect to find some hints in the sonnets of the major interests of Southampton's early life; his military ambitions, his comradeship with Essex, the romance of his marriage. There are none."[27] But none of these events belongs to Southampton's early life, the years before he came of age. He did not see military action until the Azores expedition of July 1597, though he tried and was not allowed to join the Cádiz raid in March 1596. His marriage to Elizabeth Vernon took place in August 1598. His active comradeship with Essex was in the Azores in 1597, in Ireland in 1599, and in the uprising of 1601. Though Southampton knew and admired Essex in his younger years, a close association with him was impossible while Southampton was under age and under the rule of the chief enemy of Essex, Lord Burghley. In other words, the events that Chambers finds missing from the sonnets corroborate the fact of their early composition. For reasons that I find puzzling, it has been difficult or impossible for some critics to associate the sonnets with Shakespeare's early years as a writer. If their argument is that the sonnets are too good for early work, the answer again is—genius.

LOVE'S LABOUR'S LOST. The sonnet play, as we have seen, was written, and perhaps performed, by 1593–94. The writing of this play occurred around the same time as the writing of the sonnets. The date of composition of the poems, therefore, involves the year 1593. If the poems cover three or four years, the dates might well be 1592–95. It is impossible to be more precise, but it is certain that they represent the work of Shakespeare's earlier years.

EDWARD HUBLER: (I) "Other internal evidence points to an earlier date [than 1599 for the sonnets]. The poet refers to himself as an unestablished writer; he fears that although the sonnets will survive, his name will be forgotten. And so on. But by 1598 Shakespeare was famous and could not seriously have written in that vein."[28] (II) "I have assumed an early date for the sonnets. . . . It seems proper to accept the internal evidence which places them early in Shakespeare's career. I believe they were written over a period of four or five years beginning in 1592. This conclusion is conservative enough, and accords with the opinion of reputable scholars with no axes to grind."[29]

KENNETH MUIR: "[Claes] Schaar* claims that 'the vast majority of the sonnets . . . seem to have been written between 1591–2 and 1594–5.' . . . I accept Schaar's dating as the most probable."[30]

W. H. AUDEN: "On the whole, I think an early date is a more plausible conjecture than a late one, because the experiences the sonnets describe seem to me to be more likely to befall a younger man than an older."[31]

The final pages of Q contain the least known of Shakespeare's poems, the least alluded to (it comes last in the number of references in the *Shakespeare Allusion Book*), and the least studied. "A Lover's Complaint" would not be known at all were it not for Q. The "Bath" sonnets are followed by the word FINIS, and the next page bears the half-title "A Lover's complaint [sic] / BY / William Shake-speare," followed by the first three stanzas and part of the fourth. Let us look at this neglected work.

"A Lover's Complaint"

The poem is a joke, a fact mentioned by none of its critics. The complaining lover is a woman and the joke, which

---

* Claes Shaar, *Elizabethan Sonnet Themes and the Dating of the Sonnets,* Lund Studies in English 32, Copenhagen, 1962, p. 185.

could be called black humour, is that at the end of the tale
of her betrayal by the handsome seducer, she realizes that
she wants it to happen again. Not until the last lines of the
penultimate stanza does her tone of grief and remorse
suddenly shift:

> *Ay, me! I fell, and yet do question make*
> *What I should do again for such a sake.*

She concludes with a fervent hope that the youth "Would
yet again betray the fore-betrayed"! Unlike the heroine of
the poem that is its principal model—Samuel Daniel's *The
Complaint of Rosamund* (1592), whose ghostly narrator,
a historical figure, bitterly laments her seduction by Henry
II and her poisoning by Queen Eleanor of Aquitaine—the
woman in "A Lover's Complaint," like Edith Piaf in her
well-known song, regrets nothing.

In his study of the poem (1912), J. W. Mackail argued
against Shakespeare's authorship. Mackail, who was certain it was "not the work of a beginner," called it "highly
mannered" and found in the writing a "cramped, gritty,
discontinuous quality."[32] George Rylands in 1960 considered it a "little-appreciated masterpiece" of Shakespeare's
and an early one.[33] Macdonald P. Jackson, author of a
recent study (1965), argues for its authenticity, but on the
grounds of language dates it with Shakespeare's maturer
work after 1600.[34]

It is certainly Shakespeare's poem, and the apprentice
work of a genius. Edmund Malone considered it "a beautiful poem, in every part of which the hand of Shakespeare
is visible."[35] Algernon Swinburne wrote that "it contains
two of the most exquisitely Shakespearean verses vouch-

safed to us by Shakespeare,"[36] referring to lines 288 and 289:

> *O father, what a hell of witchcraft lies*
> *In the small orb of one particular tear!*

These lines are the climax of the poem, proving again that when greatness of language is required, Shakespeare always rises to greatness.

"A Lover's Complaint" is also uneven, which for me confirms its early composition. Without specifying the lines, Swinburne also said it contains "two of the most execrably euphuistic and dysphuistic lines ever inflicted on us by man." There are a number of possible candidates for this attack, including a description of the woman's voice:

> *As often shrieking undistinguished woe*
> *In clamours of all size both high and low*

and of her eye-movements:

> *Sometimes her levelled eyes their carriage ride*
> *As they did battery to the spheres intend;*
> *Sometimes diverted, their poor balls are tied*
> *To the orbed earth; sometimes they do extend*
> *Their view right on; anon their gazes lend*
> *To every place at once . . .*

and of the young man's weeping:

> *This said, his watery eyes he did dismount,*
> *Whose sights till then were levelled on my face;*
> *Each cheek a river running from a fount*
> *With brinish current downward flowed apace.*

This is indeed euphuistic and artificial imagery, another proof of the poem's early date of composition. The influence of Lyly, as George Rylands has pointed out, "left its mark on every Elizabethan, and on Shakespeare as much as any, although he reacted against it." The use of odd, new, and coined words—one of the distinguishing features of the poem—also indicates early composition. "Young writers put all their goods in the shop window," Rylands wrote. "They coin and compound words. They accumulate images for their own sake. Shakespeare is no exception. In his early works there is considerable padding, and he follows Spenser and Sidney . . . in his employment of the compound epithet."[37] In "A Lover's Complaint" he uses a number of compounds that occur nowhere else in his writing, such as all-hurting, by-past, out-bragged, heart-wished, sad-tuned, maiden-tongued, and fore-betrayed. Nor are any of the following words in "A Lover's Complaint" found elsewhere in the work of our poet, whose vast vocabulary is unequalled in English:

maund	enpatron	annexions	ruffle (noun)
acture	sawn (for	plat	unexperient
plaintful	*seen*)	fluxive	lovered

There are three reasons for believing that Daniel's longer poem *The Complaint of Rosamund* (742 lines) served as a kind of model for "A Lover's Complaint" (329 lines): they follow the same versification, the rime royal introduced into English by Chaucer, with its stanza of seven lines in iambic pentameter, rhyming a b a b b c c; the recurrence of the word "complaint" in Shakespeare's title; and the publication of Daniel's poem in 1592, following the unauthorized appearance of some of his sonnets in Sidney's *Astrophel and Stella* (1591). Daniel's narrative poem was well thought of by his contemporaries, and praised by Spenser, Marston, and Drayton. Thomas Nashe wrote of it: "There goes more exquisite pains and purity of wit to the writing of one such rare poem as *Rosamund* than to a hundred of your duncetical sermons."[38] A comparison of Daniel's opening stanza with Shakespeare's shows that the resemblance is syntactical only; their tones are worlds apart. This is Daniel:

> *Out from the horror of infernal deeps*
> *My poor afflicted ghost comes here to plaint it,*
> *Attended with my shame that never sleeps,*
> *The spot wherewith my kind and youth did stain it.*
> *My body found a grave where to contain it,*
> *A sheet could hide my face but not my sin,*
> *For fame finds never tomb t'enclose it in.*

Shakespeare:

> *From off a hill whose concave womb reworded*
> *A plaintful story from a sistering vale,*
> *My spirits to attend this double voice accorded,*
> *And down I laid to list the sad-tuned tale.*
> *Ere long espied a fickle maid full pale,*
> *Tearing of papers, breaking rings atwain,*
> *Storming her world with sorrow's wind and rain.*

Daniel's poem is grave and serious, as befits the sad twelfth-century legend of Rosamund Clifford and her royal destruction. Its predecessors were Sackville's "Induction" to *A Mirror for Magistrates* (1563) and Churchyard's "Shore's Wife," the story of Edward IV's mistress, Jane Shore. Shakespeare occasionally echoes Sackville's Chaucerian language, in lines like "Oft did she heave her napkin to her eyne" (though "eyes" appears elsewhere in the poem), but the tone of "A Lover's Complaint" is predominantly mock-heroic. In the closing stanza, with its five O's, it is farcical:

> *O! that infected moisture of his eye,*
> *O! that false fire which in his cheek so glowed,*
> *O! that forced thunder from his heart did fly,*
> *O! that sad breath his spongy lungs bestowed,*
> *O! all that borrowed motion seeming owed . . .*

Here the poet finally makes it clear that he is parodying, or at least taking off from, a famous poem—and amusing his patron at the same time. Everyone agrees that the young seducer in the poem is very similar to the young man of the sonnets. This stanza, explaining his effect on men and women of all ages, seems to be general; yet its particularity—"in personal duty"—also suggests the effect he had on the poet:

> *That he did in the general bosom reign*
> *Of young, of old, and sexes both enchanted,*
> *To dwell with him in thoughts, or to remain*
> *In personal duty, following where he haunted;*
> *Consents bewitched ere he desire have granted,*
> *And dialogued for him what he would say,*
> *Asked their own wills, and made their wills obey.*

The last line's double entendre of "wills" foreshadows its multiple use in the later sonnets. The use of the coined verb "enpatron," in line 224, is also peculiar to this poem. Several writers have pointed out the verbal parallels with *The Complaint of Rosamund* that are to be found in *The*

Rape of Lucrece.* Shakespeare read Samuel Daniel atten-
tively, there is no doubt. The connection with "A Lover's
Complaint" has been less apparent, perhaps because the
effect of Daniel's poem on it was chiefly negative.

Shakespeare's narrative skill, at which he quickly
achieved mastery in the plays, is at its worst here. There
are four characters—five, counting the peripheral figure of
the nun whom the seducer's "parts had power to charm"
—but there need have been only three. In addition to the
woman and the seducer, there is a "reverend" old man, the
chorus-figure required to hear her tale. Though now a
shepherd, he had had a checkered youth at court, and in
business, and seems to have been a dropout:

> *Sometime a blusterer, that the ruffle knew*
> *Of court, of city, and had let go by*
> *The swiftest hours, observèd as they flew . . .*

an experienced man, well qualified "in the charity of age"
to understand and sympathize with her story. The superfluous fourth character, the odd man out, is the silent "I"
of the opening stanza ("And down I laid to list the sad-
tuned tale"), who is forgotten after the first stanza. This
is another proof that the poem is apprentice work.

"A Lover's Complaint" was not intended for publication. If Shakespeare was horrified by the publication of the
sonnets, he had another reason in "A Lover's Complaint"
for wanting Q suppressed. Perhaps this piece of apprentice-
work provided Shakespeare with an entrée to the powerful
and influential circles he needed for his career. Perhaps it
got him the commission to write the first sonnets. Mark

* Including J. W. Mackail, *op. cit.*, and Robert Adger Law, *The Complaint of Rosamund*, Texas University Series, 1947.

Van Doren cited it when he wrote that the "biography of Shakespeare is the biography of his art, his intellect, and his imagination; and if he writes better as he grows older, it is because they too have grown older, along with a heart which there is no reason for supposing to have been otherwise than normal.

> *He had the dialect and different skill,*
> *Catching all passions in his craft of will.*

This couplet from 'A Lover's Complaint' describes its author . . ."[39]

These marvellous lines (in which "different" has the meaning of "multiple") also stamp the poem as indubitably Shakespeare's. In this, the least known of his works, he describes himself more accurately than anyone has succeeded in doing in the four hundred years since.

THE POET

No! I am that I am . . .

SONNET 121

The Poet

THE POET is asked, or hired, to write a series of poems that will persuade to marriage a young man of high station, who is not yet of age. The poet accepts the job, meets the youth, and is dazzled by his extraordinary beauty. The early poems employ the flattering thesis that so rare a thing as beauty deserves to be duplicated: "From fairest creatures we desire increase . . ." They argue also that the begetting of an heir will ensure a kind of immortality for the father. After seventeen poems, not having succeeded in bringing about the marriage, and having admitted that he has come to love the golden youth, the poet drops the marriage theme and promises the young man another form of immortality—eternal life through the poems.

The writing of sonnets has, meanwhile, become a national craze, and the poet is aware that he has a first-rate subject: his beloved is a "child of state" with an important future. Can the poet be sincere? The early love poems convince us he is; the later poems revealing unkindness, disillusion, suffering, and betrayal confirm the realistic history of his love. If the precise character of the love is

221

elusive, the reason may be that the poet is not *analyzing* a complicated emotional relationship, but only expressing it. Nor is he writing for publication, though we are told by a contemporary that some sonnets have circulated among his private friends.

The poet is concerned about several rivals who are dedicating their works to the youth. One rival in particular, a writer of "great verse," is the chief source of worry, but he suddenly disappears. As the sequence continues, the poet adds a parallel series of poems to the dark-haired mistress with whom he is having a passionate affair. She deserts him for the young man, to whom the poet writes, "Take all my loves, my love, yea take them all. . . ."

After three years, he has over 150 sonnets, and we have Q. Years later, when the poet is no longer writing sonnets, the youth is charged with treason and sentenced to death. The sentence is then commuted to life-imprisonment. After two years and four months, when the head of state dies, the man—at twenty-nine no longer a youth—is released. The poet then writes what we know as sonnet 107. It is added to the portfolio of poems which, six years later, falls into the hands of a publisher who prints this work of an earlier era. The publication of the book may have distressed the poet. His friend, now powerfully placed, may have had it "stopped." If not, in the event it seems to have been received with silence. After seven years, the poet dies.

This account of Q is, I believe, in accord with the few facts we glean from the poems themselves and the known circumstances of their publication. Some might object that it is too inferential. The truth is that most of what we know of Shakespeare is inferential, except for a few documented facts, like the date of his baptism. Even his birth date is inferential; April twenty-third is an appropriate compromise, which may even be true. We do not know for certain the chronological order of Shakespeare's plays. Scholars give sound reasons for their lists, but the lists differ.

Shakespearean scholars, the subject of Professor Schoenbaum's absorbing book,[1] thrive on differences of opinion. One of the more acrimonious scholars, George Steevens, is famous as the author of the toughest proscription ever directed against Shakespearean biography:

> As all that is known with any degree of certainty concerning Shakespeare is,—*that he was born at Stratford upon Avon, married and had children there, went to London, where he commenced actor, and wrote poems and plays, returned to Stratford, made his will, died, and was buried,*—I must confess my readiness to combat every unfounded supposition respecting the particular occurrences of his life.[2]

Steevens's resolve to fight untruth is admirable, but there is a large area, extending from absolute certainty to reasonable inference, within whose boundaries truth resides. One wonders if Steevens fully perceived that his four casual words *"wrote poems and plays,"* thrown in as a detail, contain the sole and total reason for our interest in Shakespeare. The four words open up like Japanese paperflowers into the thirty-six plays, the narrative poems, the songs and sonnets, which a lifetime of study can never exhaust. Many, perhaps most, readers do not care what the factual details of Shakespeare's life may have been, as long as they can read the poems and plays.

Yet when he comes to the sonnets, the reader faces a

problem that is peculiar to these poems. Confessional, personal, and autobiographical, the sonnets offer special difficulties to the reader who wants to come to terms with them. There are those who are content to accept the poems as literary exercises, but readers who find their naked honesty and self-exposure to be unique in Shakespeare's writing cannot let the matter rest there.

George Steevens exemplifies perfectly the unsatisfactory limits of mere scholarship. His high standards of research, when it came to the sonnets, were betrayed by his own character: it is not so much that he considered the sonnets to be badly written as that he entertained a virulent dislike of their content. He therefore suppressed them, a most unscholarly thing to do. In 1793 he published a fifteen-volume edition of Shakespeare's work, in which he refused to include the sonnets, "because," he said, "the strongest act of Parliament that could be framed, would fail to compel readers into their service; notwithstanding these miscellaneous poems have derived every possible advantage from the literature and judgement of their only intelligent editor, Mr. Malone, whose implements of criticism, like the ivory rake and golden spade in Prudentius, are on this occasion *disgraced* [my italics] by the object of their culture."[3] Of the "Master-Mistress" sonnet he wrote: "It is impossible to read this fulsome panegyrick, addressed to a male object, without an equal mixture of disgust and indignation."[4] The only way in which he could edit an author whose work in part repelled him was to suppress that part and leave it to other scholars.

In every period there have been those who have rejected the sonnets. In the copy of Q in the Bibliotheca Bodmeriana at Geneva, an unknown eighteenth-century reader (perhaps the Duke of Grafton, whose armorial bookplate is stamped in the book) wrote in ink under the last sonnet, *"What a heap of wretched Infidel Stuff."* Others have primly recoiled from the poems, like Léon de Wailly in 1834: "Mais, grand Dieu! . . . *Lui* au lieu d'*elle!* . . . Est-ce que ces sonnets seraient adressés à un homme? Shakespeare! grand Shakespeare!"[5] In Victorian times Henry Hallam, the father of Tennyson's bosom friend, wrote plaintively: "It is impossible not to wish that Shakespeare had never written them."[6] In this century, in 1929, a Sydney newspaper reported that the sonnets had been banned in New Zealand,[7] and in 1930 Herbert Thurston announced, "Regretfully as we must say it, the *Sonnets* in their plain and obvious meaning point to a plague spot."[8]

Taking into account the whole story of Q, including these examples of suppression and resistance, perhaps the most extraordinary fact of all is that we have the sonnets.

SHAKE-SPEARES

SONNETS.

Neuer before Imprinted.

——————————————

——————————————

AT LONDON
By *G. Eld* for *T. T.* and are
to be folde by *Iohn Wright*, dwelling
at Chrift Church gate.
1609.

227

TO.THE.ONLIE.BEGETTER.OF.
THESE.INSVING.SONNETS.
Mr. W. H. ALL.HAPPINESSE.
AND.THAT.ETERNITIE.
PROMISED.

BY.

OVR.EVER-LIVING.POET.

WISHETH.

THE.WELL-WISHING.
ADVENTVRER.IN.
SETTING.
FORTH.

T. T.

SHAKE-SPEARES,
SONNETS.

FRom faireſt creatures we deſire increaſe,
　　That thereby beauties *Roſe* might neuer die,
But as the riper ſhould by time deceaſe,
His tender heire might beare his memory:
But thou contracted to thine owne bright eyes,
Feed'ſt thy lights flame with ſelfe ſubſtantiall fewell,
Making a famine where aboundance lies,
Thy ſelfe thy foe,to thy ſweet ſelfe too cruell:
Thou that art now the worlds freſh ornament,
And only herauld to the gaudy ſpring,
Within thine owne bud burieſt thy content,
And tender chorle makſt waſt in niggarding:
　　Pitty the world,or elſe this glutton be,
　　To eate the worlds due,by the graue and thee.

2

VVHen fortie Winters ſhall beſeige thy brow,
　　And digge deep trenches in thy beauties field,
Thy youthes proud liuery ſo gaz'd on now,
Wil be a totter'd weed of ſmal worth held:
Then being askt,where all thy beautie lies,
Where all the treaſure of thy luſty daies;
To ſay within thine owne deepe ſunken eyes,
Were an all-eating ſhame,and thriftleſſe praiſe.
How much more praiſe deſeru'd thy beauties vſe,
If thou couldſt anſwere this faire child of mine
Shall ſum my count,and make my old excuſe
Proouing his beautie by ſucceſſion thine.

B　　　　　　　　This

This were to be new made when thou art ould,
And see thy blood warme when thou feel'ft it could,

3

LOoke in thy glaffe and tell the face thou veweft,
Now is the time that face fhould forme an other,
Whofe frefh repaire if now thou not reneweft,
Thou doo'ft beguile the world, vnbleffe fome mother.
For where is fhe fo faire whofe vn-eard wombe
Difdaines the tillage of thy husbandry?
Or who is he fo fond will be the tombe,
Of his felfe loue to ftop pofterity?
Thou art thy mothers glaffe and fhe in thee
Calls backe the louely Aprill of her prime,
So thou through windowes of thine age fhalt fee,
Difpight of wrinkles this thy goulden time.
  But if thou liue remembred not to be,
  Die fingle and thine Image dies with thee.

4

VNthrifty louelineffe why doft thou fpend,
Vpon thy felfe thy beauties legacy?
Natures bequeft giues nothing but doth lend,
And being franck fhe lends to thofe are free:
Then beautious nigard why dooft thou abufe,
The bountious largeffe giuen thee to giue?
Profitles vferer why dooft thou vfe
So great a fumme of fummes yet can'ft not liue?
For hauing traffike with thy felfe alone,
Thou of thy felfe thy fweet felfe doft deceaue,
Then how when nature calls thee to be gone,
What acceptable *Audit* can'ft thou leaue?
  Thy vnuf'd beauty muft be tomb'd with thee,
  Which vfed liues th'executor to be.

5

THofe howers that with gentle worke did frame,
The louely gaze where euery eye doth dwell
Will play the tirants to the very fame,

And

And that vnfaire which fairely doth excell:
For ſeuer reſting time leads Summer on,
To hidious winter and confounds him there,
Sap checkt with froſt and luſtie leau's quite gon.
Beauty ore-ſnow'd and barenes euery where,
Then were not ſummers diſtillation left
A liquid priſoner pent in walls of glaſſe,
Beauties effect with beauty were bereft,
Nor it nor noe remembrance what it was.
    But flowers diſtil'd though they with winter meete,
    Leeſe but their ſhow, their ſubſtance ſtill liues ſweet.

6

THen let not winters wragged hand deface,
  In thee thy ſummer ere thou be diſtil'd:
Make ſweet ſome viall; treaſure thou ſome place,
With beautits treaſure ere it be ſelfe kil'd:
That vſe is not forbidden vſery,
Which happies thoſe that pay the willing lone;
That's for thy ſelfe to breed an other thee,
Or ten times happier be it ten for one,
Ten times thy ſelfe were happier then thou art,
If ten of thine ten times refigur d thee,
Then what could death doe if thou ſhould'ſt depart,
Leauing thee liuing in poſterity?
    Be not ſelfe-wild for thou art much too faire,
    To be deaths conqueſt and make wormes thine heire.

7

LOe in the Orient when the gracious light,
  Lifts vp his burning head, each vnder eye
Doth homage to his new appearing ſight,
Seruing with lookes his ſacred maieſty,
And hauing climb'd the ſteepe vp heauenly hill,
Reſembling ſtrong youth in his middle age,
Yet mortall lookes adore his beauty ſtill,
Attending on his goulden pilgrimage:
But when from high-moſt pich with wery car,

B 2

Lik

Like feeble age he reeleth from the day,
The eyes(fore dutious)now conuerted are
From his low tract and looke an other way:
   So thou,thy selfe out-going in thy noon:
   Vnlok'd on dieft vnlesse thou get a sonne.

8

MVsick to heare,why hear'st thou musick sadly,
  Sweets with sweets warre not ,ioy delights in ioy:
Why lou'st thou that which thou receauft not gladly,
Or else receau'st with pleasure thine annoy ?
If the true concord of well tuned sounds,
By vnions married do offend thine eare,
They do but sweetly chide thee, who confounds
In singlenesse the parts that thou should'st beare:
Marke how one string sweet husband to an other,
Strike each in each by mutuall ordering;
Resembling sier,and child, and happy mother,
Who all in one,one pleasing note do sing:
   Whose speechlesse song being many,seeming one,
   Sings this to thee thou single wilt proue none.

9.

IS it for feare to wet a widdowes eye,
  That thou consum'st thy selfe in single life?
Ah;if thou issulesse shalt hap to die,
The world will waile thee like a makelesse wife,
The world wilbe thy widdow and still weepe,
That thou no forme of thee hast left behind,
When euery priuat widdow well may keepe,
By childrens eyes,her husbands shape in minde:
Looke what an vnthrift in the world doth spend
Shifts but his place,for still the world inioyes it
But beauties waste, hath in the world an end,
And kept vnvsde the vser so destroyes it:
   No loue toward others in that bosome fits
   That on himselfe such murdrous shame commits.

IQ.

10

FOr fhame deny that thou bear'ſt loue to any
Who for thy ſelfe art ſo vnprouident
Graunt if thou wilt,thou art belou'd of many,
But that thou none lou ſt is moſt euident:
For thou art ſo poſſeſt with murdrous hate,
That gainſt thy ſelfe thou ſtickſt not to conſpire,
Seeking that beautious rooſe to ruinate
Which to repaire ſhould be thy chiefe deſire :
O change thy thought,that I may change my minde,
Shall hate be fairer log'd then gentle loue?
Be as thy preſence is gracious and kind,
Or to thy ſelfe at leaſt kind harted proue,
    Make thee an other ſelfe for loue of me,
    That beauty ſtill may liue in thine or thee.

11

AS faſt as thou ſhalt wane ſo faſt thou grow'ſt,
In one of thine,from that which thou departeſt,
And that freſh bloud which yongly thou beſtow'ſt,
Thou maiſt call thine,when thou from youth conuerteſt,
Herein liues wiſdome,beauty,and increaſe,
Without this follie,age,and could decay,
If all were minded ſo,the times ſhould ceaſe,
And threeſcoore yeare would make the world away:
Let thoſe whom nature hath not made for ſtore,
Harſh,featureleſſe,and rude , barrenly perriſh,
Looke whom ſhe beſt indow'd,ſhe gaue the more;
Which bountious guift thou ſhouldſt in bounty cherriſh,
    She caru'd thee for her ſeale,and ment therby,
    Thou ſhouldſt print more,not let that coppy die.

12

VVHen I doe count the clock that tels the time,
    And ſee the braue day ſunck in hidious night,
When I behold the violet paſt prime,
And ſable curls or ſiluer'd ore with white :
When lofty trees I ſee barren of leaues,
Which erſt from heat did canopie the herd

B 3   And

235

And Sommers greene all girded vp in sheaues
Borne on the beare with white and bristly beard:
Then of thy beauty do I question make
That thou among the wastes of time must goe,
Since sweets and beauties do them-selues forsake,
  And die as fast as they see others grow,
    And nothing gainst Times sieth can make defence
    Saue breed to braue him, when he takes thee hence.

13

O That you were your selfe, but loue you are
  No longer yours, then you your selfe here liue,
Against this cumming end you should prepare,
And your sweet semblance to some other giue.
So should that beauty which you hold in lease
Find no determination, then you were
You selfe again after your selfes decease,
When your sweet issue your sweet forme should beare.
Who lets so faire a house fall to decay,
Which husbandry in honour might vphold,
Against the stormy gusts of winters day
And barren rage of deaths eternall cold?
    O none but vnthrifts, deare my loue you know,
    You had a Father, let your Son say so.

14

NOt fron the stars do I my iudgement plucke,
  And yet me thinkes I haue Astronomy,
But not to tell of good, or euil lucke,
Of plagues, of dearths, or seasons quallity,
Nor can I fortune to breefe mynuits tell;
Pointing to each his thunder, raine and winde,
Or say with Princes if it shal go wel
By oft predict that I in heauen finde,
But from thine eies my knowledge I deriue,
And constaut stars in them I read such art
As truth and beautie shal together thriue
If from thy selfe, to store thou wouldst conuert:

Or

Or elſe ofthee this I prognoſticate,
Thy end is Truthes and Beauties doome and date.

15

WHen I conſider euery thing that growes
Holds in perfection but a little moment.
That this huge ſtage preſenteth nought but ſhowes
Whereon the Stars in ſecret influence comment.
When I perceiue that men as plants increaſe,
Cheared and checkt euen by the ſelfe-ſame skie:
Vaunt in their youthfull ſap, at height decreaſe,
And were their braue ſtate out of memory.
Then the conceit of this inconſtant ſtay,
Sets you moſt rich in youth before my ſight,
Where waſtfull time debateth with decay
To change your day of youth to ſullied night,
    And all in war with Time for loue of you
    As he takes from you, I ingraſt you new.

16

BVt wherefore do not you a mightier waie
Make warre vppon this bloudie tirant time?
And fortifie your ſelfe in your decay
With meanes more bleſſed then my barren rime?
Now ſtand you on the top of happie houres,
And many maiden gardens yet vnſet,
With vertuous wiſh would beare your liuing flowers,
Much liker then your painted counterfeit:
So ſhould the lines of life that life repaire
Which this (Times penſel or my pupill pen)
Neither in inward worth nor outward faire
Can make you liue your ſelfe in eies of men,
    To giue away your ſelfe, keeps your ſelfe ſtill,
    And you muſt liue drawne by your owne ſweet skill.

17

WHo will beleeue my verſe in time to come
If it were fild with your moſt high deſerts?

B 4   Though

237

Though yet heauen knowes it is but as a tombe
Which hides your life , and shewes not halfe your parts:
If I could write the beauty of your eyes,
And in fresh numbers number all your graces,
The age to come would say this Poet lies,
Such heauenly touches nere toucht earthly faces.
So should my papers (yellowed with their age)
Be scorn'd,like old men of lesse truth then tongue,
And your true rights be termd a Poets rage,
And stretched miter of an Antique song.
    But were some childe of yours aliue that time,
    You should liue twise in it,and in my rime.

18.

SHall I compare thee to a Summers day?
Thou art more louely and more temperate:
Rough windes do shake the darling buds of Maie,
And Sommers lease hath all too short a date:
Sometime too hot the eye of heauen shines,
And often is his gold complexion dimm'd,
And euery faire from faire some-time declines,
By chance,or natures changing course vntrim'd:
But thy eternall Sommer shall not fade,
Nor loose possession of that faire thou ow'st,
Nor shall death brag thou wandr'st in his shade,
When in eternall lines to time thou grow'st,
    So long as men can breath or eyes can see,
    So long liues this,and this giues life to thee,

19

DEuouring time blunt thou the Lyons pawes,
And make the earth deuoure her owne sweet brood,
Plucke the keene teeth from the fierce Tygers yawes,
And burne the long liu'd Phænix in her blood,
Make glad and sorry seasons as thou fleet'st,
And do what ere thou wilt swift-footed time
To the wide world and all her fading sweets:
But I forbid thee one most hainous crime,

O carue not with thy howers my loues faire brow,
Nor draw noe lines there with thine antique pen,
Him in thy course vntainted doe allow,
For beauties patterne to succeding men.
 Yet doe thy worst ould Time dispight thy wrong,
 My loue shall in my verse euer liue young.

20

A Womans face with natures owne hand painted,
 Haste thou the Master Mistris of my passion,
A womans gentle hart but not acquainted
With shifting change as is false womens fashion,
An eye more bright then theirs, lesse false in rowling:
Gilding the obiect where-vpon it gazeth,
A man in hew all *Hews* in his controwling,
Which steales mens eyes and womens soules amaseth.
And for a woman wert thou first created,
Till nature as she wrought thee fell a dotinge,
And by addition me of thee defeated,
By adding one thing to my purpose nothing.
 But since she prickt thee out for womens pleasure,
 Mine be thy loue and thy loues vse their treasure.

21

SO is it not with me as with that Muse,
 Stird by a painted beauty to his verse,
Who heauen it selfe for ornament doth vse,
And euery faire with his faire doth reherse,
Making a coopelment of proud compare
With Sunne and Moone, with earth and seas rich gems:
With Aprills first borne flowers and all things rare,
That heauens ayre in this huge rondure hems,
O let me true in loue but truly write,
And then beleeue me, my loue is as faire,
As any mothers childe, though not so bright
As those gould candells fixt in heauens ayer:
 Let them say more that like of heare-say well,
 I will not prayse that purpose not to sell.

C

22

239

22

MY glaſſe ſhall not perſwade me I am ould,
So long as youth and thou are of one date,
But when in thee times forrwes I behould,
Then look I death my daies ſhould expiate.
For all that beauty that doth couer thee,
Is but the ſeemely rayment of my heart,
Which in thy breſt doth liue, as thine in me,
How can I then be elder then thou art?
O therefore loue be of thy ſelfe ſo wary,
As I not for my ſelfe, but for thee will,
Bearing thy heart which I will keepe ſo chary
As tender nurſe her babe from faring ill,
　　Preſume not on thy heart when mine is ſlaine,
　　Thou gau'ſt me thine not to giue backe againe.

23

AS an vnperfect actor on the ſtage,
Who with his feare is put beſides his part,
Or ſome fierce thing repleat with too much rage,
Whoſe ſtrengths abondance weakens his owne heart;
So I for feare of truſt, forget to ſay,
The perfect ceremony of loues right,
And in mine owne loues ſtrength ſeeme to decay,
Ore-charg'd with burthen of mine owne loues might:
O let my books be then the eloquence,
And domb preſagers of my ſpeaking breſt,
Who pleade for loue, and look for recompence,
More then that tonge that more hath more expreſt.
　　O learne to read what ſilent loue hath writ,
　　To heare wit eies belongs to loues fine wiht.

24

MIne eye hath play'd the painter and hath ſteeld,
Thy beauties forme in table of my heart,
My body is the frame wherein ti's held,
And perſpectiue it is beſt Painters art.
For through the Painter muſt you ſee his skill,

To

240

To finde where your true Image pictur'd lies,
Which in my bosomes shop is hanging stil,
That hath his windowes glazed with thine eyes:
Now see what good-turnes eyes for-eies haue done,
Mine eyes haue drawne thy shape,and thine for me
Are windowes to my brest, where-through the Sun
Delights to peepe,to gaze therein on thee
    Yet eyes this cunning want to grace their art
    They draw but what they see,know not the hart.

25

LEt those who are in fauor with their stars,
  Of publike honour and proud titles bost,
Whilst I whome fortune of such tryumph bars
Vnlookt for ioy in that I honour most;
Great Princes fauorites their faire leaues spread,
But as the Marygold at the suns eye,
And in them-selues their pride lies buried,
For at a frowne they in their glory die.
The painefull warrier famosed for worth,
After a thousand victories once foild,
Is from the booke of honour rased quite,
And all the rest forgot for which he toild:
    Then happy I that loue and am beloued
    Where I may not remoue,nor be remoued.

26

LOrd of my loue,to whome in vassalage
  Thy merrit hath my dutie strongly knit;
To thee I send this written ambassage
To witnesse duty, not to shew my wit.
Duty so great,which wit so poore as mine
May make seeme bare,in wanting words to shew it;
But that I hope some good conceipt of thine
In thy soules thought(all naked) will bestow it:
Til whatsoeuer star that guides my mouing,
Points on me gratiously with faire aspect,
And puts apparrell on my tottered louing,

To show me worthy of their sweet respect,
  Then may I dare to boast how I doe loue thee,
  Til then, not show my head where thou maist proue me

27

WEary with toyle, I hast me to my bed,
  The deare repose for lims with trauaill tired,
But then begins a iourny in my head
To worke my mind, when boddies work's expired.
For then my thoughts (from far where I abide)
Intend a zelous pilgrimage to thee;
And keepe my drooping eye-lids open wide,
Looking on darknes which the blind doe see.
Saue that my soules imaginary sight
Presents their shaddoe to my sightles view,
Which like a iewell (hunge in gastly night)
Makes blacke night beautious, and her old face new.
  Loe thus by day my lims, by night my mind,
  For thee, and for my selfe, noe quiet finde.

28

HOw can I then returne in happy plight
  That am debard the benifit of rest?
When daies oppression is not eazd by night,
But day by night and night by day oprest.
And each (though enimes to ethers raigne)
Doe in consent shake hands to torture me,
The one by toyle, the other to complaine
How far I toyle, still farther off from thee.
I tell the Day to please him thou art bright,
And do'st him grace when clouds doe blot the heauen:
So flatter I the swart complexiond night,
When sparkling stars twire not thou guil'st th' eauen.
  But day doth daily draw my sorrowes longer, (stronger
  And night doth nightly make greefes length seeme

29

WHen in disgrace with Fortune and mens eyes,
  I all alone beweepe my out-cast state,

                        And

And trouble deafe heauen with my bootleffe cries,
And looke vpon my felfe and curfe my fate.
Wifhing me like to one more rich in hope,
Featur'd like him, like him with friends poffeft,
Defiring this mans art, and that mans skope,
With what I moft inioy contented leaft,
Yet in thefe thoughts my felfe almoft defpifing,
Haplye I thinke on thee, and then my ftate,
(Like to the Larke at breake of daye arifing)
From fullen earth fings himns at Heauens gate,
    For thy fweet loue remembred fuch welth brings,
    That then I skorne to change my ftate with Kings.

30

VVHen to the Seffions of fweet filent thought,
    I fommon vp remembrance of things paft,
I figh the lacke of many a thing I fought,
And with old woes new waile my deare times wafte:
Then can I drowne an eye(vn-vf'd to flow)
For precious friends hid in deaths dateles night,
And weepe a frefh loues long fince canceld woe,
And mone th'expence of many a vannifht fight.
Then can I greeue at greeuances fore-gon,
And heauily from woe to woe tell ore
The fad account of fore-bemoned mone,
Which I new pay, as if not payd before.
    But if the while I thinke on thee (deare friend)
    All loffes are reftord, and forrowes end.

31

Thy bofome is indeared with all hearts,
    Which I by lacking haue fuppofed dead,
And there raignes Loue and all Loues louing parts,
And all thofe friends which I thought buried.
How many a holy and obfequious teare
Hath deare religious loue ftolne from mine eye,
As intereft of the dead, which now appeare,
But things remou'd that hidden in there lie.

        C 2   To

Thou art the graue where buried loue doth liue,
Hung with the tropheis of my louers gon,
Who all their parts of me to thee did giue,
That due of many, now is thine alone.
 Their images I lou'd, I view in thee,
 And thou(all they)haft all the all of me.

32

IF thou furuiue my well contented daie,
 When that churle death my bones with duft fhall couer
And fhalt by fortune once more re-furuay:
Thefe poore rude lines of thy deceafed Louer:
Compare them with the bett'ring of the time,
And though they be out-ftript by euery pen,
Referue them for my loue, not for their rime,
Exceeded by the hight of happier men.
Oh then voutfafe me but this louing thought,
Had my friends Mufe growne with this growing age,
A dearer birth then this his loue had brought:
To march inranckes of better equipage:
 But fince he died and Poets better proue,
 Theirs for their ftile ile read, his for his loue.

33

FVll many a glorious morning haue I feene,
 Flatter the mountaine tops with foueraine eie,
Kiffing with golden face the meddowes greene;
Guilding pale ftreames with heauenly alcumy:
Anon permit the bafeft cloudes to ride,
With ougly rack on his celeftiall face,
And from the foi-lorne world his vifage hide
Stealing vnfeene to weft with this difgrace:
Euen fo my Sunne one early morne did fhine,
With all triumphant fplendor on my brow,
But out alack, he was but one houre mine,
The region cloude hath mask'd him from me now.
 Yet him for th s,my loue no whit difdaineth,
 Suns of the world may ftaine, whē heauens fun ftainteh.

34

244

34

VVHy didſt thou promiſe ſuch a beautious day,
  And make me trauaile forth without my cloake,
To let baſe cloudes ore-take me in my way,
Hiding thy brau'ry in their rotten ſmoke.
Tis not enough that through the cloude thou breake,
To dry the raine on my ſtorme-beaten face,
For no man well of ſuch a ſalue can ſpeake,
That heales the wound, and cures not the diſgrace:
Nor can thy ſhame giue phiſicke to my griefe,
Though thou repent , yet I haue ſtill the loſſe,
Th'offenders ſorrow lends but weake reliefe
To him that beares the ſtrong offenſes loſſe.
    Ah but thoſe teares are pearle which thy loue ſheeds,
    And they are ritch,and ranſome all ill deeds.

35

NO more bee greeu'd at that which thou haſt done,
  Roſes haue thornes,and ſiluer fountaines mud,
Cloudes and eclipſes ſtaine both Moone and Sunne,
And loathſome canker liues in ſweeteſt bud.
All men make faults,and euen I in this,
Authorizing thy treſpas with compare,
My ſelfe corrupting ſaluing thy amiſſe,
Excuſing their ſins more then their ſins are;
For to thy ſenſuall fault I bring in ſence,
Thy aduerſe party is thy Aduocate,
And gainſt my ſelfe a lawfull plea commence,
Such ciuill war is in my loue and hate,
    That I an acceſſary needs muſt be,
    To that ſweet theefe which ſourely robs from me,

36

LEt me confeſſe that we two muſt be twaine,
  Although our vndeuided loues are one:
So ſhall thoſe blots that do with me remaine,
Without thy helpe , by me be borne alone.
In our two loues there is but one reſpect,

                                        Though

245

Though in our liues a seperable spight,
Which though it alter not loues sole effect,
Yet doth it steale sweet houres from loues delight,
I may not euer-more acknowledge thee,
Least my bewailed guilt should do thee shame,
Nor thou with publike kindnesse honour me,
Vnlesse thou take that honour from thy name:
    But doe not so,I loue thee in such sort,
    As thou being mine,mine is thy good report.

37

AS a decrepit father takes delight,
    To see his actiue childe do deeds of youth,
So I, made lame by Fortunes dearest spight
Take all my comfort of thy worth and truth.
For whether beauty,birth,or wealth,or wit,
Or any of these all,or all,or more
Intitled in their parts,do crowned sit,
I make my loue ingrafted to this store:
So then I am not lame,poore, nor dispis'd,
Whilst that this shadow doth such substance giue,
That I in thy abundance am suffic'd,
And by a part of all thy glory liue:
    Looke what is best,that best I wish in thee,
    This wish I haue,then ten times happy me.

38

HOw can my Muse want subiect to inuent
    While thou dost breath that poor'st into my verse,
Thine owne sweet argument,to excellent,
For euery vulgar paper to rehearse:
Oh giue thy selfe the thankes if ought in me,
Worthy perusal stand against thy sight,
For who's so dumbe that cannot write to thee,
When thou thy selfe dost giue inuention light?
Be thou the tenth Muse,ten times more in worth
Then those old nine which rimers inuocate,
And he that calls on thee,let him bring forth

                              Eternall

Eternal numbers to out-liue long date.
 If my flight Muse doe please these curious daies,
 The paine be mine, but thine shal be the praise.

39

OH how thy worth with manners may I singe,
 When thou art all the better part of me?
What can mine owne praise to mine owne selfe bring;
And what is't but mine owne when I praise thee,
Euen for this, let vs deuided liue,
And our deare loue loose name of single one,
That by this seperation I may giue:
That due to thee which thou deseru'st alone:
Oh absence what a torment wou!dst thou proue,
Were it not thy soure leisure gaue sweet leaue,
To entertaine the time with thoughts of loue,
VVhich time and thoughts so sweetly dost deceiue.
 And that thou teachest how to make one twaine,
 By praising him here who doth hence remaine.

40

TAke all my loues, my loue, yea take them all,
 What hast thou then more then thou hadst before?
No loue, my loue, that thou maist true loue call,
All mine was thine, before thou hadst this more:
Then if for my loue, thou my loue recciuest,
I cannot blame thee, for my loue thou vsest,
But yet be blam'd, if thou this selfe deceauest
By wilfull taste of what thy selfe refusest.
I doe forgiue thy robb'rie gentle theefe
Although thou steale thee all my pouerty:
And yet loue knowes it is a greater griefe
To beare loues wrong, then hates knowne iniury.
 Lasciuious grace in whom all il wel showes,
 Kill me with spights yet we must not be foes.

41

THose pretty wrongs that liberty commits,
 When I am some-time absent from thy heart,

D   Thy

Thy beautie,and thy yeares full well befits,
For still temptacion followes where thou art.
Gentle thou art,and therefore to be wonne,
Beautious thou art,therefore to be assailed.
And when a woman woes,what womans sonne,
Will sourely leaue her till he haue preuailed.
Aye me,but yet thou mighst my seate forbeare,
And chide thy beauty,and thy straying youth,
Who lead thee in their ryot euen there
Where thou art forst to breake a two-fold truth:
　　Hers by thy beauty tempting her to thee,
　　Thine by thy beautie beeing false to me.

42

THat thou hast her it is not all my griefe,
　　And yet it may be said I lou'd her deerely,
That she hath thee is of my wayling cheefe,
A losse in loue that touches me more neerely.
Louing offendors thus I will excuse yee,
Thou doost loue her,because thou knowst I loue her,
And for my sake euen so doth she abuse me,
Suffring my friend for my sake to approoue her,
If I loose thee,my losse is my loues gaine,
And loosing her,my friend hath found that losse,
Both finde each other,and I loose both twaine,
And both for my sake lay on me this crosse,
　　But here's the ioy,my friend and I are one,
　　Sweete flattery,then she loues but me alone.

43

WHen most I winke then doe mine eyes best see,
　　For all the day they view things vnrespected,
But when I sleepe,in dreames they looke on thee,
And darkely bright,are bright in darke directed.
Then thou whose shaddow shaddowes doth make bright,
How would thy shadowes forme,forme happy show,
To the cleere day with thy much cleerer light,
When to vn-seeing eyes thy shade shines so?

How

248

How would (I say) mine eyes be blessed made,
By looking on thee in the liuing day?
When in dead night their faire imperfect shade,
Through heauy sleepe on sightlesse eyes doth stay?
   All dayes are nights to see till I see thee,
   And nights bright daies when dreams do shew thee me.

44

IF the dull substance of my flesh were thought,
Iniurious distance should not stop my way,
For then dispight of space I would be brought,
From limits farre remote, where thou doost stay,
No matter then although my foote did stand
Vpon the farthest earth remoou'd from thee,
For nimble thought can iumpe both sea and land,
As soone as thinke the place where he would be.
But ah, thought kills me that I am not thought
To leape large lengths of miles when thou art gone,
But that so much of earth and water wrought,
I must attend, times leasure with my mone.
   Receiuing naughts by elements so sloe,
   But heauie teares, badges of eithers woe.

45

THe other two, slight ayre, and purging fire,
Are both with thee, where euer I abide,
The first my thought, the other my desire,
These present absent with swift motion slide.
For when these quicker Elements are gone
In tender Embassie of loue to thee,
My life being made of foure, with two alone,
Sinkes downe to death, opprest with melancholie.
Vntill liues composition be recured,
By those swift messengers return'd from thee,
Who euen but now come back againe assured,
Of their faire health, recounting it to me.
   This told, I ioy, but then no longer glad,
   I send them back againe and straight grow sad.

D 2   Mine

46

Mine eye and heart are at a mortall warre,
How to deuide the conquest of thy sight,
Mine eye,my heart their pictures sight would barre,
My heart,mine eye the freeedome of that right,
My heart doth plead that thou in him doost lye,
(A closet neuer pearst with christall eyes)
But the defendant doth that plea deny,
And sayes in him their faire appearance lyes.
To side this title is impannelled
A quest of thoughts,all tennants to the heart,
And by their verdict is determined
The cleere eyes moyitie,and he deare hearts part.
   As thus,mine eyes due is their outward part,
   And my hearts right,their inward loue of heart.

47

Betwixt mine eye and heart a league is tooke,
And each doth good turnes now vnto the other,
When that mine eye is famisht for a looke,
Or heart in loue with sighes himselfe doth smother;
With my loues picture then my eye doth feast,
And to the painted banquet bids my heart:
An other time mine eye is my hearts guest,
And in his thoughts of loue doth share a part.
So either by thy picture or my loue,
Thy selfe away,are present still with me,
For thou nor farther then my thoughts canst moue,
And I am still with them,and they with thee.
   Or if they sleepe, thy picture in my sight
   Awakes my heart,to hearts and eyes delight.

48

How carefull was I when I tooke my way,
Each trifle vnder truest barres to thrust,
That to my vse it might vn-vsed stay
From hands of falsehood,in sure wards of trust?
But thou,to whom my iewels trifles are,

Most

Most worthy comfort, now my greatest griefe,
Thou best of deerest, and mine onely care,
Art left the prey of euery vulgar theefe.
Thee haue I not lockt vp in any chest,
Saue where thou art not, though I feele thou art,
Within the gentle closure of my brest,
From whence at pleasure thou maist come and part,
    And euen thence thou wilt be stolne I feare,
    For truth prooues theeuish for a prize so deare.

49

AGainst that time (if euer that time come)
  When I shall see thee frowne on my defects,
When as thy loue hath cast his vtmost summe,
Cauld to that audite by aduis'd respects,
Against that time when thou shalt strangely passe,
And scarcely greete me with that sunne thine eye,
When loue conuerted from the thing it was
Shall reasons finde of setled grauitie.
Against that time do I insconce me here
Within the knowledge of mine owne desart,
And this my hand, against my selfe vpreare,
To guard the lawfull reasons on thy part,
    To leaue poore me, thou hast the strength of lawes,
    Since why to loue, I can alledge no cause.

50

HOw heauie doe I iourney on the way,
  When what I seeke (my wearie trauels end)
Doth teach that ease and that repose to say
Thus farre the miles are measurde from thy friend.
The beast that beares me, tired with my woe,
Plods duly on, to beare that waight in me,
As if by some instinct the wretch did know
His rider lou d not speed being made from thee:
The bloody spurre cannot prouoke him on,
That some-times anger thrusts into his hide,
Which heauily he answers with a grone,

More sharpe to me then spurring to his side,
    For that same grone doth put this in my mind,
    My greefe lies onward and my ioy behind.

51

THus can my loue excuse the slow offence,
    Of my dull bearer, when from thee I speed,
From where thou art, why shoulld I hast me thence,
Till I returne of posting is noe need.
O what excuse will my poore beast then find,
When swift extremity can seeme but slow,
Then should I spurre though mounted on the wind,
In winged speed no motion shall I know,
Then can no horse with my desire keepe pace,
Therefore desire (of perfects loue being made)
Shall naigh noe dull flesh in his fiery race,
But loue, for loue, thus shall excuse my iade,
    Since from thee going he went wilfull slow,
    Towards thee ile run, and giue him leaue to goe.

52

SO am I as the rich whose blessed key,
    Can bring him to his sweet vp-locked treasure,
The which he will not eu'ry hower suruay,
For blunting the fine point of seldome pleasure.
Therefore are feasts so sollemne and so rare,
Since sildom comming in the long yeare set,
Like stones of worth they thinly placed are,
Or captaine Iewells in the carconet.
So is the time that keepes you as my chest,
Or as the ward-robe which the robe doth hide,
To make some speciall instant speciall blest,
By new vnfoulding his imprison'd pride.
    Blessed are you whose worthinesse giues skope,
    Being had to tryumph, being lackt to hope.

53

VVHat is your substance, whereof are you made,
    That millions of strange shaddowes on you tend?
                            Since

Since euery one,hath euery one,one shade,
And you but one,can euery shaddow lend:
Describe *Adonis* and the counterfet,
Is poorely immitated after you,
On *Hellens* cheeke all art of beautie set,
And you in *Grecian* tires are painted new:
Speake of the spring,and foyzon of the yeare,
The one doth shaddow of your beautie show,
The other as your bountie doth appeare,
And you in euery blessed shape we know.
　　In all externall grace you haue some part,
　　But you like none,none you for constant heart.

54

OH how much more doth beautie beantious seeme,
　By that sweet ornament which truth doth giue,
The Rose lookes faire, but fairer we it deeme
For that sweet odor,which doth in it liue:
The Canker bloomes haue full as deepe a die,
As the perfumed tincture of the Roses,
Hang on such thornes,and play as wantonly,
When sommers breath their masked buds discloses:
But for their virtue only is their show,
They liue vnwoo'd, and vnrespected fade,
Die to themselues . Sweet Roses doe not so,
Of their sweet deathes, are sweetest odors made:
　　And so of you,beautious and louely youth,
　　When that shall vade,by verse distils your truth.

55

NOt marble, nor the guilded monument,
　Of Princes shall out-liue this powrefull rime,
But you shall shine more bright in these contents
Then vnswept stone, besmeer'd with sluttish time.
When wastefull warre shall *Statues* ouer-turne,
And broiles roote out the worke of masonry,
Nor *Mars* his sword, nor warres quick fire shall burne
The liuing record of your memory.

　　　　　　　　　　　　　　　　Gainst

Gainſt death,and all obliuious emnity
Shall you pace forth, your praiſe ſhail ſtil finde roome,
Euen in the eyes of all poſterity
That weare this world out to the ending doome.
  So til the iudgement that your ſelfe ariſe,
  You liue in this,and dwell in louers eies.

56

Sweet loue renew thy force , be it not ſaid
  Thy edge ſhould blunter be then apetite,
Which but too daie by feeding is alaied,
To morrow ſharpned in his former might.
So loue be thou,although too daie thou fill
Thy hungrie eies,euen till they winck with fulneſſe,
Too morrow ſee againe,and doe not kill
The ſpirit of Loue,with a perpetual dulneſſe:
Let this ſad *Intrim* like the Ocean be
Which parts the ſhore,where twc contracted new,
Come daily to the banckes,that when they ſee.
Returne of loue,more bleſt may be the view.
  As cal it Winter,which being ful of care,
  Makes Sŏmers welcome,thrice more wiſh'd,more rare :

57

BEing your ſlaue what ſhould I doe but tend,
  Vpon the houres,and times of your deſire?
I haue no precious time at al to ſpend;
Nor ſeruices to doe til you require.
Nor dare I chide the world without end houre,
Whilſt I(my ſoueraine)watch the clock for you,
Nor thinke the bitterneſſe of abſence ſowre,
VVhen you haue bid your ſeruant once adieue.
Nor dare I queſtion with my iealious thought,
VVhere you may be,or your affaires ſuppoſe,
But like a ſad ſlaue ſtay and thinke of nought
Saue where you are , how happy you make thoſe.
  So true a foole is loue,that in your Will,
  (Though you doe any thing)he thinkes no ill.

58

58

THat God forbid,that made me first your slaue,
  I should in thought controule your times of pleasure,
Or at your hand th' account of houres to craue,
Being your vassail bound to staie your leisure.
Oh let me suffer(being at your beck)
Th' imprison'd absence of your libertie,
And patience tame,to sufferance bide each check,
Without accusing you of iniury.
Be where you list,your charter is so strong,
That you your selfe may priuiledge your time
To what you will,to you it doth belong,
Your selfe to pardon of selfe-doing crime.
    I am to waite,though waiting so be hell,
    Not blame your pleasure be it ill or well.

59

IF their bee nothing new,but that which is,
  Hath beene before , how are our braines beguild,
Which laboring for inuention beare amisse
The second burthen of a former child ?
Oh that record could with a back-ward looke,
Euen of fiue hundreth courses of the Sunne,
Show me your image in some antique booke,
Since minde at first in carrecter was done.
That I might see what the old world could say,
To this composed wonder of your frame,
Whether we are mended,or where better they,
Or whether reuolution be the same.
    Oh sure I am the wits of former daies,
    To subiects worse haue giuen admiring praise.

60

LIke as the waues make towards the pibled shore,
  So do our minuites hasten to their end,
Each changing place with that which goes before,
In sequent toile all forwards do contend.
Natiuity once in the maine of light,

E   Crawls

Crawles to maturity,wherewith being crown'd,
Crooked eclipſes gainſt his glory fight,
And time that gaue,doth now his gift confound.
Time doth transſixe the floriſh ſet on youth,
And delues the paralels in beauties brow,
Feedes on the rarities of natures truth,
And nothing ſtands but for his ſieth to mow.
    And yet to times in hope,my verſe ſhall ſtand
    Praiſing thy worth,diſpight his cruell hand.

61

I S it thy wil;thy Image ſhould keepe open
  My heauy eie:ids to the weary night?
Doſt thou deſire my ſlumbers ſhould be broken,
While ſhadowes like to thee do mocke my ſight?
Is it thy ſpirit that thou ſend'ſt from thee
So farre from home into my deeds to prye,
To find out ſhames and idle houres in me,
The skope and tenure of thy Ielouſie.
O no,thy loue though much,is not ſo great,
It is my loue that keepes mine eie awake,
Mine owne true loue that doth my reſt defeat,
To plaie the watch-man euer for thy ſake.
    For thee watch I,whilſt thou doſt wake elſewhere,
    From me farre of, with others all to neere.

62

S Inne of ſelfe-loue poſſeſſeth al mine eie,
  And all my ſoule,and al my euery part;
And for this ſinne there is no remedie,
It is ſo grounded inward in my heart.
Me thinkes no face ſo gratious is as mine,
No ſhape ſo true,no truth of ſuch account,
And for my ſelfe mine owne worth do define,
As I all other in all worths ſurmount.
But when my glaſſe ſhewes me my ſelfe indeed
Beated and chopt with tand antiquitie,
Mine owne ſelfe loue quite contrary I read

Selfe

Selfe,so selfe louing were iniquity,
  T'is thee(my selfe)that for my selfe I praise,
  Painting my age with beauty of thy daies,

63

AGainst my loue shall be as I am now
  With times iniurious hand chrusht and ore-worne,
When houres haue dreind his blood and fild his brow
With lines and wrincles,when his youthfull morne
Hath trauaild on to Ages steepie night,
And all those beauties whereof now he's King
Are vanishing,or vanisht out of sight,
Stealing away the treasure of his Spring.
For such a time do I now fortifie
Against confounding Ages cruell knife,
That he shall neuer cut from memory
My sweet loues beauty,though my louers life.
  His beautie shall in these blacke lines be seene,
  And they shall liue, and he in them still greene.

64

WHen I haue seene by times fell hand defaced
  The rich proud cost of outworne buried age
When sometime loftie towers I see downe rased,
And brasse eternall slaue to mortall rage,
When I haue seene the hungry Ocean gaine
Aduantage on the Kingdome of the shoare,
And the firme soile win of the watry maine,
Increasing store with losse, and losse with store,
When I haue seene such interchange of state,
Or state it selfe confounded, to decay,
Ruine hath taught me thus to ruminate
That Time will come and take my loue away.
  This thought is as a death which cannot choose
  But weepe to haue,that which it feares to loose.

65

SInce brasse,nor stone,nor earth,nor boundlesse sea,
  But sad mortallity ore-swaies their power,

E 2   How

257

How with this rage shall beautie hold a plea,
Whose action is no stronger then a flower?
O how shall summers hunny breath hold out,
Against the wrackfull siedge of battring dayes,
When rocks impregnable are not so stoute,
Nor gates of steele so strong but time decayes?
O fearefull meditation, where alack,
Shall times best Iewell from times chest lie hid?
Or what strong hand can hold his swift foote back,
Or who his spoile or beautie can forbid?
　　O none, vnlesse this miracle haue might,
　　That in black inck my loue may still shine bright.

66

TYr'd with all these for restfull death I cry,
　As to behold desert a begger borne,
And needie Nothing trimd in iollitie,
And purest faith vnhappily forsworne,
And gilded honor shamefully misplast,
And maiden vertue rudely strumpeted,
And right perfection wrongfully disgrac'd,
And strength by limping sway disabled,
And arte made tung-tide by authoritie,
And Folly (Doctor-like) controuling skill,
And simple-Truth miscalde Simplicitie,
And captiue-good attending Captaine ill.
　　Tyr'd with all these, from these would I be gone,
　　Saue that to dye, I leaue my loue alone.

67

AH wherefore with infection should he liue,
　And with his presence grace impietie,
That sinne by him aduantage should atchiue,
And lace it selfe with his societie?
Why should false painting immitate his cheeke,
And steale dead seeing of his liuing hew?
Why should poore beautie indirectly seeke,
Roses of shaddow, since his Rose is true

Why

Why should he liue, now nature banckrout is,
Beggerd of blood to blush through liuely vaines,
For she hath no exchecker now but his,
And proud of many, liues vpon his gaines?
  O him she stores, to show what welth she had,
  In daies long since, before these last so bad.

68

THus is his cheeke the map of daies out-worne,
  When beauty liu'd and dy'ed as flowers do now,
Before these bastard signes of faire were borne,
Or durst inhabit on a liuing brow:
Before the goulden tresses of the dead,
The right of sepulchers, were shorne away,
To liue a scond life on second head,
Ere beauties dead fleece made another gay:
In him those holy antique howers are seene,
Without all ornament, it selfe and true,
Making no summer of an others greene,
Robbing no ould to dresse his beauty new,
  And him as for a map doth Nature store,
  To shew faulse Art what beauty was of yore.

69

THose parts of thee that the worlds eye doth view,
  Want nothing that the thought of hearts can mend:
All toungs (the voice of soules) giue thee that end,
Vttring bare truth, euen so as foes Commend.
Their outward thus with outward praise is crownd,
But those same toungs that giue thee so thine owne,
In other accents doe this praise confound
By seeing farther then the eye hath showne.
They looke into the beauty of thy mind,
And that in guesse they measure by thy deeds,
Then churls their thoughts (although their eies were kind)
To thy faire flower ad the rancke smell of weeds,
  But why thy odor matcheth not thy show,
  The solye is this, that thou doest common grow.

E 3   That

70

THat thou are blam'd shall not be thy defect,
For slanders marke was euer yet the faire,
The ornament of beauty is suspect,
A Crow that flies in heauens sweetest ayre.
So thou be good, slander doth but approue,
Their worth the greater beeing woo d of time,
For Canker vice the sweetest buds doth loue,
And thou present'st a pure vnstayined prime.
Thou hast past by the ambush of young daies,
Either not assayld, or victor beeing charg'd,
Yet this thy praise cannot be soe thy praise,
To tye vp enuy, euermore inlarged,
  If some suspect of ill maskt not thy show,
  Then thou alone kingdomes of hearts shouldst owe.'

71

NOe Longer mourne for me when I am dead,
Then you shall heare the surly sullen bell
Giue warning to the world that I am fled
From this vile world with vildest wormes to dwell:
Nay if you read this line, remember not,
The hand that writ it, for I loue you so,
That I in your sweet thoughts would be forgot,
If thinking on me then should make you woe.
O if (I say) you looke vpon this verse,
When I (perhaps) compounded am with clay,
Do not so much as my poore name reherse;
But let your loue euen with my life decay.
  Least the wise world should looke into your mone,
  And mocke you with me after I am gon.

72

O Least the world should taske you to recite,
What merit liu'd in me that you should loue
After my death (deare loue) for get me quite,
For you in me can nothing worthy proue.
Vnlesse you would deuise some vertuous lye,

To

260

To doe more for me then mine owne defert,
And hang more praife vpon deceafed I,
Then nigard truth would willingly impart:
O leaft your true loue may feeme falce in this,
That you for loue fpeake well of me vntrue,
My name be buried where my body is,
And liue no more to fhame nor me, nor you.
　　For I am fhamd by that which I bring forth,
　　And fo fhould you, to loue things nothing worth.

73

THat time of yeeare thou maift in me behold,
　　When yellow leaues, or none, or few doe hange
Vpon thofe boughes which fhake againft the could,
Bare rn'wd quiers, where late the fweet birds fang.
In me thou feeft the twi-light of fuch day,
As after Sun-fet fadeth in the Weft,
Which by and by blacke night doth take away,
Deaths fecond felfe that feals vp all in reft.
In me thou feeft the glowing of fuch fire,
That on the afhes of his youth doth lye,
As the death bed, whereon it muft expire,
Confum'd with that which it was nurrifht by.
　　This thou perceu'ft, which makes thy loue more ftrong,
　　To loue that well, which thou muft leaue ere long.

74

BVt be contented when that fell areft,
　　With out all bayle fhall carry me away,
My life hath in this line fome intereft,
Which for memoriall ftill with thee fhall ftay.
When thou reueweft this, thou doeft reuew,
The very part was confecrate to thee,
The earth can haue but earth, which is his due,
My fpirit is thine the better part of me,
So then thou haft but loft the dregs of life,
The pray of wormes, my body being dead,
The coward conqueft of a wretches knife,

To

261

To bafe of thee to be remembred,
  The worth of that, is that which it containes,
  And that is this, and this with thee remaines.

75

SO are you to my thoughts as food to life,
  Or as fweet feafon'd fhewers are to the ground;
And for the peace of you I hold fuch ftrife,
As twixt a mifer and his wealth is found.
Now proud as an inioyer, and anon
Doubting the filching age will fteale his treafure,
Now counting beft to be with you alone,
Then betterd that the world may fee my pleafure,
Some-time all ful with feafting on your fight,
And by and by cleane ftarued for a looke,
Poffeffing or purfuing no delight
Saue what is had, or muft from you be tooke.
  Thus do I pine and furfet day by day,
  Or gluttoning on all, or all away,

76

VVHy is my verfe fo barren of new pride?
  So far from variation or quicke change?
Why with the time do I not glance afide
To new found methods, and to compounds ftrange?
Why write I ftill all one, euer the fame,
And keepe inuention in a noted weed,
That euery word doth almoft fel my name,
Shewing their birth, and where they did proceed?
O know fweet loue I alwaies write of you,
And you and loue are ftill my argument:
So all my beft is dreffing old words new,
Spending againe what is already fpent:
  For as the Sun is daily new and old,
  So is my loue ftill telling what is told,

77

THy glaffe will fhew thee how thy beauties were,
  Thy dyall how thy pretious mynuits wafte,

The

262

The vacant leaues thy mindes imprint will beare,
And of this booke,this learning maiſt thou taſte.
The wrinckles which thy glaſſe will truly ſhow,
Of mouthed graues will giue thee memorie,
Thou by thy dyals ſhady ſtealth maiſt know,
Times theeuiſh progreſſe to eternitie.
Looke what thy memorie cannot containe,
Commit to theſe waſte blacks,and thou ſhalt finde
Thoſe children nurſt,deliuerd from thy braine,
To take a new acquaintance of thy minde.
　　Theſe offices,ſo oft as thou wilt looke,
　　Shall profit thee, and much inrich thy booke.

78

SO oft haue I inuok'd thee for my Muſe,
And found ſuch faire aſſiſtance in my verſe,
As euery *Alien* pen hath got my vſe,
And vnder thee their poeſie diſperſe.
Thine eyes, that taught the dumbe on high to ſing,
And heauie ignorance aloft to flie,
Haue added fethers to the learneds wing,
And giuen grace a double Maieſtie.
Yet be moſt proud of that which I compile,
Whoſe influence is thine,and borne of thee,
In others workes thou dooſt but mend the ſtile,
And Arts with thy ſweete graces graced be.
　　But thou art all my art,and dooſt aduance
　　As high as learning,my rude ignorance.

79

WHilſt I alone did call vpon thy ayde,
　My verſe alone had all thy gentle grace,
But now my gracious numbers are decayde,
And my ſick Muſe doth giue an other place.
I grant (ſweet loue)thy louely argument
Deſerues the trauaile of a worthier pen,
Yet what of thee thy Poet doth inuent,
He robs thee of,and payes it thee againe,

F　　　　　　　　　　　　　　　　He

263

He lends thee vertue,and he ſtole that word,
From thy behauiour,beautie doth he giue
And found it in thy cheeke: he can affoord
No praiſe to thee,but what in thee doth liue.
   Then thanke him not for that which he doth ſay,
   Since what he owes thee,thou thy ſelfe dooſt pay.

80

O How I faint when I of you do write,
  Knowing a better ſpirit doth vſe your name,
And in the praiſe thereof ſpends all his might,
To make me toung-tide ſpeaking of your fame.
But ſince your worth(wide as the Ocean is)
The humble as the proudeſt ſaile doth beare,
My ſawſie barke (inferior farre to his)
On your broad maine doth wilfully appeare.
Your ſhalloweſt helpe will hold me vp a floate,
Whilſt he vpon your ſoundleſſe deepe doth ride,
Or (being wrackt) I am a worthleſſe bote,
He of tall building,and of goodly pride.
   Then If he thriue and I be caſt away,
   The worſt was this,my loue was my decay.

81

OR I ſhall liue your Epitaph to make,
  Or you ſuruiue when I in earth am rotten,
From hence your memory death cannot take,
Although in me each part will be forgotten.
Your name from hence immortall life ſhall haue,
Though I (once gone) to all the world muſt dye,
The earth can yeeld me but a common graue,
When you intombed in mens eyes ſhall lye,
Your monument ſhall be my gentle verſe,
Which eyes not yet created ſhall ore-read,
And toungs to be, your beeing ſhall rehearſe,
When all the breathers of this world are dead,
   You ſtill ſhall liue (ſuch vertue hath my Pen)
   Where breath moſt breaths,euen in the mouths of men.
               I grant

82

I Grant thou wert not married to my Muse,
And therefore maiest without attaint ore-looke
The dedicated words which writers vse
Of their faire subiect,blessing euery booke.
Thou art as faire in knowledge as in hew,
Finding thy worth a limmit past my praise,
And therefore art inforc'd to seeke anew,
Some fresher stampe of the time bettering dayes.
And do so loue,yet when they haue deuisde,
What strained touches Rhethorick can lend,
Thou truly faire,wert truly simpathizde,
In true plaine words ,by thy true telling friend.
    And their grosse painting might be better vs'd,
    Where cheekes need blood,in thee it is abus'd.

83

I Neuer saw that you did painting need,
And therefore to your faire no painting set,
I found (or thought I found) you did exceed,
The barren tender of a Poets debt :
And therefore haue I slept in your report,
That you your selfe being extant well might show,
How farre a moderne quill doth come to short,
Speaking of worth,what worth in you doth grow,
This silence for my sinne you did impute,
Which shall be most my glory being dombe,
For I impaire not beautie being mute,
When others would giue life,and bring a tombe.
    There liues more life in one of your faire eyes,
    Then both your Poets can in praise deuise.

84

WHo is it that sayes most,which can say more,
    Then this rich praise,that you alone,are you,
In whose confine immured is the store,
Which should example where your equall grew,
Leane penurie within that Pen doth dwell,

F 2   That

That to his subiect lends not some small glory,
But he that writes of you,if he can tell,
That you are you,so dignifies his story.
Let him but coppy what in you is writ,
Not making worse what nature made so cleere,
And such a counter-part shall fame his wit,
Making his stile admired euery where.
    You to your beautious blessings adde a curse,
    Being fond on praise,which makes your praises worse.

85

MY toung-tide Muse in manners holds her still,
   While comments of your praise richly compil'd,
Reserue their Character with goulden quill,
And precious phrase by all the Muses fil'd.
I thinke good thoughts,whilst other write good wordes,
And like vnlettered clarke still crie Amen,
To euery Himne that able spirit affords,
In polisht forme of well refined pen.
Hearing you praisd,I say'tis so,'tis true,
And to the most of praise adde some-thing more,
But that is in my thought,whose loue to you
(Though words come hind-most)holds his ranke before,
    Then others,for the breath of words respect,
    Me for my dombe thoughts,speaking in effect.

86

VVAs it the proud full saile of his great verse,
   Bound for the prize of (all to precious) you,
That did my ripe thoughts in my braine inhearce,
Making their tombe the wombe wherein they grew?
Was it his spirit,by spirits taught to write,
Aboue a mortall pitch,that struck me dead ?
No,neither he,nor his compiers by night
Giuing him ayde,my verse astonished.
He nor that affable familiar ghost
Which nightly gulls him with intelligence,
As victors of my silence cannot boast,

                      I was

I was not sick of any feare from thence,
But when your countinance fild vp his line,
Then lackt I matter, that infeebled mine.

87

FArewell thou art too deare for my poſſeſſing,
And like enough thou knowſt thy eſtimate,
The Chater of thy worth giues thee releaſing:
My boinds in thee are all determinate.
For how do I hold thee but by thy granting,
And for that ritches where is my deſeruing?
The cauſe of this faire guiſt in me is wanting,
And ſo my pattent back againe is ſweruing.
Thy ſelfe thou gau'ſt, thy owne worth then not knowing,
Or mee to whom thou gau'ſt it, elſe miſtaking,
So thy great guiſt vpon miſpriſion growing,
Comes home againe, on better iudgement making.
    Thus haue I had thee as a dreame doth flatter,
    In ſleepe a King, but waking no ſuch matter.

88

VVHen thou ſhalt be diſpode to ſet me light,
And place my merrit in the eie of ſkorne,
Vpon thy ſide, againſt my ſelfe ile fight,
And proue thee virtuous, though thou art forſworne:
With mine owne weakeneſſe being beſt acquainted,
Vpon thy part I can ſet downe a ſtory
Of faults conceald, wherein I am attainted:
That thou in looſing me ſhalt win much glory.
And I by this wil be a gainer too,
For bending all my louing thoughts on thee,
The iniuries that to my ſelfe I doe,
Doing thee vantage, duble vantage me.
    Such is my loue, to thee I ſo belong,
    That for thy right, my ſelfe will beare all wrong.

89

SAy that thou didſt forſake mee for ſome falt,
And I will comment vpon that offence,

F 3   The

267

ſpeake of my lameneſſe, and I ſtraight will halt:
Againſt thy reaſons making no defence.
Thou canſt not(loue)diſgrace me halfe ſo ill,
To ſet a forme vpon deſired change,
As ile my ſelfe diſgrace,knowing thy wil,
I will acquaintance ſtrangle and looke ſtrange:
Be abſent from thy walkes and in my tongue,
Thy ſweet beloued name no more ſhall dwell,
Leaſt I(too much prophane)ſhould do it wronge:
And haplie of our old acquaintance tell.
　For thee,againſt my ſelfe ile vow debate,
　For I muſt nere loue him whom thou doſt hate.

90

THen hate me when thou wilt, if euer,now,
Now while the world is bent my deeds to croſſe,
Ioyne with the ſpight of fortune,make me bow,
And doe not drop in for an after loſſe:
Ah doe not,when my heart hath ſcapte this ſorrow,
Come in the rereward of a conquerd woe,
Giue not a windy night a rainie morrow,
To linger out a purpoſd ouer-throw.
If thou wilt leaue me, do not leaue me laſt,
When other pettie grieſes haue done their ſpight,
But in the onſet come,ſo ſtall I taſte
At firſt the very worſt of fortunes might.
　And other ſtraines of woe, which now ſeeme woe,
　Compar'd with loſſe of thee,will not ſeeme ſo.

91

SOme glory in their birth,ſome in their skill,
Some in their wealth, ſome in their bodies force,
Some in their garments though new-fangled ill:
Some in their Hawkes and Hounds,ſome in their Horſe.
And euery humor hath his adiunct pleaſure,
Wherein it findes a ioy aboue the reſt,
But theſe perticulers are not my meaſure,
All theſe I better in one generall beſt.

Thy

Thy loue is bitter then high birth to me,
Richer then wealth, prouder then garments coſt,
Of more delight then Hawkes or Horſes bee:
And hauing chee, of all mens pride I boaſt.
　　Wretched in this alone, that thou maiſt take,
　　All this away, and me moſt wretched make.

92

BVt doe thy worſt to ſteale thy ſelfs away,
　For tearme of life thou art aſſured mine,
And life no longer then thy loue will ſtay,
For it depends vpon that loue of thine.
Then need I not to feare the worſt of wrongs,
When in the leaſt of them my life hath end,
I ſee, a better ſtate to me belongs
Then that, which on thy humor doth depend.
Thou canſt not vex me with inconſtant minde,
Since that my life on thy reuolt doth lie,
Oh what a happy title do I finde,
Happy to haue thy loue, happy to die!
　　But whats ſo bleſſed faire that feares no blot,
　　Thou maiſt be falce, and yet I know it not.

93

SO ſhall I liue, ſuppoſing thou art true,
　Like a deceiued husband, ſo loues face,
May ſtill ſeeme loue to me, though alter'd new:
Thy lookes with me, thy heart in other place.
For their can liue no hatred in thine eye,
Therefore in that I cannot know thy change,
In manies lookes, the falce hearts hiſtory
Is writ in moods and frounes and wrinckles ſtrange.
But heauen in thy creation did decree,
That in thy face ſweet loue ſhould euer dwell,
What ere thy thoughts, or thy hearts workings be,
Thy lookes ſhould nothing thence, but ſweetneſſe tell,
　　How like *Eaues* apple doth thy beauty grow,
　　If thy ſweet vertue anſwere not thy ſhow.

94

94

THey that haue powre to hurt,and will doe none,
That doe not do the thing,they moſt do ſhowe,
Who mouing others,are themſelues as ſtone,
Vnmooued,could,and to temptation ſlow:
They rightly do inherrit heauens graces,
And husband natures ritches from expence,
They are the Lords and owners of their faces,
Others,but ſtewards of their excellence:
The ſommers flowre is to the ſommer ſweet,
Though to it ſelfe,it onely liue and die,
But if that flowre with baſe infection meete,
The baſeſt weed out-braues his dignity:
   For ſweeteſt things turne ſowreſt by their deedes,
   Lillies that feſter, ſmell far worſe then weeds.

95

HOw ſweet and louely doſt thou make the ſhame,
Which like a canker in the fragrant Roſe,
Doth ſpot the beautie of thy budding name?
Oh in what ſweets doeſt thou thy ſinnes incloſe!
That tongue that tells the ſtory of thy daies,
(Making laſciuious comments on thy ſport)
Cannot diſpraiſe,but in a kinde of praiſe,
Naming thy name, bleſſes an ill report.
Oh what a manſion haue thoſe vices got,
Which for their habitation choſe out thee,
Where beauties vaile doth couer euery blot,
And all things turnes to faire,that eies can ſee!
   Take heed(deare heart)of this large priuiledge,
   The hardeſt knife ill vſ'd doth looſe his edge.

96

SOme ſay thy fault is youth,ſome wantoneſſe,
Some ſay thy grace is youth and gentle ſport,
Both grace and faults are lou'd of more and leſſe:
Thou makſt faults graces,that to thee reſort:
As on the finger of a throned Queene,

The

270

The baseft Iewell wil be well efteem'd:
So are thofe errors that in thee are feene,
To truths tranflated, and for true things deem'd.
How many Lambs might the fterne Wolfe betray,
If like a Lambe he could his lookes tranflate.
How many gazers mighft thou lead away,
If thou wouldft vfe the ftrength of all thy ftate?
   But doe not fo, I loue thee in fuch fort,
   As thou being mine, mine is thy good report.

97

HOw like a Winter hath my abfence beene
From thee, the pleafure of the fleeting yeare?
   What freezings haue I felt, what darke daies feene?
What old Decembers bareneffe euery where?
And yet this time remou'd was fommers time,
The teeming Autumne big with ritch increafe,
Bearing the wanton burthen of the prime,
Like widdowed wombes after their Lords deceafe:
Yet this aboundant iffue feem'd to me,
But hope of Orphans, and vn-fathered fruite,
For Sommer and his pleafures waite on thee,
And thou away, the very birds are mute.
   Or if they fing, tis with fo dull a cheere,
   That leaues looke pale, dreading the Winters neere.

98

FRom you haue I beene abfent in the fpring,
When proud pide Aprill (dreft in all his trim)
Hath put a fpirit of youth in euery thing:
That heauie *Saturne* laught and leapt with him.
Yet nor the laies of birds, nor the fweet fmell
Of different flowers in odor and in hew,
Could make me any fummers ftory tell:
Or from their proud lap pluck them where they grew:
Nor did I wonder at the Lillies white,
Nor praife the deepe vermillion in the Rofe,
They weare but fweet, but figures of delight:

G   Drawne

Drawne after you, you patterne of all thofe.
  Yet feem'd it Winter ftill, and you away,
  As with your fhaddow I with thefe did play.

99

THe forward violet thus did I chide,
  Sweet theefe whence didft thou fteale thy fweet that
If not from my loues breath, the purple pride,   (fmels.
Which on thy foft cheeke for complexion dwells?
In my loues veines thou haft too grofely died,
The Lillie I condemned for thy hand,
And buds of marierom had ftolne thy haire,
The Rofes fearefully on thornes did ftand,
Our blufhing fhame, an other white difpaire:
A third nor red, nor white, had ftolne of both,
And to his robbry had annext thy breath,
But for his theft in pride of all his growth
A vengfull canker eate him vp to death.
  More flowers I noted, yet I none could fee,
  But fweet, or culler it had ftolne from thee.

100

VVHere art thou Mufe that thou forgetft fo long,
  To fpeake of that which giues thee all thy might?
Spendft thou thy furie on fome worthleffe fonge,
Darkning thy powre to lend bafe fubiects light.
Returne forgetfull Mufe, and ftraight redeeme,
In gentle numbers time fo idely fpent,
Sing to the eare that doth thy laies efteeme,
And giues thy pen both skill and argument.
Rife refty Mufe, my loues fweet face furuay,
If time haue any wrincle grauen there,
If any, be a *Satire* to decay,
And make times fpoiles difpifed euery where.
  Giue my loue fame fafter then time wafts life,
  So thou preuenft his fieth, and crooked knife.

101

OH truant Mufe what fhalbe thy amends,

                                   For

272

For thy negleƈt of truth in beauty di'd?
Both truth and beauty on my loue depends:
So doſt thou too,and therein dignifi'd:
Make anſwere Muſe,wilt thou not haply ſaie,
Truth needs no collour with his collour fixt,
Beautie no penſell,beauties truth to lay:
But beſt is beſt,if neuer intermixt.
Becauſe he needs no praiſe,wilt thou be dumb?
Excuſe not ſilence ſo,for't lies in thee,
To make him much out-liue a gilded tombe:
And to be praiſd of ages yet to be.
    Then do thy office Muſe,I teach thee how,
    To make him ſeeme long hence,as he ſhowes now.

102

MY loue is ſtrengthned though more weake in ſee-
   I loue not leſſe,thogh leſſe the ſhow appeare, (ming
That loue is marchandiz'd,whoſe ritch eſteeming,
The owners tongue doth publiſh euery where.
Our loue was new,and then but in the ſpring,
When I was wont to greet it with my laies,
As *Philomell* in ſummers front doth ſinge,
And ſtops his pipe in growth of riper daies:
Not that the ſummer is leſſe pleaſant now
Then when her mournefull himns did huſh the night,
But that wild muſick burthens euery bow,
And ſweets growne common looſe their deare delight.
    Therefore like her, I ſome-time hold my tongue:
    Becauſe I would not dull you with my ſonge.

103

ALack what pouerty my Muſe brings forth,
   That hauing ſuch a skope to ſhow her pride,
The argument all bare is of more worth
Then when it hath my added praiſe beſide.
Oh blame me not if I no more can write!
Looke in your glaſſe and there appeares a face,
That ouer-goes my blunt inuention quite,
Dulling my lines,and doing me diſgrace.
        G 2   Were

Were it not sinfull then striuing to mend,
To marre the subiect that before was well,
For to no other passe my verses tend,
Then of your graces and your gifts to tell.
      And more,much more then in my verse can sit,
      Your owne glasse showes you,when you looke in it.

104

TO me faire friend you neuer can be old,
      For as you were when first your eye I eyde,
Such seemes your beautie still:Three Winters colde,
Haue from the forrests shooke three summers pride,
Three beautious springs to yellow *Autumne* turn'd,
In processe of the seasons haue I seene,
Three Aprill perfumes in three hot Iunes burn'd,
Since first I saw you fresh which yet are greene.
Ah yet doth beauty like a Dyall hand,
Steale from his figure,and no pace perceiu'd,
So your sweete hew,which me thinkes still doth stand,
Hath motion,and mine eye may be deceaued.
      For feare of which,heare this thou age vnbred,
      Ere you were borne was beauties summer dead.

105

LEt not my loue be cal'd Idolatrie,
      Nor my beloued as an Idoll show,
Since all alike my songs and praises be
To one,of one,still such,and euer so.
Kinde is my loue to day,to morrow kinde,
Still constant in a wondrous excellence,
Therefore my verse to constancie confin'de,
One thing expressing,leaues out difference.
Faire,kinde,and true,is all my argument,
Faire,kinde and true,varrying to other words,
And in this change is my inuention spent,
Three theams in one,which wondrous scope affords.
      Faire,kinde,and true,haue often liu'd alone.
      Which three till now,neuer kept seate in one.

                                        When

106

WHen in the Chronicle of wasted time,
  I see discriptions of the fairest wights,
And beautie making beautifull old rime,
In praise of Ladies dead,and louely Knights,
Then in the blazon of sweet beauties best,
Of hand,of foote,of lip,of eye,of brow,
I see their antique Pen would haue exprest,
Euen such a beauty as you maister now.
So all their praises are but prophesies
Of this our time,all you prefiguring,
And for they look'd but with deuining eyes,
They had not still enough your worth to sing :
  For we which now behold these present dayes,
  Haue eyes to wonder,but lack toungs to praise.

107

NOt mine owne feares,nor the prophetick soule,
  Of the wide world,dreaming on things to come,
Can yet the lease of my true loue controule,
Supposde as forfeit to a confin'd doome.
The mortall Moone hath her eclipse indur'de,
And the sad Augurs mock their owne presage,
Incertenties now crowne them-selues assur'de,
And peace proclaimes Oliues of endlesse age.
Now with the drops of this most balmie time,
My loue lookes fresh,and death to me subscribes,
Since spight of him Ile liue in this poore rime,
While he insults ore dull and speachlesse tribes.
  And thou in this shalt finde thy monument,
  When tyrants crests and tombs of brasse are spent.

108

VVHat's in the braine that Inck may character,
  Which hath not figur'd to thee my true spirit,
What's new to speake,what now to register,
That may expresse my loue,or thy deare merit?
Nothing sweet boy,but yet like prayers diuine,
        G 3   I must

I muſt each day ſay ore the very ſame,
Counting no old thing old,thou mine,I thine,
Euen as when firſt I hallowed thy faire name.
So that eternall loue in loues freſh caſe,
Waighes not the duſt and iniury of age,
Nor giues to neceſſary wrinckles place,
But makes antiquitie for aye his page,
      Finding the firſt conceit of loue there bred,
      Where time and outward forme would ſhew it dead,

109

O Neuer ſay that I was falſe of heart,
      Though abſence ſeem'd my flame to quallifie,
As eaſie might I from my ſelfe depart,
As from my ſoule which in thy breſt doth lye :
That is my home of loue, if I haue rang'd,
Like him that trauels I returne againe,
Iuſt to the time,not with the time exchang'd,
So that my ſelfe bring water for my ſtaine,
Neuer beleeue though in my nature raign'd,
All frailties that beſiege all kindes of blood,
That it could ſo prepoſterouſlie be ſtain'd,
To leaue for nothing all thy ſumme of good :
      For nothing this wide Vniuerſe I call,
      Saue thou my Roſe,in it thou art my all.

110

A Las 'tis true,I haue gone here and there,
      And made my ſelfe a motley to the view,
Gor'd mine own thoughts, ſold cheap what is moſt deare,
Made old offences of affections new.
Moſt true it is,that I haue lookt on truth
Aſconce and ſtrangely: But by all aboue,
Theſe blenches gaue my heart an other youth,
And worſe eſſaies prou'd thee my beſt of loue,
Now all is done,haue what ſhall haue no end,
Mine appetite I neuer more will grin'de
On newer proofe,to trie an older friend,
A God in loue,to whom I am confin'd.

                                        Then

276

Then giue me welcome,next my heauen the beſt,
Euen to thy pure and moſt moſt louing breſt.

111

O For my ſake doe you wiſh fortune chide,
  The guiltie goddeſſe of my harmfull deeds,
That did not better for my life prouide,
Then publick meanes which publick manners breeds.
Thence comes it that my name receiues a brand,
And almoſt thence my nature is ſubdu'd
To what it workes in,like the Dyers hand,
Pitty me then,and wiſh I were renu'de,
Whilſt like a willing pacient I will drinke,
Potions of Eyſell gainſt my ſtrong infection,
No bitterneſſe that I will bitter thinke,
Nor double pennance to correct correction.
    Pittie me then deare friend,and I aſſure yee,
    Euen that your pittie is enough to cure mee.

112

YOur loue and pittie doth th'impreſſion fill,
  Which vulgar ſcandall ſtampt vpon my brow,
For what care I who calles me well or ill,
So you ore-greene my bad,my good alow?
You are my All the world,and I muſt ſtriue,
To know my ſhames and praiſes from your tounge,
None elſe to me,nor I to none aliue,
That my ſteel'd ſence or changes right or wrong,
In ſo profound *Abiſme* I throw all care
Of others voyces,that my Adders ſence,
To cryttick and to flatterer ſtopped are:
Marke how with my neglect I doe diſpence.
    You are ſo ſtrongly in my purpoſe bred,
    That all the world beſides me thinkes y'are dead.

113

SInce I left you,mine eye is in my minde,
  And that which gouernes me to goe about,
Doth part his function,and is partly blind,

Seemes

Seemes feeing, but effectually is out:
For it no forme deliuers to the heart
Of bird, of flowre, or shape which it doth lack,
Of his quick obiects hath the minde no part,
Nor his owne vision houlds what it doth catch:
For if it see the rud'st or gentlest sight,
The most sweet-fauor or deformedst creature,
The mountaine, or the sea, the day, or night:
The Croe, or Doue, it shapes them to your feature.
　Incapable of more repleat, with you,
　My most true minde thus maketh mine vntrue.

114

OR whether doth my minde being crown'd with you
Drinke vp the monarks plague this flattery?
Or whether shall I say mine eie saith true,
And that your loue taught it this *Alcumie*?
To make of monsters, and things indigest,
Such cherubines as your sweet selfe resemble,
Creating euery bad a perfect best
As fast as obiects to his beames assemble:
Oh tis the first, tis flatry in my seeing,
And my great minde most kingly drinkes it vp,
Mine eie well knowes what with his gust is greeing,
And to his pallat doth prepare the cup.
　If it be poison'd, tis the lesser sinne,
　That mine eye loues it and doth first beginne.

115

THose lines that I before haue writ doe lie,
Euen those that said I could not loue you deerer,
Yet then my iudgement knew no reason why,
My most full flame should afterwards burne cleerer.
But reckening time, whose milliond accidents
Creepe in twixt vowes, and change decrees of Kings,
Tan sacred beautie, blunt the sharp'st intents,
Diuert strong mindes to th' course of altring things:
Alas why fearing of times tiranie,

　　　　　　　　　　Might

278

Might I not then fay now I loue you beſt,
When I was certaine ore in-certainty,
Crowning the preſent,doubting of the reſt:
    Loue is a Babe , then might I not ſay ſo
    To giue full growth to that which ſtill doth grow.

119

LEt me not to the marriage of true mindes
    Admit impediments,loue is not loue
Which alters when it alteration findes,
Or bends with the remouer to remoue.
O no,it is an euer fixed marke
That lookes on tempeſts and is neuer ſhaken;
It is the ſtar to euery wandring barke,
Whoſe worths vnknowne,although his higth be takeň.
Lou's not Times foole,though roſie lips and cheeks
Within his bending ſickles compaſſe come,
Loue alters not with his breeſe houres and weekes,
But beares it out euen to the edge of doome:
    If this be error and vpon me proued,
    I neuer writ,nor no man euer loued.

117

ACcuſe me thus,that I haue ſcanted all,
    Wherein I ſhould your great deſerts repay,
Forgot vpon your deareſt loue to call,
Where o al bonds do tie me day by day,
That I haue frequent binne with vnknown mindes,
And giuen to time your owne deare purchaſ'd right,
That I haue hoyſted ſaile to al the windes
Which ſhould tranſport me fartheſt from your ſight.
Booke both my wilfulneſſe and errors downe,
And on iuſt proofe ſurmiſe,accumilate,
Bring me within the leuel of your frowne,
But ſhoote not at me in your wakened hate:
    Since my appeale ſaies I did ſtriue to prooue
    The conſtancy and virtue of your loue

H   118

118

Like as to make our appetites more keene
With eager compounds we our pallat vrge,
As to preuent our malladies vnseene,
We sicken to shun sicknesse when we purge.
Euen so being full of your nere cloying sweetnesse,
To bitter sawces did I frame my feeding;
And sicke of wel-fare found a kind of meetnesse,
To be diseas'd ere that there was true needing.
Thus pollicie in loue t'anticipate
The ills that were,not grew to faults assured,
And brought to medicine a healthfull state
Which rancke of goodnesse would by ill be cured.
   But thence I learne and find the lesson true,
   Drugs poyson him that so fell sicke of you.

119

WHat potions haue I drunke of *Syren* teares
Distil'd from Lymbecks foule as hell within,
Applying feares to hopes,and hopes to feares,
Still loosing when I saw my selfe to win?
What wretched errors hath my heart committed,
Whilst it hath thought it selfe so blessed neuer?
How haue mine eies out of their Spheares bene fitted
In the distraction of this madding feuer?
O benefit of ill, now I find true
That better is, by euil still made better.
And ruin'd loue when it is built anew
Growes fairer then at first,more strong,far greater.
   So I returne rebukt to my content,
   And gaine by ills thrise more then I haue spent.

120

THat you were once vnkind be-friends mee now,
And for that sorrow , which I then didde feele,
Needes must I vnder my transgression bow,
Vnlesse my Nerues were brasse or hammered steele.
For if you were by my vnkindnesse shaken

As

As I by yours , y'haue paſt a hell of Time,
And I a tyrant haue no leaſure taken
To waigh how once I ſuffered in your crime.
O that our night of wo might haue remembred
My deepeſt ſence,how hard true ſorrow hits,
And ſoone to you,as you to me then tendred
The humble ſalue,which wounded boſomes fits!
   But that your treſpaſſe now becomes a fee,
   Mine ranſoms yours,and yours muſt ranſome mee.

121

TIS better to be vile then vile eſteemed,
  When not to be,receiues reproach of being,
And the iuſt pleaſure loſt,which is ſo deemed,
Not by our feeling,but by others ſeeing.
For why ſhould others falſe adulterat eyes
Giue ſalutation to my ſportiue blood?
Or on my frailties why are frailer ſpies;
Which in their wils count bad what I think good?
Noe, I am that I am,and they that leuell
At my abuſes,reckon vp their owne,
I may be ſtraight though they them-ſelues be beuel
By their rancke thoughtes,my deedes muſt not be ſhown
   Vnleſſe this generall euill they maintaine,
   All men are bad and in their badneſſe raigne.

122.

THy guift,,thy tables,are within my braine
  Full characterd with laſting memory,
Which ſhall aboue that idle rancke remaine
Beyond all date euen to eternity.
Or at the leaſt,ſo long as braine and heart
Haue facultie by nature to ſubſiſt,
Til each to raz'd obliuion yeeld his part
Of thee,thy record neuer can be miſt:
That poore retention could not ſo much hold,
Nor need I tallies thy deare loue to skore,
Therefore to giue them from me was I bold,

H 2

To truſt thoſe tables that receaue thee more,
　Ʈo keepe an adiunckt to remember thee,
　Were to import forgetfulneſſe in mee.

123

NO! Time, thou ſhalt not boſt that I doe change,
　Thy pyramyds buylt vp with newer might
To me are nothing nouell,nothing ſtrange,
They are but dreſſings of a former ſight:
Our dates are breefe,and therefor we admire,
What thou doſt foyſt vpon vs that is ould,
And rather make them borne to our deſire,
Then thinke that we before haue heard them tould:
Thy regiſters and thee I both defie,
Not wondring at the preſent,nor the paſt,
For thy records,and what we ſee doth lye,
Made more or les by thy continuall haſt:
　This I doe vow and this ſhall euer be,
　I will be true diſpight thy ſyeth and thee.

124

YF my deare loue were but the childe of ſtate,
　It might for fortunes baſterd be vnfathered,
As ſubiect to times loue,or to times hate,
Weeds among weeds,or flowers with flowers gatherd.
No it was buylded far from accident,
It ſuffers not in ſmilinge pomp,nor falls
Vnder the blow of thralled diſcontent,
Whereto th'inuiting time our faſhion calls:
It feares not policy that *Heriticke,*
Which workes on leaſes of ſhort numbred howers,
But all alone ſtands hugely pollitick,
That it nor growes with heat,nor drownes with ſhowres.
　To this I witnes call the foles of time,
　Which die for goodnes,who haue liu'd for crime.

125

VVEr't ought to me I bore the canopy,
　With my extern the outward honoring,

Or

Or layd great bases for eternity,
Which proues more short then wast or ruining?
Haue I not seene dwellers on forme and fauor
Lose all,and more by paying too much rent
For compound sweet;Forgoing simple sauor,
Pittifull thriuors in their gazing spent.
Noe,let me be obsequious in thy heart,
And take thou my oblacion,poore but free,
Which is not mixt with seconds,knows no art,
But mutuall render onely me for thee.
   Hence,thou subbornd*Informer*, a trew soule
   When most impeacht,stands least in thy controule.

126

O Thou my louely Boy who in thy power,
  Doest hould times sickle glasse,his sickle,hower:
Who hast by wayning growne,and therein shou'st,
Thy louers withering,as thy sweet selfe grow'st.
If Nature(soueraine misteres ouer wrack)
As thou goest onwards still will plucke thee backe,
She keepes thee to this purpose,that her skill.
May time disgrace,and wretched mynuit kill.
Yet feare her O thou minnion of her pleasure,
She may detaine,but not still keepe her tresure!
Her *Audite*(though delayd)answer'd must be,
And her *Quietus* is to render thee.
    (   )
    (   )

127

IN the ould age blacke was not counted faire,
  Or if it weare it bore not beauties name:
But now is blacke beauties successiue heire,
And Beautie slanderd with a bastard shame,
For since each hand hath put on Natures power,
Fairing the foule with Arts fauise borrow'd face,
Sweet beauty hath no name no holy boure,
But is prophan'd,if not liues in disgrace.

H 3

Therefore

Therefore my Mifterffe eyes are Rauen blacke,
Her eyes fo futed,and they mourners feeme,
At fuch who not borne faire no beauty lack,
Slandring Creation with a falfe efteeme,
    Yet fo they mourne becomming of their woe,
    That euery toung faies beauty fhould looke fo.

128

HOw oft when thou my mufike mufike playft,
  Vpon that bleffed wood whofe motion founds
With thy fweet fingers when thou gently fwayft,
The wiry concord that mine eare confounds,
Do I enuie thofe Iackes that nimble leape,
To kiffe the tender inward of thy hand,
Whilft my poore lips which fhould that harueft reape,
At the woods bouldnes by thee blufhing ftand.
To be fo tikled they would change their ftate,
And fituation with thofe dancing chips,
Ore whome their fingers walke with gentle gate,
Making dead wood more bleft then liuing lips,
    Since faufie Iackes fo happy are in this,
    Giue them their fingers,me thy lips to kiffe.

129

TH'expence of Spirit in a wafte of fhame
  Is luft in action,and till action , luft
Is periurd,murdrous,blouddy full of blame,
Sauage,extreame,rude,cruell,not to truft,
Inioyd no fooner but difpifed ftraight,
Paft reafon hunted, and no fooner had
Paft reafon hated as a fwollowed bayt,
On purpofe layd to make the taker mad.
Made In purfut and in poffeffion fo,
Had,hauing,and in queft,to haue extreame,
A bliffe in proofe and proud and very wo,
Before a ioy propofd behind a dreame,
    All this the world well knowes yet none knowes well,
    To fhun the heauen that leads men to this hell.

My

284

130

MY Miſtres eyes are nothing like the Sunne,
Currall is farre more red,then her lips red,
If ſnow be white,why then her breſts are dun:
If haires be wiers,black wiers grow on her head:
I haue ſeene Roſes damaskt,red and white,
But no ſuch Roſes ſee I in her cheekes,
And in ſome perfumes is there more delight,
Then in the breath that from my Miſtres reekes.
I loue to heare her ſpeake,yet well I know,
That Muſicke hath a farre more pleaſing ſound:
I graunt I neuer ſaw a goddeſſe goe,
My Miſtres when ſhee walkes treads on the ground.
    And yet by heauen I thinke my loue as rare,
    As any ſhe beli'd with falſe compare.

131

THou art as tiranous,ſo as thou art,
As thoſe whoſe beauties proudly make them cruell:
For well thou know'ſt to my deare doting hart
Thou art the faireſt and moſt precious Iewell.
Yet in good faith ſome ſay that thee behold,
Thy face hath not the power to make loue grone;
To ſay they erre,I dare not be ſo bold,
Although I ſweare it to my ſelfe alone.
And to be ſure that is not falſe I ſweare
A thouſand grones but thinking on thy face,
One on anothers necke do witneſſe beare
Thy blacke is faireſt in my iudgements place.
    In nothing art thou blacke ſaue in thy deeds,
    And thence this ſlaunder as I thinke proceeds.

132

THine eies I loue,and they as pittying me,
Knowing thy heart torment me with diſdaine,
Haue put on black,and louing mourners bee,
Looking with pretty ruth vpon my paine,

And

And truly not the morning Sun of Heauen
Better becomes the gray cheeks of th'Eaſt,
Nor that full Starre that vſhers in the Eauen
Doth halfe that glory to the ſober Weſt
As thoſe two morning eyes become thy face:
O let it then as well beſeeme thy heart
To mourne for me ſince mourning doth thee grace,
And ſute thy pitty like in euery part.
 Then will I ſweare beauty her ſelfe is blacke,
 And all they foule that thy complexion lacke.

133

BEſhrew that heart that makes my heart to groane
For that deepe wound it giues my friend and me;
I'ſt not ynough to torture me alone,
But ſlaue to ſlauery my ſweet'ſt friend muſt be.
Me from my ſelfe thy cruell eye hath taken,
And my next ſelfe thou harder haſt ingroſſed,
Of him,my ſelfe,and thee I am forſaken,
A torment thrice three-fold thus to be croſſed :
Priſon my heart in thy ſteele boſomes warde,
But then my friends heart let my poore heart bale,
Who ere keepes me,let my heart be his garde,
Thou canſt not then vſe rigor in my Iaile.
 And yet thou wilt,for I being pent in thee,
 Perforce am thine and all that is in me.

134

SO now I haue confeſt that he is thine,
 And I my ſelfe am morgag'd to thy will,
My ſelfe Ile forfeit,ſo that other mine,
Thou wilt reſtore to be my comfort ſtill:
But thou wilt not,nor he will not be free,
For thou art couetous,and he is kinde,
He learnd but ſuretie-like to write for me,
Vnder that bond that him as faſt doth binde.
The ſtatute of thy beauty thou wilt take,
Thou vſurer that put'ſt forth all to vſe,

And

And ſue a friend,came debter for my ſake,
So him I looſe through my vnkinde abuſe.
 Him haue I loſt, thou haſt both him and me,
 He paies the whole,and yet am I not free.

135

WHo euer hath her wiſh,thou haſt thy *Will,*
 And *Will* too boote,and *Will* in ouer-plus,
More then enough am I that vexe thee ſtill,
To thy ſweet will making addition thus.
Wilt thou whoſe will is large and ſpatious,
Not once vouchſafe to hide my will in thine,
Shall will in others ſeeme right gracious,
And in my will no faire acceptance ſhine:
The ſea all water,yet receiues raine ſtill,
And in aboundance addeth to his ſtore,
So thou beeing rich in *Will* adde to thy *Will,*
One will of mine to make thy large *Will* more.
 Let no vnkinde,no faire beſeechers kill,
 Thinke all but one,and me in that one *Will.*

136

IF thy ſoule check thee that I come ſo neere,
 Sweare to thy blind ſoule that I was thy *Will,*
And will thy ſoule knowes is admitted there,
Thus farre for loue, my loue-ſute ſweet fullfill.
Will, will fulfill the treaſure of thy loue,
I fill it full with wils,and my will one,
In things of great receit with eaſe we prooue,
Among a number one is reckon'd none.
Then in the number let me paſſe vntold,
Though in thy ſtores account I one muſt be,
For nothing hold me ſo it pleaſe thee hold,
That nothing me,a ſome-thing ſweet to thee.
 Make but my name thy loue,and loue that ſtill,
 And then thou loueſt me for my name is *Will.*

137

THou blinde foole loue,what dooſt thou to mine eyes,
     I   That

That they behold and fee not what they fee :
They know what beautie is,fee where it lyes,
Yet what the beft is,take the worft to be.
If eyes corrupt by ouer-partiall lookes,
Be anchord in the baye where all men ride,
Why of eyes falfehood haft thou forged hookes.
Whereto the iudgement of my heart is tide?
Why fhould my heart thinke that a feuerall plot,
Which my heart knowes the wide worlds common place?
Or mine eyes feeing this,fay this is not
To put faire truth vpon fo foule a face,
    In things right true my heart and eyes haue erred,
    And to this falfe plague are they now tranfferred.

138

WHen my loue fweares that fhe is made of truth,
    I do beleeue her though I know fhe lyes,
That fhe might thinke me fome vntuterd youth,
Vnlearned in the worlds falfe fubtilties.
Thus vainely thinking that fhe thinkes me young,
Although fhe knowes my dayes are paft the beft,
Simply I credit her falfe fpeaking tongue,
On both fides thus is fimple truth fuppreft :
But wherefore fayes fhe not fhe is vniuft ?
And wherefore fay not I that I am old ?
O loues beft habit is in feeming truft,
And age in loue,loues not t'haue yeares told.
    Therefore I lye with her,and fhe with me,
    And in our faults by lyes we flattered be.

139

OCall not me to iuftifie the wrong,
    That thy vnkindneffe layes vpon my heart,
Wound me not with thine eye but with thy toung,
Vfe power with power,and flay me not by Art,
Tell me thou lou'ft elfe-where;but in my fight,
Deare heart forbeare to glance thine eye afide,
What needft thou wound with cunning when thy might

l2

Is more then my ore-preſt defence can bide?
Let me excuſe thee ah my loue well knowes,
Her prettie lookes haue beene mine enemies,
And therefore from my face ſhe turnes my foes,
That they elſe-where might dart their iniuries :
   Yet do not ſo,but ſince I am neere ſlaine,
   Kill me out-right with lookes,and rid my paine.

140

BE wiſe as thou art cruell,do not preſſe
  My toung tide patience with too much diſdaine :
Leaſt ſorrow lend me words and words expreſſe,
The manner of my pittie wanting paine.
If I might teach thee witte better it weare,
Though not to loue,yet loue to tell me ſo,
As teſtie ſick-men when their deaths be neere,
No newes but health from their Phiſitions know.
For if I ſhould diſpaire I ſhould grow madde,
And in my madneſſe might ſpeake ill of thee,
Now this ill wreſting world is growne ſo bad,
Madde ſlanderers by madde eares beleeued be.
   That I may not be ſo, nor thou be lyde,   (wide.
   Beare thine eyes ſtraight , though thy proud heart goe

141

IN faith I doe not loue thee with mine eyes,
 For they in thee a thouſand errors note,
But 'tis my heart that loues what they diſpiſe,
Who in diſpight of view is pleaſd to dote.
Nor are mine eares with thy toungs tune delighted,
Nor tender feeling to baſe touches prone,
Nor taſte, nor ſmell, deſire to be inuited
To any ſenſuall feaſt with thee alone :
But my fiue wits,nor my fiue ſences can
Diſwade one fooliſh heart from ſeruing thee,
Who leaues vnſwai'd the likeneſſe of a man,
Thy proud hearts ſlaue and vaſſall wretch to be :
   Onely my plague thus farre I count my gaine,
   That ſhe that makes me ſinne,awards me paine.

I 2   Lone

142

LOue is my sinne, and thy deare vertue hate,
Hate of my sinne, grounded on sinfull louing,
O but with mine, compare thou thine owne state,
And thou shalt finde it merrits not reprouing,
Or if it do, not from those lips of thine,
That haue prophan'd their scarlet ornaments,
And seald false bonds of loue as oft as mine,
Robd others beds reuenues of their rents.
Be it lawfull I loue thee as thou lou'st those,
Whome thine eyes wooe as mine importune thee,
Roote pittie in thy heart that when it growes,
Thy pitty may deserue to pittied bee.
   If thou doost seeke to haue what thou doost hide,
   By selfe example mai'st thou be denide.

143

LOe as a carefull huswife runnes to catch,
One of her fethered creatures broake away,
Sets downe her babe and makes all swift dispatch
In pursuit of the thing she would haue stay:
Whilst her neglected child holds her in chace,
Cries to catch her whose busie care is bent,
To follow that which flies before her face:
Not prizing her poore infants discontent;
So runst thou after that which flies from thee,
Whilst I thy babe chace thee a farre behind,
But if thou catch thy hope turne back to me:
And play the mothers part kisse me, be kind.
   So will I pray that thou maist haue thy *Will*,
   If thou turne back and my loude crying still.

144

TWo loues I haue of comfort and dispaire,
Which like two spirits do sugiest me still,
The better angell is a man right faire:
The worser spirit a woman collour'd il.
To win me soone to hell my femall euill,

Tempteth

290

Tempteth my better angel from my sight,
And would corrupt my saint to be a diuel:
Wooing his purity with her fowle pride.
And whether that my angel be turn'd finde,
Suspect I may,yet not directly tell,
But being both from me both to each friend,
I geffe one angel in an others hel.

　　Yet this shal I nere know but liue in doubt,
　　Till my bad angel fire my good one out.

145

THofe lips that Loues owne hand did make,
　　Breath'd forth the sound that said I hate,
To me that languisht for her fake:
But when she saw my wofull state,
Straight in her heart did mercie come,
Chiding that tongue that euer sweet,
Was vsde in giuing gentle dome:
And tought it thus a new to greete:
I hate she alterd with an end,
That follow'd it as gentle day,
Doth follow night who like a fiend
From heauen to hell is flowne away.

　　I hate,from hate away she threw,
　　And fau'd my life saying not you.

146

POore foule the center of my sinfull earth,
　　My sinfull earth thefe rebbell powres that thee array,
Why dost thou pine within and suffer dearth
Painting thy outward walls so costlie gay?
Why so large cost hauing so short a leafe,
Dost thou vpon thy fading mansion spend?
Shall wormes inheritors of this excesse]
Eate vp thy charge?is this thy bodies end?
Then foule liue thou vpon thy seruants losse,
And let that pine to aggrauat thy store;
Buy tearmes diuine in selling houres of drosse:

1 3　　　　　　　　　　　　Within

Within be fed, without be rich no more,
  So fhalt thou feed on death,that feeds on men,
  And death once dead,ther's no more dying then.

147

MY loue is as a feauer longing ftill,
  For that which longer nurfeth the difeafe,
Feeding on that which doth preferue the ill,
Th'vncertaine ficklie appetite to pleafe:
My reafon the Phifition to my loue,
Angry that his prefcriptions are not kept
Hath left me,and I defperate now approoue,
Defire is death,which Phifick did except.
Paft cure I am,now Reafon is paft care,
And frantick madde with euer-more vnreft,
My thoughts and my difcourfe as mad mens are,
At randon from the truth vainely expreft.
  For I haue fworne thee faire,and thought thee bright,
  Who art as black as hell,as darke as night.

148

O Me ! what eyes hath loue put in my head,
  Which haue no correfpondence with true fight,
Or if they haue,where is my iudgment fled,
That cenfures falfely what they fee aright ?
If that be faire whereon my falfe eyes dote,
What meanes the world to fay it is not fo ?
If it be not,then loue doth well denote,
Loues eye is not fo true as all mens:no,
How can it ? O how can loues eye be true,
That is fo vext with watching and with teares?
No maruaile then though I miftake my view,
The funne it felfe fees not, till heauen cleeres.
  O cunning loue,with teares thou keepft me blinde,
  Leaft eyes well feeing thy foule faults fhould finde.

149

CAnft thou O cruell,fay I loue thee not,
  When I againft my felfe with thee pertake :

Doe

Doe I not thinke on thee when I forgot
Am of my felfe, all tirant for thy fake?
Who hateth thee that I doe call my friend,
On whom froun'ft thou that I doe faune vpon,
Nay if thou lowrft on me doe I not fpend
Reuenge vpon my felfe with prefent mone?
What merrit do I in my felfe refpect,
That is fo proude thy feruice to difpife,
When all my beft doth worfhip thy defect,
Commanded by the motion of thine eyes.
    But loue hate on for now I know thy minde,
    Thofe that can fee thou lou'ft,and I am blind.

150

OH from what powre haft thou this powrefull might,
VVith infufficiency my heart to fway,
To make me giue the lie to my true fight,
And fwere that brightneffe doth not grace the day?
Whence haft thou this becomming of things il,
That in the very refufe of thy deeds,
There is fuch ftrength and warrantife of skill,
That in my minde thy worft all beft exceeds?
Who taught thee how to make me loue thee more,
The more I heare and fee iuft caufe of hate,
Oh though I loue what others doe abhor,
VVith others thou fhouldft not abhor my ftate.
    If thy vnworthineffe raifd lone in me,
    More worthy I to be belou'd of thee.

151

LOue is too young to know what confcience is,
Yet who knowes not confcience is borne of loue,
Then gentle cheater vrge not my amiffe,
Leaft guilty of my faults thy fweet felfe proue.
For thou betraying me, I doe betray
My nobler part to my grofe bodies treafon,
My foule doth tell my body that he may,
Triumph in loue,flefh ftaies no farther reafon,

                                      But

But ryfing at thy name doth point out thee,
As his triumphant prize,proud of this pride,
He is contented thy poore drudge to be
To ftand in thy affaires,fall by thy fide.
    No want of confcience hold it that I call,
    Her loue, for whofe deare loue I rife and fall.

152

IN louing thee thou know'ft I am forfworne,
  But thou art twice forfworne to me loue fwearing,
In act thy bed-vow broake and new faith torne,
In vowing new hate after new loue bearing:
But why of two othes breach doe I accufe thee,
When I breake twenty:I am periur'd moft,
For all my vowes are othes but to mifufe thee:
And all my honeft faith in thee is loft.
For I haue fworne deepe othes of thy deepe kindneffe:
Othes of thy loue,thy truth,thy conftancie,
And to inlighten thee gaue eyes to blindneffe,
Or made them fwere againft the thing they fee.
    For I haue fworne thee faire:more periurde eye,
    To fwere againft the truth fo foule a lie.

153

CVpid laid by his brand and fell a fleepe,
  A maide of *Dyans* this aduantage found,
And his loue-kindling fire did quickly fteepe
In a could vallie-fountaine of that ground:
Which borrowd from this holie fire of loue,
A dateleffe liuely heat ftill to indure,
And grew a feething bath which yet men proue,
Againft ftrang malladies a foueraigne cure:
But at my miftres eie loues brand new fired,
The boy for triall needes would touch my breft,
I fick withall the helpe of bath defired,
And thether hied a fad diftemperd gueft.
    But found no cure,the bath for my helpe lies,
    Where *Cupid* got new fire;my miftres eye.

154

154

THe little Loue-God lying once a ſleepe,
 Laid by his ſide his heart inflaming brand,
Whilſt many Nymphes that vou'd chaſt life to keep,
Came tripping by,but in her maiden hand,
The fayreſt votary tooke vp that fire,
Which many Legions of true hearts had warm'd,
And ſo the Generall of hot deſire,
Was ſleeping by a Virgin hand diſarm'd.
This brand ſhe quenched in a coole Well by,
Which from loues fire tooke heat perpetuall,
Growing a bath and healthfull remedy,
For men diſeaſd,but I my Miſtriſſe thrall,
    Came there for cure and this by that I proue,
    Loues fire heates water,water cooles not loue.

FINIS.

K   A

A Louers complaint.

BY

WILLIAM SHAKE-SPEARE.

FRom off a hill whose concaue wombe reworded,
A plaintfull story from a sistring vale
My spirrits t'attend this doble voyce accorded,
And downe I laid to list the sad tun'd tale,
Ere long espied a fickle maid full pale
Tearing of papers breaking rings a twaine,
Storming her world with sorrowes, wind and raine.

Vpon her head a plattid hiue of straw,
Which fortified her visage from the Sunne,
Whereon the thought might thinke sometime it saw
The carkas of a beauty spent and donne,
Time had not sithed all that youth begun,
Nor youth all quit, but spight of heauens fell rage,
Some beauty peept, through lettice of sear'd age.

Oft did she heaue her Napkin to her eyne,
Which on it had conceited charecters:
Laundring the silken figures in the brine,
That seasoned woe had pelleted in teares,
And often reading what contents it beares:
As often shriking vndistinguisht wo,
In clamours of all size both high and low.

Some-times her leueld eyes their carriage ride,
As they did battry to the spheres intend:
Sometime diuerted their poore balls are tide,
To th'orbed earth; sometimes they do extend,
Their view right on, anon their gases lend,

To

To euery place at once and no where fixt,
The mind and fight diftractedly commxit.

Her haire nor loofe nor ti'd in formall plat,
Proclaimd in her a careleſſe hand of pride;
For ſome vntuck'd deſcended her ſheu'd hat,
Hanging her pale and pined cheeke beſide,
Some in her threeden fillet ſtill did bide,
And trew to bondage would not breake from thence,
Though ſlackly braided in loofe negligence.

A thouſand fauours from a maund ſhe drew,
Of amber chriſtall and of bedded Iet,
Which one by one ſhe in a riuer threw,
Vpon whoſe weeping margent ſhe was ſet,
Like vſery applying wet to wet,
Or Monarches hands that lets not bounty fall,
Where want cries ſome;but where exceſſe begs all.

Of folded ſchedulls had ſhe many a one,
Which ſhe peruſ d,ſighd,tore and gaue the flud,
Crackt many a ring of Poſied gold and bone,
Bidding them find their Sepulchers in mud,
Found yet mo letters ſadly pend in blood,
With ſleided ſilke,feate and affectedly
Enſwath'd and ſeald to curious ſecrecy.

Theſe often bath'd ſhe in her fluxiue eies,
And often kiſt,and often gaue to teare,
Cried O falſe blood thou regiſter of lies,
What vnapproued witnes dooſt thou beare!
Inke would haue ſeem'd more blacke and damned heare!
This ſaid in top of rage the lines ſhe rents,
Big diſcontent,ſo breaking their contents.

A reuerend man that graz'd his cattell ny,

K 2   ſome

Sometime a bluſ'erer that the ruffle knew
Of Court of Cittie, and had let go by
The ſwifteſt houres obſerued as they flew,
Towards this afflicted fancy faſtly drew:
And priuiledg'd by age deſires to know
In breeſe the grounds and motiues of her wo.

So ſlides he downe vppon his greyned bat;
And comely diſtant ſits he by her ſide,
When hee againe deſires her, being ſatte,
Her greeuance with his hearing to deuide:
If that from him there may be ought applied
Which may her ſuffering extaſie aſſwage
Tis promiſt in the charitie of age .

Father ſhe ſaies, though in mee you behold
The iniury of many a blaſting houre;
Let it not tell your Iudgement I am old,
Not age, but ſorrow, ouer me hath power;
I might as yet haue bene a ſpreading flower
Freſh to my ſelfe, if I had ſelfe applyed
Loue to my ſelfe, and to no Loue beſide.

But wo is mee, too early I atttended
A youthfull ſuit it was to gaine my grace;
O one by natures outwards ſo commended,
That maidens eyes ſtucke ouer all his face,
Loue lackt a dwelling and made him her place.
And when in his faire parts ſhee didde abide,
Shee was new lodg'd and newly Deified.

His browny locks did hang in crooked curles,
And euery light occaſion of the wind
Vpon his lippes their ſilken parcels hurles,
Whats ſweet to do, to do wil aptly find,
Each eye that ſaw him did inchaunt the minde;

For

298

For on his visage was in little drawne,
What largenesse thinkes in parradise was sawne.

Smal shew of man was yet vpon his chinne,
His phenix downe began but to appeare
Like vnshorne veluet, on that termlesse skin
Whose bare out-brag'd the web it seem'd to were.
Yet shewed his visage by that cost more deare,
And nice affections wauering stood in doubt
If best were as it was, or best without.

His qualities were beautious as his forme,
For maiden tongu'd he was and thereof free;
Yet if men mou'd him, was he such a storme
As oft twixt May and Aprill is to see,
When windes breath sweet, vnruly though they bee.
His rudenesse so with his authoriz'd youth,
Did liuery falsenesse in a pride of truth.

Wel could hee ride, and often men would say
That horse his mettell from his rider takes
Proud of subiection, noble by the swaie,   (makes
What rounds, what bounds, what course what stop he
And controuersie hence a question takes,
Whether the horse by him became his deed,
Or he his mannad'g, by'th wel doing Steed.

But quickly on this side the verdict went,
His reall habitude gaue life and grace
To appertainings and to ornament,
Accomplisht in him-selfe not in his case:
All ayds them-selues made fairer by their place,
Can for addicions, yet their purpos'd trimme
Feec'd not his grace but were al grac'd by him.

So on the tip of his subduing tongue.
                    K 3   All

                        299

All kinde of arguments and question deepe,
Al replication prompt,and reason strong
For his aduantage still did wake and sleep,
To make the weeper laugh,the laugher weepe
He hadthe dialect and different skil,
Catching al passions in his craft of will.

That hee didde in the general bosome raigne
Of young, of old,and sexes both inchanted,
To dwel with him in thoughts,or to remaine
In personal duty,following where he haunted,
Consent's bewitcht , ere he desire haue granted,
And dialogu'd for him what he would say,
Askt their own wils and made their wils obey.

Many there were that did his picture gette
To serue their eies,and in it put their mind,
Like fooles that in th' imagination set
The goodly obiects which abroad they find
Of lands and mansions,theirs in thought assign'd,
And labouring in moe pleasures to bestow them,
Then the true gouty Land-lord which doth owe them.

So many haue that neuer toucht his hand
Sweetly suppos'd them mistresse of his heart:
My wofull selfe that did in freedome stand,
And was my owne fee simple(not in part)
What with his art in youth and youth in art
Threw my affections in his charmed power,
Reseru'd the stalke and gaue him al my flower.

Yet did I not as some my equals did
Demaund of him,nor being desired yeelded,
Finding my selfe in honour so forbidde,
With safest distance I mine honour sheelded,
Experience for me many bulwarkes builded

Of

300

Of proofs new bleeding which remaind the foile
Of this false Iewell, and his amorous spoile.

But ah who euer shun'd by precedent,
The destin'd ill she must her selfe assay,
Or forc'd examples gainst her owne content
To put the by-past perrils in her way?
Counsaile may stop a while what will not stay:
For when we rage, aduise is often seene
By blunting vs to make our wits more keene.

Nor giues it satisfaction to our blood,
That wee must curbe it vppon others proofe,
To be forbod the sweets that seemes so good,
For feare of harmes that preach in our behoofe;
O appetite from iudgement stand aloofe!
The one a pallate hath that needs will taste,
Though reason weepe and cry it is thy last.

For further I could say this mans vntrue,
And knew the patternes of his foule beguiling,
Heard where his plants in others Orchards grew,
Saw how deceits were guilded in his smiling,
Knew vowes, wer e euer brokers to defiling,
Thought Characters and words meerly but art
And bastards of his foule adulterat heart.

And long vpon these termes I held my Citty,
Till thus hee gan besiege me : Gentle maid
Haue of my suffering youth some feeling pitty
And be not of my holy vowes affraid,
Thats to ye sworne to none was euer said,
For feasts of loue I haue bene call'd vnto
Till now did nere inuite nor neuer vovv.

All my offences that abroad you see
K 4   Are

301

Are errors of the blood none of the mind:
Loue made them not, with acture they may be,
Where neither Party is nor trew nor kind,
They sought their shame that so their shame did find,
And so much lesse of shame in me remaines,
By how much of me their reproch containes,

Among the many that mine eyes haue seene,
Not one whose flame my hart so much as warmed,
Or my affection put to th, smallest teene,
Or any of my leisures euer Charmed,
Harme haue I done to them but nere was harmed,
Kept hearts in liueries, but mine owne was free,
And raignd commaunding in his monarchy.

Looke heare what tributes wounded fancies sent me,
Of palyd pearles and rubies red as blood:
Figuring that they their passions likewise lent me
Of greefe and blushes, aptly vnderstood
In bloodlesse white, and the encrimson'd mood,
Effects of terror and deare modesty,
Encampt in hearts but fighting outwardly.

And Lo behold these tallents of their heir,
With twisted mettle amorously empleacht
I haue receau'd from many a seueral faire,
Their kind acceptance, wepingly beseecht,
With th'annexions of faire gems inricht,
And deepe brain'd sonnets that did amplifie
Each stones deare Nature, worth and quallity.

The Diamond? why twas beautifull and hard,
Whereto his inuis'd properties did tend,
The deepe greene Emrald in whose fresh regard,
Weake sights their sickly radience do amend.
The heauen hewd Saphir and the Opall blend

With

With obiects manyfold ; each feuerall ftone,
With wit well blazond fmil'd or made fome mone,

Lo all thefe trophies of affections hot,
Of penfiu'd and fubdew'd defires the tender,
Nature hath chargd me that I hoord them not,
Bur yeeld them vp where I my felfe muft render:
That is to you my origin and ender :
For thefe of force muft your oblations be,
Since I their Aulter, you en patrone me.

Oh then aduance(of yours)that phrafeles hand,
Whofe white weighes downe the airy fcale of praife,
Take all thefe fimilies to your owne command,
Hollowed with fighes that burning lunges did raife:
What me your minifter for you obaies
Workes vnder you,and to your audit comes
Their diftract parcells,in combined fummes.

Lo this deuice was fent me from a Nun,
Or Sifter fanctified of holieft note,
Which late her noble fuit in court did fhun,
Whofe rareft hauings made the bloffoms dote,
For fhe was fought by fpirits of ritcheft cote,
But kept cold diftance,and did thence remoue,
To fpend her liuing in eternall loue.

But oh my fweet what labour ift to leaue,
The thing we haue not,maftring what not ftriues,
Playing the Place which did no forme receiue,
Playing patient fports in vnconftraind giues,
She that her fame fo to her felfe contriues,
The fcarres of battaile fcapeth by the flight,
And makes her abfence valiant,not her might.

Oh pardon me in that my boaft is true,
L   The

The accident which brought me to her eie,
Vpon the moment did her force subdewe,
And now she would the caged cloister flie:
Religious loue put out religions eye:
Not to be tempted would she be enur'd,
And now to tempt all liberty procure.

How mightie then you are, Oh heare me tell,
The broken bosoms that to me belong,
Haue emptied all their fountaines in my well:
And mine I powre your Ocean all amonge:
I strong ore-them and you ore me being strong,
Must for your victorie vs all congest,
As compound loue to phisick your cold brest.

My parts had powre to charme a sacred Sunne,
Who disciplin'd I dieted in grace,
Beleeu'd her eies, when they t' assaile begun,
All vowes and consecrations giuing place:
O most potentiall loue, vowe, bond, nor space
In thee hath neither sting, knot, nor confine
For thou art all and all things els are thine.

When thou impressest what are precepts worth
Of stale example? when thou wilt inflame,
How coldly those impediments stand forth
Of wealth of filliall feare, lawe, kindred fame,   (shame
Loues armes are peace, gainst rule, gainst sence, gainst
And sweetens in the suffring pangues it beares,
The *Alloes* of all forces, shockes and feares.

Now all these hearts that doe on mine depend,
Feeling it breake, with bleeding groanes they pine,
And supplicant their sighes to you extend
To leaue the battrie that you make gainst mine,
Lending soft audience, to my sweet designe,

                                                And

And credent foule,to that ftrong bonded oth,
That fhall preferre and vndertake my troth.

This faid,his watrie eies he did difmount,
Whofe fightes till then were leaueld on my face,
Each cheeke a riuer running from a fount,
With brynifh currant downe-ward flowed a pace:
Oh how the channell to the ftreame gaue grace!
Who glaz'd with Chriftall gate the glowing Rofes,
That flame through water which their hew inclofes,

Oh father,what a hell of witch-craft lies,
In the fmall orb of one perticular teare?
But with the invndation of the eies:
What rocky heart to water will not weare?
What breft fo cold that is not warmed heare,
Or cleft effect,cold modefty hot wrath:
Both fire from hence,and chill extincture hath.

For loe his paffion but an art of craft,
Euen there refolu'd my reafon into teares,
There my white ftole of chaftity I daft,
Shooke off my fober gardes,and ciuill feares,
Appeare to him as he to me appeares:
All melting,though our drops this diffrence bore,
His poifon'd me, and mine did him reftore.

In him a plenitude of fubtle matter,
Applied to Cautills,all ftraing formes receiues,
Of burning blufhes,or of weeping water,
Or founding palenefle: and he takes and leaues,
In eithers aptnefle as it beft deceiues:
To blufh at fpeeches ranck , to weepe at woes
Or to turne white and found at tragick fhowes.

That not a heart which in his leuell came,
L 2   Could

305

Cou'd scape the haile of his all hurting ayme,
Shewing faire Nature is both kinde and tame :
And vaild in them did winne whom he would maime,
Against the thing he sought, he would exclaime,
When he most burnt in hart-wisht luxurie,
He preacht pure maide, and praisd cold chastitie.

Thus meerely with the garment of a grace,
The naked and concealed feind he couerd,
That th'vnexperient gaue the tempter place,
Which like a Cherubin aboue them houerd,
Who young and simple would not be so louerd.
Aye me I fell, and yet do question make,
What I should doe againe for such a sake.

O that infected moysture of his eye,
O that false fire which in his cheeke so glowd,
O that forc'd thunder from his heart did flye,
O that sad breath his spungie lungs bestowed,
O all that borrowed motion seeming owed,
Would yet againe betray the fore-betrayed,
And new peruert a reconciled Maide.

FINIS.

Sources and Notes

PREFACE

1. Sir John Suckling, *Brennoralt, or the Discontented Colonel,*
circa 1640 (in *Works,* ed. A. Hamilton Thompson, 1910).
Words and phrases from a few sonnets were borrowed or adapted
by the Cavalier poet, presumably from Benson's 1640 edition.
See J. Munro, *Shakespeare Allusion Book,* 1909, I, p. 386.
2. Robert Giroux, "The Book Known as Q," the third Archibald
Smith lecture, delivered 28 April 1981, published by the Baylor
School, Chattanooga, Tennessee.

POEMS I

1. E. K. Chambers, *William Shakespeare: A Study of the Facts
and Problems,* 1930, I, p. 550.
2. George Rylands, "Shakespeare the Poet," in *A Companion to
Shakespeare Studies,* eds. H. Granville Barker and G. B. Harrison,
1960, p. 102.
3. Edward Capell, Unpublished preface to his corrected text of
Lintott's 1711 edition, called the "Capell Ms.," 1766. Cited by
Rollins (see note 8), II, 38.
4. J. W. Mackail, *The Approach to Shakespeare,* 1930, p. 113.
5. Paul Morgan, " 'Our Will Shakespeare' and Lope de Vega: An
Unrecorded Contemporary Document," in *Shakespeare Survey*
16 (1963), pp. 118–20.
6. Frank Mathew, *An Image of Shakespeare,* 1922, p. 114.
7. J. M. Robertson, *The Problems of Shakespeare's Sonnets,*
1926, p. 121.
8. Hyder Edward Rollins, ed., *A New Variorum Edition of
Shakespeare: The Sonnets,* 1944, II, p. 327.
9. H. J. Gottlieb, *Robert Burton's Knowledge of English Poetry,*
1937, p. 14n.

10.   George Steevens, ed., *Twenty of the Plays of Shakespeare,* 1780 edition, IV.
11.   Edmund Malone, *Supplement to the Edition of Shakespeare's Plays Published in 1778,* with notes by George Steevens, 1780 edition.
12.   *Ibid.*
13.   Chambers, *op. cit.,* I, p. 559.
14.   W. H. Auden, "Shakespeare's Sonnets," in *Forewords and Afterwords,* 1973, p. 105. First printed in *The Listener,* 30 April and 7 May 1964.
15.   A. Kent Hieatt, *Short Time's Endless Monument,* 1960, pp. 83–109.
16.   Alastair Fowler, *Triumphal Forms,* 1970, pp. 174–97.
17.   Leslie Hotson, *Mr. W. H.,* 1964, p. 269.
18.   John Dover Wilson, *The Works of Shakespeare: The Sonnets,* 1966, p. xxxiv.
19.   W. H. Auden, *op. cit.,* p. 95.
20.   Vladimir Nabokov, *Notes on Prosody,* 1964, p. 55.
21.   John Jay Chapman, *A Glance toward Shakespeare,* 1922, p. 98.
22.   C. S. Lewis, *English Literature in the Sixteenth Century,* 1954, pp. 503 ff.
23.   Stephen Spender, "The Alike and the Other," in *The Riddle of Shakespeare's Sonnet,* ed. Edward Hubler, 1962, p. 102.
24.   Martin Seymour-Smith, *Shakespeare's Sonnets,* 1963, p. 34.
25.   Samuel Butler, *Shakespeare's Sonnets Reconsidered,* 1899, p. 122.
26.   Valéry Larbaud, Introduction to *Shakespeare: Les Sonnets,* ed. E. LeBrun, 1927, p. xxiv.
27.   William Empson, "Shakespeare's Angel," *The New Statesman* (4 October 1963), p. 447.
28.   G. B. Harrison, ed., *Shakespeare: The Complete Works,* 1952, p. 366.
29.   John Lyly, *Endimion, The Man in the Moon,* 1591, III, iv.
30.   Robert Bernard Martin, *Tennyson: The Unquiet Heart,* 1980, p. 94.
31.   Iris Murdoch, *Nuns and Soldiers,* 1980, p. 194.
32.   Marcel Proust, *Remembrance of Things Past,* tr. C. K. Scott-Moncrieff and Terence Kilmartin, addenda to Vol. II ("Cities of the Plains"), 1981, p. 1185.

33. Richard P. Blackmur, "A Poetics for Infatuation," in *The Riddle of the Sonnets, op. cit.,* p. 132.
34. C. S. Lewis, *op. cit.,* p. 505.
35. Aristotle, *Nicomachaen Ethics,* Book VIII, vi, 1158b.
36. C. S. Lewis, *op. cit.,* p. 505.
37. J. W. Mackail, *Lectures on Poetry,* 1911, p. 196.
38. Stephen Booth, *Shakespeare's Sonnets,* 1977, p. 180.
39. George Lyman Kittredge, *Shakespeare,* address at Harvard, 23 April 1916, pp. 52–53.
40. J. B. Leishman, *Themes and Variations in Shakespeare's Sonnets,* 1961, p. 203.
41. M. J. Wolff on Giovanni della Casa, in "Petrarkismus und Antipetrarkismus in Shakespeares Sonetten," *Englische Studien,* 1916, XLIX, pp. 172–80.
42. Edgar I. Fripp, *Shakespeare, Man and Artist,* 1938, p. 311.
43. Colette, *La Jumelle Noire,* II, pp. 33–34.
44. Stephen Booth, *op. cit.,* p. 548.
45. *Ibid.,* p. 432.
46. John Berryman, "Despondency and Madness," in *The Freedom of the Poet,* 1976, p. 316.
47. Kenneth Muir, *Shakespeare's Sonnets,* 1979, p. i.
48. Northrop Frye, "How True a Twain," in *The Riddle of the Sonnets, op. cit.,* p. 31.
49. C. J. Sisson, "The Mythical Sorrows of Shakespeare," British Academy Proceedings, 1934, p. 9.
50. Kenneth Muir, *op. cit.,* p. 122.

THE PATRON

1. E. A. B. Barnard, *New Links with Shakespeare,* 1930, cites the Archbishop of Canterbury (Lord Davidson of Lambeth), p. 96.
2. Stephen Booth, *op. cit.,* p. 547.
3. G. P. V. Akrigg, *Shakespeare and the Earl of Southampton,* 1968, p. 131.
4. John Bruce, ed., *Correspondence of King James I with Sir Robert Cecil & Others,* 1861, p. 71.
5. King James Bible, dedicatory epistle of the translators, 1612, opening para.

6. Charlotte Carmichael Stopes, *The Life of Henry, Third Earl of Southampton, Shakespeare's Patron,* 1922, p. 16.
7. Cecil Papers, 164, 82.
8. William Murdin, ed., *A Collection of State Papers,* 1759, p. 792.
9. Calendar of State Papers (Domestic), 1581–90, p. 680.
10. Public Records Office, State Papers, 12/33/71.
11. Statute of Merton (1236), cited by Joel Hurstfield, *The Queen's Wards,* 1958, p. 142.
12. Landsdowne Ms., lxxi, p. 72.
13. John Clapham, *Narcissus,* printed by John Scarlet, 1591, S.T.C. 5349.
14. Charlotte Stopes, *op. cit.,* p. 41.
15. G. P. V. Akrigg, *op. cit.,* p. 193.
16. J. Dover Wilson, *The Essential Shakespeare,* 1932, p. 64.
17. *Henslowe's Diary,* ed. by R. S. A. Foakes and R. T. Rickert, 1961, pp. 16 ff.
18. *Apollinis et Musarum Euktika Eidyllia,* 1592. Reprinted in *Elizabethan Oxford,* Publications of the Oxford Historical Society, VIII, p. 294.
19. Nicholas Rowe, *Works of Shakespeare,* "Some Account of the Life," I, prefatory material.
20. Angus Heriot, *The Castrati in Opera,* "Nicolino (Grimaldi, Nicolo)," 1956, pp. 123–28.
21. William Empson, *Some Versions of Pastoral,* "They That Have Power," 1935, 1974, p. 107.
22. J. Dover Wilson, *op. cit.*
23. E. K. Chambers, *op. cit.,* I, p. 61.
24. Arthur Collins, ed. *Letters and Memorials of State (The Sidney Papers),* 1746, II, p. 62.
25. Historical Manuscripts Commission, De L'Isle Mss., II, p. 176.
26. Arthur Collins, *op. cit.,* p. 348.
27. Historical Manuscripts Commission, *op. cit.,* p. 312.
28. Arthur Collins, *op. cit.,* p. 87.
29. Calendar of State Papers (Domestic), 1598–1601, p. 90.
30. Salisbury Mss., XIV, p. 107.
31. John Nichols, ed., *The Progresses of Queen Elizabeth,* 1788–1821, II, p. 701.
32. Calendar of State Papers (Ireland), 1599–1600, p. 62.

33. W. B. Devereux, *Lives and Letters of the Devereux, Earls of Essex*, 1853, II, p. 45.

34. Calendar State Papers (Ireland), 1599–1600, pp. 100–1.

35. Salisbury Mss., XI, pp. 72–73.

36. Arthur Collins, *op. cit.*, II, p. 127.

37. *Ibid.*, p. 132.

38. John Nichols, *op. cit.*, III (from Lambard family ms.), p. 552.

39. William Empson, "Shakespeare's Angel," *The New Statesman*, 4 October 1963, pp. 447–48.

40. Thomas Middleton, *Blurt, Master Constable*, 1602, II, ii.

41. Ben Jonson, *Poetaster*, 1601, II, ii.

42. John Florio, *A World of Words*, 1598, p. 12.

43. Thomas Nashe, *Works*, ed. by R. B. McKerrow, I, p. 243.

44. Rutland Ms., I, p. 321.

45. Cecil Papers, 83, 62.

46. William Empson, *op. cit.*, p. 447.

47. *Roxburghe Ballads*, VIII, pp. 135–37.

48. Thomas B. Howell, *State Trials*, I, p. 202.

49. John Florio, *A World of Words*, dedication entered with text, 3 March 1596; published 1598.

THE PEDANT

1. John Florio, *Second Fruits*, epistle dedicatory, 1591.

2. Michael Angelo Florio, *Apologia di M. Michel Agnolo Fiorentino*, 1557, p. 34.

3. John Florio, *A World of Words*, "Address to the Reader," 1598.

4. John Florio, *His First Fruits*, 1578, ch. 15, p. 18.

5. *Ibid.*, ch. 14, p. 12a.

6. *Ibid.*, ch. 11, p. 10a.

7. Calendar of State Papers (Foreign), 1584–85, letter of Ambassador Mauvissière to Walsingham, 10–20 August 1584, p. 15.

8. *Ibid.*, p. 16.

9. John Florio, *First Fruits*, ch. 15, p. 17a.

10. John Florio, *Second Fruits*, ch. 2, p. 23.

11. Giordano Bruno, *La Cena de le Ceneri*, 1584. Reprinted in tr. by E. A. Gosselin and L. S. Lerner as *The Ash Wednesday Supper*, 1977, p. 127.

12.   John Florio, *First Fruits,* ch. 27, p. 50.
13.   Edmund Malone, *op. cit.*
14.   John Florio, *A World of Words, op cit.,* dedication.
15.   E. Arber, 1875–94, III, p. 60.
16.   Frances Yates, *John Florio,* 1934, p. 126.
17.   *Ibid.*
18.   Public Records Office, State Papers, 12/219/78.
19.   *Ibid.*
20.   Sir Edward Coke, Reports, 1826, III, p. 246.
21.   Lansdowne Ms., 827, f. 24v.
22.   *Ibid.*
23.   William Minto, *Characteristics of English Poets,* 1885, p. 371.
24.   M. H. Spielmann, *The Title-Page of the First Folio: A Comparative Study of the Droeshout Portrait and the Stratford Monument,* 1924, p. 14.
25.   William Minto, *op. cit.,* p. 382.
26.   E. K. Chambers, *op. cit.,* I, p. 555.
27.   Frances Yates, *John Florio,* p. 130.
28.   *Ibid.,* p. 314.
29.   *Ibid.,* p. 240.
30.   T. S. Eliot, *Selected Essays,* New Ed., 1950, p. 126.

THE PLAY

1.   Charles Gildon, *Critical Remarks,* Rowe's ed., 1710, VII, p. 308.
2.   Samuel Johnson, ed., [Shakespeare's] *Plays,* 1765, I.
3.   Mark Van Doren, *Shakespeare,* 1939, p. 64.
4.   George Kittredge, *op. cit.*
5.   Sir Walter Cope, in E. K. Chambers, *Elizabethan Stage,* IV, p. 139.
6.   Frances Yates, *A Study of "Love's Labour's Lost,"* 1936, p. 99.
7.   G. P. V. Akrigg, *op. cit.,* p. 30.
8.   Walter Pater, *Appreciations,* 1889, p. 167.
9.   Sir Philip Sidney, *An Apology for Poetry,* 1595.
10.   Richard David, *Shakespeare Survey 4,* 1951, pp. 129–33.
11.   William Warburton, *Works of Shakespear* (ed. with Alexander Pope), 1747, II, pp. 227–28.

12. Samuel Johnson, *op. cit.*
13. Edmund Malone, *op. cit.*
14. Frances A. Yates, *A Study of "Love's Labour's Lost," op. cit.*, p. 14.
15. John Florio, *First Fruits,* ch. 4, p. 4.
16. Gerald Eades Bentley, *Shakespeare: A Biographical Handbook,* 1961, p. 155.
17. Sir Walter Cope, *op. cit.* (Chambers), p. 139.
18. Dudley Carleton, *ibid.*
19. Revels Account, cited in Chambers, *William Shakespeare,* II, p. 331.
20. *Ibid.,* p. 331.

THE PUBLISHER

1. Leona Rostenberg, "Thomas Thorpe, Publisher of Shakespeare's Sonnets," Papers of the Bibliographical Society of America, 54, 1960, pp. 16–37.
2. John Healey, tr., *The Discovery of a New World,* 1609, dedication of translator to author.
3. Frances Yates, *John Florio,* 1934, p. 285.
4. Thomas Thorpe, dedicatory letter to Pembroke in *The City of God,* tr. by John Healey, 1610.
5. Northrop Frye, "How True a Twain," in *The Riddle of Shakespeare's Sonnets, op. cit.,* p. 28.
6. T. S. Eliot, "The Frontiers of Criticism," *On Poetry and Poets,* 1957, p. 104.
7. Ivor R. W. Cook, letter to editor, *Times Literary Supplement,* 18 May 1973, p. 556.

THE POEMS II

1. William Wordsworth, in a note written by 1803, in Anderson's *Works of British Poets,* II, Folger Shakespeare Library, Washington, D.C.
2. W. H. Auden, *op. cit.,* p. 103.
3. A. L. Rowse, *The Poems of Shakespeare's Dark Lady,* 1978, p. 6.
4. *Ibid.,* p. 6.

5. *Ibid.*, p. 13.

6. Edmund Malone, *Supplement* (to the 1778 edition of Shakespeare's *Plays*), 1780.

7. Mark Eccles, "Barnabe Barnes," in *Thomas Lodge and Other Elizabethans,* ed. by C. J. Sisson, 1933, pp. 167 and 174.

8. Hyder Edward Rollins, *op. cit.*, II, p. 291.

9. Robert Cartwright, *The Footsteps of Shakespeare*, 1859, pp. 8 ff.

10. E. K. Chambers, *op. cit.*, I, p. 563.

11. Peter Quennell, *Shakespeare: A Biography*, 1963, p. 126.

12. W. H. Auden, *op. cit.*, p. 97.

13. Garrett Mattingly, "The Date of Shakespeare's Sonnet CVII," *PMLA*, 1933, vol. 48, pp. 705–21.

14. Dedicatory Epistle to Authorized Version, 1612.

15. Gervase Markham, *Honour in Her Perfection*, 1624.

16. John Donne, *Sermons: Selected Passages,* ed. Logan Pearsall Smith, 1919, p. 48.

17. C. J. Sisson, "The Mythical Sorrows of Shakespeare," *British Academy Proceedings*, 1934.

18. Garrett Mattingly, *op. cit.*, p. 721.

19. G. P. V. Akrigg, *op. cit.*, p. 254n.

20. Hyder Edward Rollins, *op. cit.*, II, p. 53.

21. *Ibid.*, p. 326.

22. Hermann Conrad, *Jahrbuch,* 1884, XIX, pp. 176–264. Cited in Rollins, II, p. 63.

23. Horace Davis, cited in R. M. Alden's *Sonnets,* 1916, pp. 447 ff.

24. John Berryman, "Shakespeare at Thirty," *The Freedom of the Poet,* 1976, p. 44.

25. Hyder Edward Rollins, *op. cit.*, II, p. 326.

26. S. Schoenbaum, *William Shakespeare: A Documentary Life,* 1974, p. 134.

27. E. K. Chambers, *William Shakespeare,* II, p. 565.

28. Edward Hubler, ed., *The Riddle of Shakespeare's Sonnets,* 1962, p. 6.

29. Edward Hubler, *The Sense of Shakespeare's Sonnets,* 1952, p. 5.

30. Kenneth Muir, *Shakespeare's Sonnets,* 1979, p. 4.

31. W. H. Auden, *op. cit.*, p. 91.

32.   J. W. Mackail, "A Lover's Complaint," *Essays and Studies of the English Association,* 1912, III, p. 51.
33.   George Rylands, *op. cit.,* p. 102.
34.   MacDonald P. Jackson, *Shakespeare's "A Lover's Complaint," Its Date and Authenticity,* 1965, University of Auckland Bulletin 72, English Series, 13, pp. 7–39.
35.   Edmund Malone, *op. cit.*
36.   Algernon Swinburne, *A Study of Shakespeare,* 1879, p. 61.
37.   George Rylands, *op. cit.,* pp. 94, 106.
38.   Thomas Nashe, *op. cit.,* I, p. 92.
39.   Mark Van Doren, *op. cit.,* 1939, p. 10.

THE POET

1.   S. Schoenbaum, *Shakespeare's Lives,* 1970.
2.   George Steevens, *Supplement,* ed. by Edmund Malone, 1780, I, p. 654.
3.   George Steevens, ed., *Plays,* 1793, I, p. vii.
4.   George Steevens, *Supplement.*
5.   Léon de Wailly, *Revue des Deux Mondes,* IV, 1834, p. 688.
6.   Henry Hallam, *Introduction to the Literature of Europe,* III, 1839, pp. 289–91.
7.   *T.P.'s Weekly,* New Zealand (7 September 1929), p. 569.
8.   Herbert Thurston, "The Mr. W.H. of Shakespeare's Sonnets," *Month,* CLVI (1930), p. 425.

The First Lines of the Sonnets

Index

[NOTE: "S" in the items that follow refers to Shakespeare; "LLL" refers to *Love's Labour's Lost*]

Florio, John (*continued*)
  Chambrun, 115; and Danver
  brothers, 118–19, 150; and
  "Phaeton" sonnet, 120–1;
  Daniel and, 123–4; literary
  friends of, 125; second marriage,
  death, and will of, 125, 127;
  and Queen Anne, 125, 127, 158;
  and Montaigne, 127; and
  Thorpe, 150–1, 155–8, 161;
  see also under items throughout
Florio, Michael Angelo, 106–7,
  156
Forman, Simon, 179–80
France, Southampton and, 86, 88,
  118; embassy of, in London,
  108–10
friend (male), in sonnets, viii,
  7, 12, 21–3, 26, 28, 173–4; and
  suppression of Q, 7, 222; Southampton as, 23, 190; and *Sonnet
  81,* 184; as patron, 187; *see
  also* Southampton *and* young
  man
Fripp, Edgar I., 49, 207
Frizer, Ingram, and Marlowe, 189
Frye, Northrop, 52, 162, 168

Ganymede, 98–9
Gildon, Charles, and LLL, 133
Giovanni Florio, 115
Golden Fleece, 125
Gottlieb, H. J., 8
Grafton, Duke of, and sonnets, 225
Greene, Robert, attack of, on S,
  viii–ix, 22, 41, 48–9, 122, 135,
  137, 207
Greville, Sir Fulke, 112
Grey, Lady Jane, 106
Grimaldi, Nicolo, 81
Grose, Lawrence, Sheriff, 118–19
Gryse, William, 109–10

Hakluyt, Richard, and Florio, 125
Hall, A., and Marlowe, 189
Hall, Joseph, 155–6, 158–9
Hallam, Arthur, Tennyson and, 25
Hallam, Henry, and sonnets, 225
Hamlet, 127, 176, 181

Harbage, Alfred, 143, 198
Harrison, G. B., 24, 198
Harry the Sixth, 74, 79
Harvey, Sir William, 165, 167
Hathaway, Anne, 15, 21
Haughton, William, viii
Healey, John, 155–6, 159, 161
Heminge, John, 59, 67, 83, 162
Heneage, Thomas, marriage of, 208
Henry V, and Essex, 90–1
Henry VI, 83, 105, 122
Henry VII, chapel of, 196
Henry VIII, 67–8
Henslowe, Philip, 74, 79
Herbert, Henry, 106, 156
Herbert, Philip, 162
Herbert, William, Florio and, 127,
  156, 158; as patron of Thorpe,
  161–2; dedications to, 161–2
Herford, C. H., 14n
Hero and Leander, 153, 187–8,
  190
Hicks, Michael, letter to, 76–7
Hieatt, A. K., and numerology, 13
Hilliard, Nicholas, 69, 201
*Histriomastix, or the Playwright
  Whipt,* Thorpe and, 159
Holofernes, identification of,
  144–6, 149–50
homosexuality, in sonnets, 13,
  19–23, 25, 30, 50–1; South-
  ampton and, 21, 98–100; in
  other works, 24; *see also* love
Hotson, Leslie, 14
Hubler, Edward, 26n, 209
Hunning, James, 118
Hunsdon, Lord Chamberlain, 180

"I Am that I Am," 30, 41, 219
Idea's Mirrour, 200
immortality, as theme, 17, 45,
  167–8, 221
"Induction," 214
"ingle," 98
Irving, Henry, and LLL, 133

Jackson, Macdonald, 211
Jacobean Journal, 198
Jacobean Pageant, 198

327

Index

sonnets *(continued)*
  bowdlerized, Benson and, 5–6,
  169; and *A Passionate Pilgrim*,
  6, 30, 162, 174; couplets of,
  9–10; term of composition of,
  14, 46, 199–200, 209–10; as
  commissioned work, 16; on
  acting and theatre, 48; and
  Southampton, 66–7, 69, 78–9,
  89, 98, 141, 149, 167, 184–5,
  187, 190–1, 201, 208–9, *see
  also under Sonnet numbers;*
  and LLL, 131–2, 138–41, 149–
  50, *see also under Sonnet numbers;* allusions in, 194, 198;
  Elizabethans and, 200; difficulties of, 224; rejection and ban-
  ning of, 224–5; allusions to,
  see under Q; publication of, *see*
  Q *and* Shakespeare; dating of,
  see dating; suppression of, *see
  under* Q; patron and, *see* patron;
  see also linked sonnets, *Sonnets,
  and under items throughout*
Sonnets, New Variorum edition
  of, xi, 7, 199, 207; Aspley and,
  159, 162; facsimile of, 227–306;
  dedication in, *see under* Q;
  suppression of, *see under* Q;
  Thorpe and, *see* Thorpe, and Q;
  see also Q *and* sonnets
Sonnets 1–17, as "Marriage" sonnets, 35–6; and Southampton,
  79, 81
Sonnets 1–20, and love, 25
Sonnets 18–28, as love poems,
  36–7
Sonnets 40–42, Nashe and, 206
Sonnets 40–52, as "Double Betrayal," 37–8
Sonnets 78–86, 47; and rival poets,
  39, 184
Sonnets 109–12, as "Vulgar Scandal," 41
Sonnets 110–12, and Greene
  attack, 206–7; dates of, 207
Sonnets 127–52, to raven-haired
  mistress, 14, 42–3

Sonnets 133 and *134,* Nashe and,
  206
Sonnets 153 and *154,* as "Bath"
  sonnets, 14, 43
Southampton, Countess of, 68–9,
  72, 74–5, 78, 208; and "Marriage" sonnets, 78, 167; *see also*
  Vernon, Elizabeth
Southampton, Earl of, 1st, 68
Southampton, Earl of, 2nd, 69, 72
Southampton, Earl of, 3rd, 67–8,
  81, 101, 147–8, 206; and homosexuality, 21, 98–100; and
  Empson, 23, 98, 100; as "young
  man," 55, *see also* young man;
  S and, 55, 57, 59, 66–7, 69, 78–
  9, 81, 83, 85, 96–8, 100, 105–6,
  113–14, 123, 128, 144, 148–9,
  158, 184–7; dedicatory letters
  to, 60–1, 190; as patron, 60,
  67, 69, 78–9, 81, 83, 96, 100,
  113–14, 128, 144, 148, 150,
  185, 187, 190–1, 201; in Tower
  of London, 64–6, 128, 194, 222;
  and James I, 65–6, 97, 194;
  painting of, 66, 69, 201; financial difficulties of, 66, 76–7, 81,
  86, 119–20; release of and
  favors to, 66–7, 196, 201, 222;
  origin and early life of, 67, 69,
  72–4, 98, 208–9; becomes earl,
  72; at Cambridge, 73–4; and
  marriage plans, 74–6, 78, 80–1,
  101, 142–3; letter of, to Hicks,
  76–7; Sandford poem about, 80;
  and 1,000 pounds, 82–3; and
  France, 86, 88, 118; and soldier-
  ing, 86, 89–92, 97, 208; and
  card game, 87; marriage and
  imprisonment of, 88–9, 92–3,
  208; daughter and sons of, 89,
  96–7; death of, 97; description
  of, 98–9, 184; and Edmonds,
  99–100; extravagances and
  benefactions of, 101; and Danvers brothers, 115, 117–20, 150;
  and LLL, 131, 139–42, 148–50;
  essay of, 140–1; and Thomas
  Wright, 159, 161; and mother's

ROBERT GIROUX *is a book editor, a book publisher, and a lifelong common reader—in short, a bookman. He has been associated with Farrar, Straus and Giroux since 1955 and has worked with some of the most eminent writers of our time.*

Fripp
Auden
Blair Leishman